UNDERCURRENTS

UNDERCURRENTS

FROM OCEANOGRAPHER TO UNIVERSITY PRESIDENT

John V. Byrne

President Emeritus
Oregon State University

OREGON STATE UNIVERSITY PRESS • CORVALLIS

Library of Congress Cataloging-in-Publication Data

Names: Byrne, John Vincent, 1928- author.
Title: Undercurrents : From Oceanographer to University President / John V.
    Byrne, President Emeritus, Oregon State University.
Description: Corvallis OR : Oregon State University Press, 2018. | Includes
    bibliographical references and index.
Identifiers: LCCN 2017054227 | ISBN 9780870719141 (paperback)
Subjects: LCSH: Byrne, John Vincent, 1928- | College presidents—United States—
    Oregon—Biography. | Oregon State University—Presidents_Biography. |
    Oceanographers—United States—Biography. | BISAC: BIOGRAPHY &
    AUTOBIOGRAPHY / Educators. | BIOGRAPHY & AUTOBIOGRAPHY /
    Science & Technology.
Classification: LCC LD4346.O417 B95 2018 | DDC 378.0092—dc23
LC record available at https://lccn.loc.gov/2017054227

∞ This paper meets the requirements of ANSI/NISO Z39.48-1992
(Permanence of Paper).

Oregon State University Press
121 The Valley Library
Corvallis OR 97331-4501
541-737-3166 • fax 541-737-3170
www.osupress.oregonstate.edu

To SMB, best friend and spouse,
for more than six decades of
support, guidance, and love

Contents

This was taken two weeks after retiring as president of Oregon State University. Notice the relaxed look. (*Gazette-Times*, Corvallis, Oregon)

Preface

Undercurrents tells of my time as president of Oregon State University and my life, mainly career, leading up to the presidency. I had originally thought of writing two separate memoirs, but a friend convinced me to write one, reasoning that decisions made as president were influenced by my prior development. *Undercurrents* covers my early life, formal education, time in industry, academe, and government. It is based mainly on my memory of events. Others may remember them differently. I relied heavily on the Oregon State University archives and *OSU Fact Books* for details related to the eleven years during which I served as president.

From my account of the years leading up to the presidency and events during those years, the discerning reader may recognize characteristics of my personality. It is my hope that *Undercurrents* tells not only of the decisions I made, but also reveals to the reader how and why I made those decisions. In short, how I tried to live my life and how I actually lived it. A complete draft of the initial version of this memoir is on file in the Oregon State University Archives.

—*John V. Byrne*

This is me at age ten sitting on a pony outside Hewitt Elementary School, Rockville Centre, New York. Fortunately, the pony never moved. (Byrne collection)

CHAPTER 1

The Early Years (1928–1947)

Gnarly rocks with footprints

I HAVE THE SAME NAME as my paternal grandfather, John Vincent Byrne. It's an Irish name. Byrne as a last name can be troublesome to some people here in America. They don't know how to pronounce it (*burn*) or spell it. You have no idea how many people mistakenly spell it B-R-Y-N-E (brine, salty). I frequently tell folks, "I'm John V. Byrne, that's B-Y-R-N-E. It's the seventh most common last name in Dublin." Someone told me that once, and I have accepted it without confirmation. In Ireland, you don't have to spell Byrne for people. The Irish wouldn't think of spelling it any other way.

My wife's maiden name is O'Connor, another good Irish name. She claims to have descended from the O'Connors who were early kings of Ireland, and that the Byrnes were "come-latelies." My standard response to that, "Sure. The O'Connors had things so screwed up, the Byrnes had to come over to straighten things out." So she has Irish blood, too. That's good, I suppose.

My father was Frank E (no period) Byrne. When people asked him what the E stood for, he would say Erandino. I think he was kidding. I never did learn if he had a middle name. He had two sisters, Ruth and Inez, and two brothers, Dave and Jack, all of whom grew up in Brooklyn. Of everyone in the family, my dad carried on Irish traditions more than anyone. He made it a practice to march with other Irish-Americans in the St. Patrick's Day Parade on Fifth Avenue. He was proud to be American, to be a New Yorker, and to be Irish.

My mother, Kathleen Barry, married Frank Byrne in 1922. They met at Cannon Mills Inc. in downtown Manhattan, where they both worked.

My mother quit when she became pregnant with me, but my father worked for Cannon Mills from the time he was sixteen until he retired at sixty-five as the company treasurer.

I was told my mother was in labor with me for more than twenty-four hours. I guess the labor lasted so long because they were both Christian Scientists and they tried to have me without medical intervention. I was an only child.

While I was growing up, our family practiced Christian Science. I never had professional medical attention for anything other than going to the dentist on a regular basis. The tenets of Mary Baker Eddy, the founder of Christian Science, were our tenets. Grandma Byrne was a Christian Science practitioner, and every medical case was brought to her attention for Christian Science treatment. I had the usual childhood diseases, mumps, chicken pox, measles; all received the Christian Science treatment. I turned to medical treatments while in graduate school and eventually dropped my Christian Science beliefs as our children grew up. I think being brought up as a Christian Scientist was important in forming my generally positive philosophy of life. For that I am grateful.

I was born at home in Hempstead, New York, on Long Island, and we lived there until I was four. One early memory I have is of being held by my father during an exceptional electrical storm, hearing him *ooh*ing and *aah*ing at how beautiful the lightning and thunder were. Another memory is staying overnight with my maternal grandparents, PopPop and Marnie. They lived in Mineola, across the railroad tracks from Roosevelt Field, where Charles Lindberg took off on his flight across the Atlantic in 1927. PopPop and Marnie kept the "funnies" from the weekend newspapers for me to look at, and after supper (we had supper, not dinner) we played cards, dominoes, or dice games. There was a certain amount of gambling using chips. Marnie's sister, Aunt Louise, and her son, Henny, lived next door. Henny, who must have been in his thirties, came over to play games with us. He had been gassed in the First World War, and apparently that affected his speech and possibly his mental abilities. He was a lovely, loving man. I liked him and never made fun of him. I was told some of my cousins did make fun of him. I think generally I was a good little boy.

We moved to Rockville Centre, also on Long Island, in 1932. Our house on Oakdale Road had just been built in a new neighborhood. There were woods of oaks and other trees behind our house. The house had two stories, with three bedrooms upstairs and a maid's room in the rear on the first floor. We never had a maid, so that room became a play-room for me. We lived in that house for nine years. I went to the Hewitt Elementary School, played in the woods behind our house, and grew up with the kids in the neighborhood. It seemed that because it was a new neighborhood, there were lots of kids—nineteen of us by my count.

We were a tight group, much like *Our Gang* of the movies. The big kids were the older brothers and sisters of us, the little kids. We learned a lot from the big kids: how to play football and stickball and capture-the-flag. There were no organized Little League–type programs in those days; we made up our own games. When we weren't outside playing games, we listened to the radio: *Jack Armstrong—All American Boy, Tom Mix, The Lone Ranger.* Saturday afternoons we went to the movies, all black and white, with a double feature, a newsreel, cartoons, and a thrilling serial chapter that always ended with the hero or heroine in a situation they couldn't possibly survive—but by the next Saturday they had escaped and were back again for more adventures.

During the summer, baseball was our game, played on the "baseball diamond" we created in the vacant lot at the end of Willets Court. From lumber odds and ends we "borrowed" from one of the new homesites, we built a beautiful backstop and painted it green. A hit onto or over the dirt road at the end of the lot was a home run. Touch football and stick-ball were played in the street on Willets Court because it was a dead-end street. We spent a lot of time in the woods next to our neighborhood. There were paths we gave names to: Skunk Trail, Mystery Trail, Monkey Tree Trail. The names had meaning. Someone had actually seen, or smelled, a skunk on one path; Mystery Trail was a path that seemed to go in a circle, so why it existed was a mystery. Monkey Tree Trail led to a huge silver beech we climbed on.

On Hempstead Road, the main road to downtown Rockville Centre, we set up a lemonade stand, but cars were traveling too fast and few bothered to stop. Once, within the neighborhood, a car did stop when a group of us was gathered there for one reason or another. It was a big sedan. The front door opened and a man called us over. We knew we shouldn't go near a stranger in an unfamiliar car, but we figured if we were together in a group, we'd be all right. We thought we were pretty tough anyway. The man showed us all sorts of neat kid things, baseball bats, gloves and balls, footballs, roller skates. He told us any of those things could be ours. All we had to do was sell eight *Saturday Evening Posts* or *Collier's* magazines for X number of weeks. Several of us saw what an outstanding opportunity that was and were provided with canvas bags marked "Saturday Evening Post" on the side and eight copies of the magazine.

The man told us he would be back in a week to collect the money we made, and he would leave next week's issues of the magazines. It never worked out for us, or for him. Three or four kids each trying to sell the same magazine in a small neighborhood was overkill at best. I think we each sold two or three magazines, probably to our parents, and that was about it. We never did collect any of the gloves, bats, or balls.

When I was about eight years old, I was beginning to be aware of the world around me. World War I hadn't been so long ago, and my father had a couple of books about the war, including descriptions of air warfare. Sonny Higginson and I were both taken with the romance of the flying machines: SPADs, Nieuports, Sopwith Camels. We saw pulp magazines of "Heroes of the Air" on newsstands and imagined ourselves flying those machines. I have a clear memory of spending an afternoon in Sonny's bedroom drawing pictures of World War I airplanes, pencils on plain white paper. It must have been my first creative art experience.

It was the time of the Great Depression, and my father was fortunate to have a job. He never graduated from high school and started at Cannon Mills as a box boy, but he took courses at night school, developed a fine reputation among credit managers in New York, and eventually became manager of the credit department and treasurer of the company. Because of his job, we never felt the anguish of the unemployed, but the Depression was all around us. I remember men coming to the back door of our home in Rockville Centre and asking if there were any chores they could do in exchange for a meal. My mother would say, "No, but let me fix a meal for you anyway." They sat on our back steps, ate their meal, and then thanked my mother profusely.

Life was different in the early thirties. There were no supermarkets, only individual markets for meat, bread and bakery goods, and groceries. Cottage cheese was called "pot cheese" and was available from the grocer, who dipped it from a large pot. Cheddar was called "store cheese" and was cut from a large wheel. The grocer picked out our boxed groceries from shelves behind a counter.

Bakery goods were delivered by truck, and the driver came to the door with a basket of samples. After we decided what we wanted, he went back to the truck to get it. Once purchased, bread was stored in a bread box. Milk came in a glass bottle and was also delivered and left on the doorstep before we were up for breakfast. It wasn't homogenized, so the cream rose to the top. In cold weather, the cream froze and pushed the cap out of the top of the bottle.

We boys often wore knickers, frequently dropped down to our ankles. They were often made of corduroy and "whistled" as you walked. We called them "whistle britches." Scotch tape hadn't been invented yet, so string or ribbon was used to hold the paper on a package. Sometimes straight pins were used temporarily to hold the paper in place until the string had been tied. School desks were fastened to the floor. The tops of the desk could be flipped up and the desk opened. Books, papers, pens, and pencils were left in the desk under the top. In the upper right corner of the part of the desktop that didn't lift up was an inkwell, or at least the hole for an inkwell. A "blotter" was used to soak up excess ink after writing was complete. Blotters were also used in banks where inkwells were present. Ballpoint pens became commercial in the late thirties, replacing liquid ink, and consequently inkwells and blotters disappeared.

Hewitt Elementary School was a half mile or so from where we lived. As I grew older, I was allowed to ride my bike to school. We left our bikes outside the school, unlocked. Ethel Getman, my third-grade teacher, was new to Hewitt School. Most of the kids wanted to have another very popular teacher, but I was lucky to be in Miss Getman's class. She was terrific. I felt that she really cared for each one of us, made each of us feel important, and caused us to want to learn. My first memories of music were in her class. More than anything else, Miss Getman helped me realize for the first time that learning new things could be fun.

My seventh-grade homeroom and English teacher, Morris Ottman, treated us as mature students. He explained complicated things in terms we could understand. He required us to make public speeches to the class. Warren Thompson, one of the Oakdale Road gang, was very good at giving these talks; he was relaxed, articulate, a pleasure to listen to. When I asked him his secret, he said, "It's easy. Read an interesting article in the *Readers' Digest* a couple of times and just tell the class what you read." Thanks to Warren Thompson and Morris Ottman, I have enjoyed public speaking and writing ever since.

Mr. Ottman also emphasized diagramming sentences. I learned to parse almost any grammatically correct sentence the human brain could put together. I was good at it, which later got me into trouble with my ninth-grade English teacher. She was trying to show us how to diagram a reasonably complex sentence with compound clauses. She struggled and eventually botched it. I made the tactless error of correcting her in front of the class, to which she replied, "John Byrne, I wish you had never come to this school!" In spite of this experience, I have always enjoyed diagramming sentences. I guess I learned something about tact, too.

We lived with our bicycles, rode them to school, rode them around the neighborhood, took them apart, and tried to put them back together. One day we raced against each other using the same bike. Someone had a stopwatch, and we thought it would be fun to see who was fastest. We laid out a rectangular course using the paved roads of the neighborhood and the nearest dirt road just out of the neighborhood. From the starting point on Vanderveer Court, you could see a racer at the halfway point on the dirt road. I was the last person to race. I had a plan. I remembered a story my father told me about Glenn Cunningham, a world-famous middle distance runner in the mid-1930s. Cunningham characteristically ran slowly at first, saving himself for the end of the race. I planned to do the same.

During the first half of the course, I laid back and didn't go too fast. At the halfway point, where the group of racers could see me, my speed was the slowest of all the group. At about that point, I gave it everything I had. I ended up with the fastest overall time. I'd planned ahead and followed the plan, and it worked. I guess I was competitive, too.

My best friends were Bobby Wulfing, my age, and his brother George, a couple of years older. They lived in a one-story cottage, and their ground-floor bedroom, easily accessible through a window, became a gathering place. George suffered from asthma and didn't participate in physical games with the rest of us. He developed other interests—electricity and radio—that he shared with the rest of us. He had a Hallicrafters shortwave radio, and he learned telegraphy in order to communicate with other amateur radio operators. We gathered in Bobby and George's bedroom in the evening and listened to shortwave radio broadcasts from Europe. I remember hearing a Nazi radio broadcaster claim that in the war in Europe, the British were using the same unfair tactics they had used during the American Revolution. In addition to listening to shortwave radio broadcasts, we helped George with a number of electrical experiments and learned quite a bit about electricity. Years later, when I was a freshman in college and was struggling through my physics classes, the one part I did very well on was electricity. I'm convinced it was due to what I had learned from George Wulfing.

I loved the summers. Once every summer, my father took me to Steeplechase Park at Coney Island, an amusement center that had been there when he was a kid. I loved hearing his stories of growing up as much as I did going on the rides. Most of all I loved Jones Beach, a state park that extended over miles of white sand and dune grass. Our family often went to the beach, where we bodysurfed in the ocean waves.

At Jones Beach, there was an Olympic-size swimming pool my father took me to almost every Saturday morning. It never seemed to be crowded, and he taught me how to dive off the side of the pool and swim short distances. I learned to hold my nose when I jumped off the low diving board—the same board divers practicing for the 1936 Olympic Games were using.

At night when I went to bed, my father read to me. He propped his book on the wooden reading stand he had made and read from books that have left a lifelong impression: *The Boy's King Arthur, The Swiss Family Robinson, The Will To Win* (sports stories from the magazine *Boys' Life*)—all books I've kept to this day. Later, about the time I was in high school, he gave me one of his own books, *The Go-Getter* by Peter B. Kyne. Published in 1921, it's a short book about a wounded World War I soldier who is given a task to complete before being given a job in a small lumber firm. The chore is to acquire for the owner of the company a special vase during a weekend. All sorts of obstacles to getting the vase have been set up to test his ingenuity and his persistence. He succeeds, of course. I probably read that book three or four times during high school, a couple of times while I was in college, and I still look at it from time to time. It sends a simple message about the importance of persistence.

Every summer, thousands of teenagers and preteenagers in the New York City area headed for camps in the Adirondacks or other places in the New York–New England area. During the summer of 1937, I joined them. I was nine years old. I don't know what prompted my folks to send me away for six or eight weeks, but there I was on the train headed to Forest Lake Camp in upstate New York. I was lonely and a little scared. I stayed the full eight weeks but was glad to come home when camp was over.

In third grade, all the kids at Hewitt School were introduced to the Tonette, a black plastic instrument that resembled a recorder. The Tonette was my first musical instrument. My parents were not interested in classical music, but they wanted to encourage me musically. So when I was in the fifth or sixth grade, they bought me an alto saxophone and hired a private teacher to give me a lesson at home once a week. I wasn't a very good music student, and my strongest memory of those lessons is that the instructor smelled of cigarette smoke and seemed bored by the whole enterprise. But it was a good enough introduction to music. I didn't realize it at the time, but music would become an important part of my life.

In 1939, the New York World's Fair opened. Mayor Fiorello LaGuardia and a group of New York boosters converted a garbage dump at Flushing, Long Island, into a beautiful park of fountains, greenways, and art-deco buildings. The fair boasted exhibits from numerous corporations and sixty or more foreign governments. Nazi Germany opted not to participate. The focus of the fair was on the future, new products, and ethnic cultures. It was the second-largest fair in American history, attracting more than forty-four million visitors during its two-year run. For an eleven-year-old boy, the fair was a huge playground, a place to visit as often as possible. I went to the fair many times during 1939, and I knew my way around the fairgrounds very well.

In 1940, my great-aunt Bessie, Grandma Byrne's sister, came to visit us. Like my grandmother, she was a very proper person. She lived in Maine and, although we had visited her there, this was her first time to visit us. She wanted to see the New York World's Fair. And who better to serve as her guide than the young John Byrne?

Aunt Bessie and I started our tour at the Trylon and Perisphere, the fair's art-deco icon. Then we went to the popular General Motors exhibit, saw cultural displays, and were impressed with paintings by Vermeer and other artists. We walked and walked . . . and then walked some more.

Aunt Bessie: "Haven't we been here before?"

"Yes."

"Why didn't you tell me?"

"You didn't ask me."

"I think it's time for lunch. Let's go to the nearest cafeteria. Do you know where that would be?"

"Yes."

After lunch: "John, would you get me a glass of water, please?"

"Yes, of course."

I think, after two cups of coffee, she must really be thirsty. But surprise, she used the glass of water as a finger bowl. She was a very proper lady.

The tour was a success. Aunt Bessie was happy; she had seen the New York World's Fair. It was everything she had hoped it would be—and she had an exceptional tour guide.

By 1940, our neighborhood had matured: all the houses had been built and their shrubbery and plantings were well established. The summer of 1941 was much like any other summer for us kids. We spent our days as we always had: playing Monopoly in one kid's garage during the day or perhaps pick-up baseball in the vacant lot next to the Pratt house. We spent evenings under streetlights talking, kidding each other, taking our bikes apart and reassembling them under poor light, or gathering in Bobby and George Wulfing's room to listen to shortwave radio. For the rest of the world, it was not a normal summer. World War II was well under way in Europe. The British army had been successfully evacuated from France at Dunkirk, and the Royal Air Force achieved an amazing victory in the Battle of Britain, thereby deterring a German invasion of England. London was in ruins from German bombing. Germany occupied virtually all of Europe, and Japan occupied large areas of China and was attempting to show muscle against the United States. The United States was doing what it could to support England, short of being directly involved in the war. My friends and I knew about these things, but they didn't affect us. Our parents were concerned, but we were not. Life was good for us during the summer of 1941.

I was thirteen years old, had done reasonably well at Hewitt School, and was getting ready to enter the eighth grade at South Side High School. The neighborhood group was still holding together. The difference between the big kids and the little kids was changing. Hormones were manifesting themselves; the older boys were noticing girls for reasons new to us. We had thought we had "girl friends" earlier, probably best described as "girls who were friends." The girls who were part of the neighborhood group were maturing; their shapes were changing. They were being dated by young men from outside our neighborhood. Were we missing something? A couple of us thought so. The little kids weren't so little anymore, but before serious physical explorations took place, my folks decided to move away from Rockville Centre.

CHAPPAQUA

MY FATHER had always wanted a place in the country with woods, fields, perhaps a stream or a pond. One weekend in late spring, my folks returned from a trip to Westchester County and told me we were going to move to a place they thought I would like. The house was in a hilly area about two miles from the small village of Chappaqua. There was a long driveway—actually two dirt ruts—that led from an entrance between two stone gateposts with marble plaques inscribed "Stony Ledge" up to a house on a rise surrounded by a sweeping lawn of tall weeds nestled between outcrops of gray rock. Woods occupied much of the property behind the house. Stone walls, typical of New England, divided the five and a half acres that came with the house into small areas. A spring behind the garage created a small stream that ran along the side of the property, under the highway in front, and into a small pond across the street. The three-bedroom house, although only four years old, needed painting.

Chappaqua, population about thirty-five hundred, was a commuter's town about thirty miles north of New York City. Its name, we were told, was derived from an Algonquin word meaning "land of hidden waters." The town, settled by Quakers around 1730, included a meeting house built in 1753 and a number of houses built before the American Revolution. Local history claimed that after the battle of White Plains during the American Revolution, George Washington used the meeting house as an infirmary for wounded soldiers and that you could still see bloodstains on the floor. I never saw the stains, but I never really looked for them.

Wooded hills with ponds and streams characterized the countryside. The rocks exposed near our house were gray, gnarly, and in a couple of places had depressions that looked exactly like footprints. I was sure these must be the footprints of ancient Indians who were about the same physical size as us. How could it be otherwise? And the huge boulders, some as big as automobiles, scattered around the property—where did they come from? How did they get there? I learned much later that the rocks were metamorphic rocks more than 500 million years old, (Precambrian Manhattan schist and Fordham gneiss).[1] The depressions could not be footprints. Too bad—but I found the real story even more interesting. During the last Ice Age, the area around our house had been covered by a continental ice sheet.[2] A huge glacier had spread south and carried boulders and smaller rocks from someplace in the north. When the ice melted, the rocks dropped out of the glacier all over our property. Some of the boulders were buried and their tips stuck out of the ground in areas we were trying to turn into lawn. I spent a lot of my time after school, on weekends, and during the summer breaking up those rocks and digging them out of the ground.

On weekends, I worked with my father, building our own rock walls, painting the house, or cutting the grass to form a continuous lawn of ever-increasing size once the boulders were removed. The area behind the house had been an apple orchard at some time in the past. The apple trees shared the area with oaks, birches, and other kinds of trees. The ancient orchard still produced apples that mostly fell to the ground, rotted, and then seasoned the air with a wonderful ciderlike aroma. Occasionally we saw deer as we cleared brush or cut firewood in the woods. Our dog, Tubby, chased the deer through the woods, scrambling over the ancient stone walls that the deer cleared so easily. Tubby thought the property belonged to him and did not hesitate to so inform the other animals who lived there. Unfortunately, he was uneducated about skunks and suffered a hard lesson one evening when he encountered one that was also convinced of its property rights. It took much washing to eliminate the characteristic odor from Tubby's fur. We all suffered because of Tubby's indiscretion.

In 1941, downtown Chappaqua was small. It included the railroad station and a number of stores and offices at the bottom of the hill where Kings Road flattened out. The places that were important to me were the barbershop, Cadman's Pharmacy with its old-fashioned ice cream fountain and booths where teenagers gathered, the Italian diner—the only place to get that new taste sensation called "pizza pie"—and Horace Greeley High School (HGHS), an imposing structure of gray rock that appeared larger than it actually was.[3] Though it was called a high school, it included grades two through twelve, with the elementary grades located on the first floor of a separate wing. There were no middle schools in those days.

My folks had been active in the Christian Science church in Rockville Centre, so I suppose it was natural that their first connections in Chappaqua were through the church. The closest Christian Science church was in Pleasantville, about five miles south of Chappaqua. That is where the Byrnes went to church and Sunday school, and so did the Brewers, who lived near us in Chappaqua.

My mother was serious about Christian Science and eventually became the first reader of the church and a practitioner. She helped others understand and use the tenets of Christian Science, which emphasizes a positive attitude about life. My mother knew that no matter how bad conditions might seem, things would work out for the best if you practiced what you learned through Christian Science.

In the fall of 1941, I entered eighth grade. Our closest Christian Scientist neighbors, Mike and Agnes Brewer, had a daughter, Barbara, also about to enter the eighth grade. It was good to have a new friend to help introduce me to Horace Greeley High School. Barbara was a friend throughout high school.

The high school student body was small, with twenty-six of us in the graduating class of 1946. We were the Quakers, and our athletic rival was Katonah High School, at least nominally. I think we felt better or worse depending on the outcome of contests with Bedford High School, located in a town not far from Chappaqua.

As the 1941–1942 academic year started, my father thought we should lay out a high school curriculum that would prepare me for college. The US Military Academy at West Point was a short distance up the Hudson River, and it seemed to him to be a worthy institution to prepare for. My father had never graduated from high school and really didn't know much about college, but he was impressed that West Point must provide a good college education for any young man. We collected the proper materials from West Point and selected a four-year course of study that would prepare me for entrance there. In addition to the required courses in English and social studies, I would take all the mathematics and science available at HGHS, as well as French and mechanical drawing. In retrospect, this turned out to be a useful curriculum for entrance to almost any American college or university in the 1940s.

In Mrs. Twining's eighth-grade social studies class, we studied life in America during colonial times. Each student was expected to do a special project. I thought special projects were for extra credit and not a course requirement, so I didn't do one. I was wrong, but because I was new to the school and hadn't understood, she said I could have a week or two to complete a project. A week later, I turned in a large cartoon showing the mishaps that might happen to people during those colonial times. The cartoon was accepted as my special project and was posted with other projects in the hall outside the classroom. It set me up as the class cartoonist. I continued to draw cartoons of one topic or another during my time at Horace Greeley. I still sketch and even draw cartoons from time to time.

HGHS lacked some of the advantages of larger schools like Pleasantville to the south and Mount Kisco to the north. There was band, both marching and concert, but no choral or string programs. There were athletic programs: football, basketball, baseball, and track for the boys and field hockey and basketball for the girls. The school was good academically because of a number of excellent teachers: Sylvia Kurson (English), Alice Barry (social studies), Jean Fenn (French), Herbert Oakes (mathematics). Our principal, Douglas Grafflin, was new. His popularity suffered somewhat from following the beloved Robert Bell, who had recently been promoted to school superintendent.

Each of these people had a profound effect on one aspect or another of my life. Sylvia Kurson did an excellent job of teaching us how to write. I didn't realize until much later that she was regarded as one of the top ten high school English teachers in the United States. What I remember most clearly was that she required us to memorize the prologue to Chaucer's Canterbury tales—in Middle English ("Whan that Aprille with his shoures soote"). I don't know why we did that, but I discovered later that teenagers throughout the East and Midwest had memorized it, and many were able to sing it to any popular song. We sang it to the tune of "The Darktown Strutters' Ball." Andy Scheer, who was a year or two ahead of me in school, joined the marines and told me years later that he started to sing it in the shower after some sort of drill and was joined in singing it by half a dozen other marines.

Alice Barry kept us on our toes in government and history. Jean Fenn led me into my second language, French, even to the point of edging me into the starring role in one act of the play *Tovarich*, performed in French. Herbert "Herbie" Oakes was the teacher who had the greatest impact. I took classes in geometry, trigonometry, spherical trigonometry, and advanced algebra from him and enjoyed virtually every minute of them. He communicated well and had a great sense of humor. When I left high school, I had every intention of becoming a high school mathematics teacher like Herbert Oakes.

When we moved to Chappaqua in 1941, I played in the Horace Greeley High School band. I started out playing alto saxophone. Later on, when I was a junior, I took over the school's baritone saxophone. At first, band was a challenge because, as an eighth grader, I thought the wise-guy comments of the upperclassmen were hilariously funny. I couldn't help laughing, and that interfered with my ability to play. Sometimes things were more serious. In one of the concerts early in my HGHS career, I played in a saxophone quartet, with Buddy Karlebach and me on alto saxophone, Howie Peck on baritone, and someone whose name I don't remember playing tenor sax. There was no laughing during the practice sessions for those concerts. Buddy Karlebach was easily the best of us. As a high school student, he often sat in with Les Brown and His Band of Renown when they played at the Log Cabin in Armonk, New York, not far from Chappaqua.

My first experience playing published dance music happened when I was in ninth grade. Bob Mengebier, who played trumpet, invited several of us to his house on a Saturday morning to play the published arrangement of "This Love of Mine," a song made popular by Frank Sinatra when he was a sensation in New York City. Teenage girls swooned when Sinatra sang this song. They didn't swoon when we tried to play it. Even so, playing in the band was fun and an important part of my high school experience.

Life in Chappaqua during World War II

The war in Europe was a constant concern to our parents and other adults, as was the increasing tension between the United States and Japan in the Pacific. They kept a close eye on the potential involvement of the United States, primarily in Europe. The surprise Japanese attack on Pearl Harbor on December 7 changed our lives immediately, in and out of school. World War II was the dominant event of our high school years and affected our lives during the 1940s. Two of my best friends took specific action to avoid the draft, one by joining the National Guard, the other by enlisting in the navy.

Selective Service had been in effect since October 1940, and by 1941 included most men from eighteen to forty-five. My father was technically qualified for military service, but because he was forty and the head of a family, he was not drafted. He volunteered as an air-raid warden. One of his first duties was to take a census of all of the people living in his district of northwest Chappaqua and inform them how to prepare for a possible incendiary bomb attack. It was suggested that every home have a pail of sand and a shovel handy. Everyone was required to black out windows and doors in their homes and paint over their car's headlights, leaving only a small clear rectangle about one inch by two and a half inches to provide light for any nighttime driving. It was the air-raid warden's job to be sure the people in his district complied.

We changed our lifestyle when rationing went into effect early in 1942. Gasoline, tires, heating oil, sugar, and coffee were all rationed. Tin was a strategic metal, and apparently toothpaste came in tin tubes; to get a new tube of toothpaste, you had to turn in the old tube. Home heating was also a problem. To save heating fuel at our house, we sealed off the living room from the rest of the house with a heavy blanket. It was the only room in the house that was heated to a comfortable level. Heat came from burning cannel coal (soft bituminous coal) in the fireplace for a short time every night.

Commuters in our part of Chappaqua who traveled to New York City contracted for a bus to take them to and from the Chappaqua train station. This saved the rationed gasoline for individual cars. Residents who didn't live close to each other became acquainted as they rode to and from the railroad station. Every weekday morning, my father hiked about a quarter mile up the hill to Seven Bridges Road to catch the commuter bus. Frequently, I walked up the hill with him in the morning and met him at Seven Bridges Road when he returned in the evening. It was a routine we enjoyed, even when it snowed. It was a time for me to be with my father to talk about events of the day, family values, and principles to live by.

Much of high school social life continued essentially unaffected by the war, but each class made a contribution to the war effort. Our class of 1946 held a festival each year at which participants paid to play games or bought raffle tickets for donated prizes. We held auctions for donated cakes from the Band Box Restaurant, occasionally bidding the price of a cake up to forty or fifty dollars, a steep price in those days.

Gender differences were still prevalent in the courses we took: boys took shop and girls, home economics. For the war effort, the boys made models of military airplanes, both ally and enemy. Carved from soft wood and painted black, these were to be used for aircraft recognition training. The girls knitted gloves and scarves for servicemen.

Our social lives went on pretty much as before. We gathered at Cadman's Pharmacy after school, dated girls, and went to movies, dances, and athletic contests. If we didn't have an after-school activity, we gravitated to the center of town, the intersection of King Street and South Greeley Avenue. Sometimes we'd hang out there and talk to our favorite police officer, Don Tully, who was often on duty directing traffic. We thought of Officer Tully as a good friend and a great ambassador for the police department.

When I returned to Chappaqua many years later, I stopped for coffee and a sandwich at a lunch counter that didn't exist in 1946. Sitting down the counter from me was an older gentleman who looked vaguely familiar. I asked the counter attendant if that man could possibly be a former policeman named Don Tully. "I don't know anything about service on the police force, but that's Don Tully, all right," the attendant said. "He's retired from the dry cleaning establishment he used to run next door." I remembered him; I'm not sure he remembered me. Tully and I had a wonderful conversation; reminiscing with old friends you haven't seen for decades is one of the pleasant rewards in life. I hope Don Tully thought so, too.

Sometime between 1942 and 1944, our class was joined by a number of girls who had been evacuated from England. They lived with local volunteer families and fit in very well with our class. We knew it was difficult for them and made every effort to make them valued members of our class and to feel as such. They returned to their homes in England as soon as it seemed safe, even before the war was over and our class graduated.

During the summer of 1945, I commuted to New York City to take courses in typing and speed writing, a form of shorthand. I usually took a train back to Chappaqua in midafternoon. On one August day, I ran into a classmate in Grand Central Station. We boarded the train and sat together. About fifteen or twenty minutes out of Grand Central, I noticed someone two or three seats ahead reading a tabloid newspaper. When that person turned the paper so I could see the front page, I was startled by the headline in huge black letters, "U.S. DROPS ATOM BOMB ON JAPAN." In a few days, World War II ended.

Before we graduated in 1946, several HGHS students from earlier classes who had been drafted or enlisted returned to Chappaqua. Some reentered Horace Greeley to complete their high school degrees. Gene Carr was one who had served in the navy and returned to school to complete his high school degree; he became a good friend. The most heart-wrenching returnee was Alan Gowan, who had been several years ahead of me in school. Always cheery, he'd had a smile and a friendly word for all, including lowerclassmen. He had been the kind of person you couldn't help liking, even loving. He returned from the war disfigured, blind, and bitter. The first time I saw him after he returned I was shocked. I cried. He remains a vivid reminder for me of how stupid—and evil—war is.

I was never much of an athlete, although in high school I did play second-string guard on the basketball team. In a small school like Horace Greeley, you didn't have to have the dimensions of an athlete to participate. I was close to the athletic environment, however, handling the ten-yard chains during football games and serving as manager of the baseball team.

With the manager's job, I had what I thought of as awesome responsibilities. It was my task to be sure the bases and the bats were all available at the baseball diamond two blocks from the high school, for every practice and every home game. This may sound simple, but half a dozen bats in a canvas bag and three bases are both heavy and awkward to carry. If I have any skills of persuasion, they were probably developed during my tenure as the high school's baseball manager. Not every player was eager to help. Andy Scheer, the marine mentioned earlier, will forever be high on my list of helpful people. He was always ready to help carry the bases or the bats. Further, once the game was under way, I was responsible for keeping score. After the game, I called the sports editor of the local newspaper and recounted the game to him using the complete box score I had noted during the game.

I took three years of French and hit my stride in my senior year. There were seven of us in third-year French, four girls and three boys. The teacher, Mrs. Fenn, proposed putting on a play in French for the student body at the monthly all-school assembly. She wanted to highlight the French program and demonstrate that learning a foreign language could be fun. The class voted on the idea: three nays (all boys) and four ayes (all girls). Chalk one up for the ladies.

One act of Jacques Deval's *Tovarich*, presented in French, was scheduled for a winter-term assembly. Mrs. Fenn worked a deal with coach Whitey Kiel so I could miss basketball practice in order to rehearse my part in the play. In 1937, the play had been made into a movie starring Claudette Colbert and Charles Boyer. The story: a Russian couple, members of the nobility, flee to Paris during the Russian revolution and take positions as manservant and maid in the home of a wealthy Parisian family. Being of noble birth and upbringing, the manservant teaches the young man of the family how to fence and how to dress for a formal affair and otherwise serves as his mentor in the finer arts and manners of the upper classes. Our cast decided that I would play the lead, the role of the manservant, and Dotty Lobrano, one of my classmates, would be the maid.

On the big day, the auditorium was packed. Shortly into the opening scene of the play, I entered carrying a tray with a glass of water and two aspirins for the young man of the family. A loud cheer arose from the back of the auditorium where sat the basketball team. I tried not to smile or look at them. I recovered quickly and soon said the only line of the play I can still remember. As I straightened the bow tie for the young man, I said, "*Voilà, on ne le voyons pas le bouton,*" or something like that. ("There. Now one cannot see the button.") It was my first stage utterance in French and elicited an even bigger cheer from the rear of the auditorium. Somehow we got through the rest of the play, and I embraced Dotty Lobrano, my stage wife, aka Claudette Colbert, as the curtain came down. I have always considered French to be my second language.

Academically, I did all right in high school. By the time my class graduated in 1946, I probably ranked third, fourth, or fifth in a class of twenty-six. Shortly before I graduated, my folks convinced me I should attend Principia, the Christian Science college in Elsah, Illinois, so in late spring, my father and I made the trip to Elsah to see the college. The campus was nice, but we were too late; they had filled their admission quota for 1946–1947. I would have to wait until the following year, or I could attend the Principia High School, about fifty miles away in St. Louis, and wait for a vacancy in the college. It was a disappointment. We swallowed hard, decided I would not attend their high school, and returned to Chappaqua.

During the year after high school, I became a daily commuter and traveled with my father to the Big Apple, where I worked as an office boy at the accounting firm Price Waterhouse at 56 Pine Street, one block north of Wall Street. The job was interesting, but when it turned warm in early spring, I decided it was not for me and resigned. Back in Chappaqua, I stopped in at the high school to sit in with the band, playing baritone saxophone as before. The assistant principal saw me and asked if he could speak with me. He told me the head janitor had dropped a desk on his foot and would be out of commission for six weeks or so. They needed a part-time janitor, and when he saw me playing with the band, he thought I would be the perfect choice. Would I do it?

Of course I would. I loved my years at Horace Greeley. How could I refuse? So for the next six weeks, I was a janitor on the afternoon–nighttime shift, from one to ten, with an hour off for dinner. With a big bunch of keys to all of the rooms in the school, I felt important when a former teacher came up to me and asked if I could open her room for her.

Frequently after work, I drove to a diner in the neighboring town, Pleasantville, for coffee and pie. On one occasion, while returning from Pleasantville, I was passed by Chad Messenger and Dave Quimby on a motorcycle, traveling at high speed. It was quickly evident they were being pursued by a Pleasantville police car. I suspect Chad assumed that if they could evade arrest and reach the safety of Chappaqua, he would not be ticketed. They missed a turn coming into Chappaqua, lost control, and crashed. By the time I caught up to them, Dave and the Pleasantville officer were coming into sight.

I stopped, and Dave said, "John, get help. I think Chad has been hurt." I immediately drove to the police station and reported the incident to the officer on duty, who happened to be my friend Don Tully. Tully called for an ambulance, dispatched a patrol car to the scene, and began taking down my report. Several minutes later, an older adult burst into the station and stammered that a terrible accident had occurred, not realizing that Tully already had the situation under control. Chad Messenger never regained consciousness.

About this time, a dance band was being formed by Billy Higgenbothem, a trumpet player in Pleasantville. Higgenbothem wanted a four-saxophone section and had already acquired two altos and a tenor sax. He asked me if I would be interested in playing baritone sax with them. I told him I would love to join them, that I didn't own a bari sax, but I knew where I might borrow one. I would get back to him in a few days.

My next stop was the principal's office at the high school. I explained the situation to the principal, Douglas Grafflin, who said he could understand my needs and my desires, but he also understood his responsibilities as principal. He obviously wanted to help. He told me that he preferred that I wouldn't ask him to borrow the saxophone, but if I took the instrument, please take good care of it. I thought that was a cool way to handle a somewhat sticky situation. I also wondered if my helping the school as janitor might have influenced his decision. In any case, he opened a door for me to experiences and memories that have lasted a lifetime. Billy Higgenbothem's band played standard dance and swing music, mostly at high school dances. Often after most of the dancers had left for other pursuits, we continued to play because it was fun. We were getting better and were looking for new opportunities.

A new opportunity presented itself as a dance band contest at a theater in White Plains, a large town near Chappaqua. The band that played best and received the loudest applause from the audience would win. I don't remember what the prize was, but the prestige of winning was enough. Besides, we thought we had an ace in the hole. Someone in our group knew a professional arranger named Jimmy Leyden, who orchestrated music for the Glenn Miller Band, then led by Tex Benecke. Benecke had been the tenor saxophonist in the original Glenn Miller Band and had reassembled the band after World War II. Would Jimmy Leyden orchestrate a piece for us? He would, and he had just the number for us. It was called "Pattern in Lace," similar in many ways to "String of Pearls," a major hit by the original Miller band. We were ready for the contest.

White Plains in 1947 was perhaps ten times larger than Chappaqua. One of the bands in the competition was from White Plains, and we expected they would draw a large audience. The outcome of the contest, based on audience approval, was really never in doubt, but we thought with our ace in the hole, "Pattern in Lace," we had a chance of pulling an upset. It didn't happen; we came in second. Immediately after the contest, an agent approached us with an offer to sign on as the orchestra on a cruise line. The offer sounded good, but it meant each of us would have to join a musicians' union at some cost, both in money and in the control of where and when we could perform. With the advice of Jimmy Leyden and others, we said, "Thanks, but no thanks."

That could be the end of the story, but it's not. From the late 1960s through the early 1990s, Norman Leyden, brother of Jimmy Leyden, conducted the Oregon Symphony Pops. In 1994 or 1995, the orchestra came to Corvallis to present a popular music concert at Oregon State University. I was president of the university at that time, and after the concert, my wife, Shirley, and I went backstage to greet Conductor Leyden. After I told him the story of the contest in White Plains and the role his brother, Jimmy, had played, he said, "Jimmy. He's here, right next door. He's our orchestra's manager."

Jimmy was summoned; I repeated the story. "'Pattern in Lace,'" he said. "Yeah," and he spontaneously hummed the melody at the same time I did. Some connections are forever, as are good memories.

After my stint as a janitor, I needed something else to do. The large Kensico Cemetery not far from Chappaqua was the answer. Every summer, the Kensico Cemetery hired a temporary workforce, largely high school and college students, to tend to gardening, mowing, and general cleanup. I was assigned the power mower in one of the five gardener groups. For five days a week, I cut the larger areas of grass in our section of the cemetery, entertaining myself by singing songs made popular by Frank Sinatra, Peggy Lee, Doris Day, Bing Crosby, and countless others ("Heartaches," "Laura," "Swinging on a Star," "That Old Feeling," and so on). I entertained myself as if I were the master of ceremonies, introducing a song and then singing it, sometimes in my version of the style of the performer who made it famous. I was conscientious, the hours moved swiftly, and I frequently got far ahead of the other workers with the hand mowers—sometimes so far ahead that Joe Bova, the leader of the group, told me on more than one occasion, "Stop and smoka you pipe." It was a beautiful cemetery, well landscaped, and I enjoyed being outdoors. The job lasted until I was ready to leave Chappaqua for college.

Earlier in 1947, my father and I had done an abbreviated tour of small, academically high-quality colleges in New York and Massachusetts. We started at Williams College and were not particularly well received there. Our next stop was Hamilton College, where, in contrast, we were made to feel comfortable and given the impression that they really wanted me. Hamilton was a men's liberal arts college with about 750 students, many of whom were returning veterans from World War II. It was located in Clinton, New York, not far from Utica, in the center of New York State. There wasn't much in Clinton besides Hamilton College. I told my father we didn't need to look any further. Hamilton was my choice. In September, my folks drove me from Chappaqua to Clinton to deliver me to the college that would become my alma mater and my residence for most of the next four years.

I was ready to prepare to become a high school mathematics teacher—I thought.

CHAPTER 2

Hamilton College (1947–1951)

Changing direction

When I arrived at Hamilton[1] in the fall of 1947, I joined 750 others at this all-male liberal arts college. In part due to the influx of veterans of World War II, Hamilton was overcrowded. After being assigned to a temporary room, I was moved to South Dormitory, where I lived with three roommates for the rest of my freshman year. Our suite consisted of two two-person sleeping rooms opening into a spacious central study room complete with large fireplace. We never had a fire in the fireplace but did use it as a goal for our own version of hockey, for which we used a tennis ball in place of a hockey puck.

Fraternities served as the living quarters for their members, roughly 90 percent of the student body. I pledged Chi Psi and moved to the Chi Psi Lodge in my second year at Hamilton. Once I moved, my life took on different dimensions. Each resident was assigned a study room, and all of us slept in a large dormitory in what was, in reality, an attic. The windows in the dormitory were open most of the time, and when the snow arrived in November, beds close to the windows often received a dusting of snow. For three years, my study-room partner was Charlie Doran, a studious fellow and a delight to study with.

I soon discovered that the year I'd spent doing various things between high school and college distinguished me from the rest of the freshman pledge class. I was a year older than other entering freshman, and that seemed to make a difference, particularly with the older upperclassmen and veterans. As an office boy at Price Waterhouse, I'd learned skills other than "office boying." One skill that helped me with two older fraternity brothers was the ability to play pinochle, a game requiring three players.

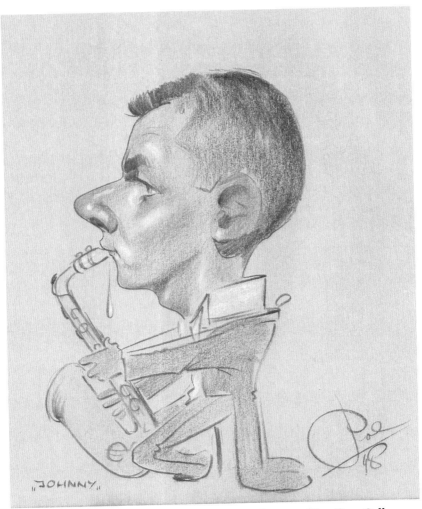

"Johnny," a caricature done while I was a freshman at Hamilton College.
(Byrne collection)

Jack Ryan and Don Parker, both army veterans, enjoyed playing pinochle, and I was the only other Chi Psi who knew anything about the game. They took me under their wings, and we played pinochle while other brothers played bridge or did nothing at all. I thought it was beneficial to have two seniors looking out for me, treating me mostly as an equal, at least serving as mentors, even though I saw them only around meal times.

The Chi Psi Lodge was my home for three years. I slept there, studied there, ate there, received mail there. I even worked there. As a freshman, I waited on tables. As a sophomore, I served as the fraternity's assistant treasurer. In my junior year, I was the treasurer. The treasurer and assistant treasurer were responsible for the business operation of the fraternity: issuing bills, paying bills, keeping the financial records. The financial system the fraternity used required me to learn double-entry bookkeeping. Learn it I did, and I learned something about the nature of people. Some brothers were prompt in paying their bills; others were always tardy, frequently with excuses as to why they were late—occasionally very late. I was learning that individuals viewed their responsibilities in very different ways.

We all took our meals in the dining room, those living in the lodge and those living elsewhere on campus. Breakfast and lunch were informal, but at dinner we were expected to wear coats and ties. Tony and Mary Erhard, our German cooks, selected the menu and prepared all our meals, sometimes traditional German food. Occasionally, Mary baked streusel kuchen (crumb cake). You were certain to get a piece if you wandered into the kitchen just after it came out of the oven, usually in midafternoon. The serving staff who worked in the kitchen became Tony and Mary's favorites. When I was a senior, I was often invited with a few others to the Erhards' apartment at the top level of the lodge to watch the Friday night boxing matches on their new television, the only set in the building.

Our social life was up to us, but the college administration tried to help by arranging exchange dances with the then all-women Cazenovia Junior College and Wells College. The first dances of the year were essentially mass blind dates. We didn't know the young ladies and they didn't know us. For some, them and us, the dances were mercifully brief, lasting only one evening; others found them too short and occasionally long-lasting relationships started.

House-party weekends were another effort by the administration to help us hone our social skills. There were three house parties each year: fall, winter, and spring. Our guests were housed in the lodge, which we evacuated for the occasion, the residents doubling up with members who lived in the dormitories. Chaperone couples were always included and stayed in the lodge for the duration of the party. Most of our guests were already friends, frequently from our hometowns. Sometimes those guests arranged blind dates for those who had failed to make our own dates. A blind date commitment for an entire weekend could be challenging, but occasionally it resulted in a positive experience. I experienced both. Success often depended on your attitude going into the weekend.

As I began my life at Hamilton, I thought of myself as being shy. I realized that I should make a conscious effort to become more outgoing. Oh,

I was a "nice guy," as a female acquaintance in high school had told me, but I didn't think I projected myself very much. I thought I needed to change, to become less shy. Stepping out of my shy persona was difficult. I thought a publicly visible activity might help, so I tried out for the cheerleading squad during spring of my freshman year and was selected. I was a cheerleader throughout my sophomore year. I must have done all right, because during my junior year I was elevated, if that's the right word, to head cheerleader. While I was in high school, I'd been impressed by West Point cheerleaders when I'd attended Army football games. I liked their style; precise, clipped, conservative. That was the style we tried to emulate under my leadership at Hamilton.

The big event of Hamilton's football season was the annual game against Union College. Usually there was a pregame bonfire at which the cheerleaders attempted to whip the Hamilton Continental supporters into a frenzy, calling for the annihilation of the Union College Dutchmen. We almost always found it necessary to redefine the words *frenzy* and *annihilation*, usually after the game. In any case, the efforts were designed to instill a spirit that would inevitably lead to a victory over the Dutchmen. No easy task, inasmuch as during my freshman year the Dutchmen defeated the Hamilton Continentals 66–24. As head cheerleader, I thought we needed to do something different to rouse Hamilton supporters, but what? My imagination failed me. The week before the game, I got a call from Gallie Crump, editor of the *Spectator*, Hamilton's student newspaper. He, too, felt we needed to do something different. Gallie had ideas that stimulated other ideas as we talked. Together we worked out a scheme that hadn't been used at Hamilton for some time: a torchlight parade starting in the Clinton town square in front of the Alexander Hamilton Inn and leading up the hill to the bonfire, everyone in pajamas, at least over warm clothes. The cheerleaders would lead the parade, the band would play, and we would have speeches by the coach and team leaders. The fraternities and other living groups would make the torches and turn out the students, and Gallie would create a big splash in the *Spectator*. At least Gallie and I whipped ourselves into a frenzy. We did it: enlisted our fraternity brothers, prepared torches, and lined up the cheerleaders, band, and speakers. The weather cooperated, and I led a parade of about two hundred pajama-clad marchers from downtown Clinton to the bonfire and the speeches. The parade was a success. We had done something different, and my "new personality" was beginning to develop. Never mind how the game turned out—the parade was a win. Gallie Crump and I were satisfied.

The social life was OK, but I was there to gain a college education and become a high school mathematics teacher. My advisor, the chairman of the physics department, laid out a curriculum for my freshman year: the required courses in English and public speaking plus courses in calculus, physics, economics, political science, education, and Spanish. The eye-openers for me were calculus and physics. I struggled mightily with those two courses and did OK in calculus and not so hot in physics. I can remember working all of most weekends on physics problems, and it wasn't until the second semester, when we got to the section on electricity, that I felt comfortable in physics. (Thank you, George Wulfing!) My average for all of the courses was probably a B-minus.

We learned to write as a result of rigorous training starting in our freshman year and were given many opportunities to speak in public. Hamilton maintained the unusual tradition of requiring all students to take courses in public speaking all four years. Thanks to Morris Ottman's seventh-grade requirement, I found the speech courses not too rigorous or intimidating. A one-hour class that met once a week meant speaking for about five minutes twice each semester. Each year a different type of speech was emphasized: freshman, general delivery; sophomore, motivational; junior, extemporaneous; senior, memorized oration. By our senior year, we were expected to be able to get the audience's attention, feel relaxed, motivate an audience, and talk on almost any topic at a moment's notice. A voluntary speech competition was held at the end of each year. I volunteered for the competition my junior year, when the competition was devoted to extemporaneous presentation. I figured I wouldn't need to prepare a talk ahead of time since I would be given a topic only a few minutes before speaking. Wrong! About a week before the event, I was given five topics, one of which would be selected by the judges the evening of the competition. Nuts! I prepared five different talks.

There were four or five of us competing. I suppose we were all a bit nervous. Five minutes before I was scheduled to speak, the head judge handed me an envelope with a single sheet of paper enclosed. The paper had one sentence: "Speak for five minutes on 'The Origin of the Planet Earth in Our Solar System.'" For a geology major, which I was by that time, this was a slow pitch over the middle of the plate. I nailed it! I took first place in the contest and won a book of my choice from the Hamilton College Bookstore.

In my sophomore year, my curriculum included solid analytic geometry and geology. Even though I was a math major at the time, I had a devil of a time with solid analytic geometry. The head of the math department called me into his office to counsel me. I was fortunate to pass, possibly with a C-minus or lower. On the other hand, I loved the course in physical geology. I didn't do particularly well in my other courses, and my grade average slipped to a C, or maybe even lower.

At some point during the second semester of my sophomore year, Winton Tolles, dean of Hamilton College, called me into his office to discuss my college career. We'd met before, when he was director of Forest Lake Camp, which I'd attended the summer I was nine years old. I remembered him; he didn't remember me. Dean Tolles pointed out that my lower grades were a red flag. At Hamilton, it was normal for grades to improve during the sophomore year, but mine had gone in the opposite direction. Why? Was I goofing off or what?

I explained that advanced calculus and solid analytic geometry were giving me grief, which was possibly affecting my other course grades, except for geology, which I found extremely interesting. The upshot of my conversation with Dean Tolles was that I changed my major from mathematics to geology.

In 1948, when I took my first geology course as a sophomore, the geology department consisted of two faculty members, Nelson C. "Rocky" Dale and Philip Oxley. Rocky Dale taught the physical geology, structural geology, mineralogy, and hard-rock courses. He had been a faculty member at Hamilton for a long time and was about to retire. Phil Oxley was working on his doctorate at Columbia University while teaching at Hamilton; he was responsible for historical geology and stratigraphy.

Dr. Dale's physical geology dealt with landforms and the processes that formed them. Some were landforms we could plainly see as we drove through the Mohawk Valley on our way home to Chappaqua. We students debated the origin of what we saw as we headed home for the semester break. It was all fun. I received my first A grade. Dr. Dale retired at the end of my junior year and was succeeded by Cecil J. Schneer, who taught mineralogy and hard-rock courses. Phil Oxley was named department chairman and shortly thereafter completed the requirements for his PhD.

Cecil Schneer and his wife, Mary, came to Hamilton and won over the geology majors. Schneer led informal Sunday-morning field trips followed by visits to his home, where Mary Schneer had apple pie waiting for us.

During the second semester, Phil Oxley taught historical geology. This course traced the evolution of the earth from the beginning of the solar system to the present day. It laid out the geological record from the

Precambrian, more than 500 million years ago, and how laymen and scientists had reasoned as they interpreted the nature of the rocks that formed the earth's crust. The course explained how the fossil record helped to define rocks of differing ages.

We took field trips to examine sedimentary rocks on the Hamilton campus and in the nearby Mohawk Valley and to collect the fossils, trilobites, eurypterids, and simple mollusks that were contained in those rocks. The advance and retreat of ancient seas that had laid down deposits of sediments, the subsidence of the crust as thousands of feet of sediments were received and piled up, and the subsequent uplifts that formed mountains—these were all new ideas for me. I found the geological story fascinating, but possibly of greater impact were the philosophical questions generated by the recognition of the age of the earth and the solar system and man's relative insignificance to the geological story.

The historical geology course was fascinating. I took detailed notes, adding color to some of my diagrams after leaving class. As I prepared for the final exam, I transferred my notes to a long sheet of butcher paper: a single diagram that started with the big bang theory on the origin of the universe on the left and proceeded geologic period by geologic period to the right, ending with the origin of man. I had translated the entire course to a single sheet of paper that stretched across much of the wall of the study room I shared with Charlie Doran. The course was a true eye-opener for me and accounted for my second A at Hamilton. After I switched my major, my grades improved markedly, and during my junior and senior years, I was making close to straight As. I learned later that the administration had cited me as an example of how important motivation can be in the evolution of a student.

Probably none of this would have happened if it hadn't been for those gnarly rocks with the "Indian footprints" next to our home in Chappaqua. Those Precambrian rocks within a hundred feet of our house opened doors for me that I didn't know existed. I doubt I would have taken any course in geology if we hadn't moved to Chappaqua when I was thirteen.

By the summer following my sophomore year, I knew I needed a chemistry course and decided I would get it out of the way during the summer. I took the train from Chappaqua to New York City five days a week to take an introductory chemistry course at Columbia University. I met some fine people, and I did well in the course. We used a chemistry text, *General Chemistry*, written by a young faculty member at the California

Institute of Technology named Linus Pauling, whom I came to know personally much later.

SUMMER FIELDWORK

HAMILTON COLLEGE didn't offer a summer field geology course, but Columbia offered one in conjunction with the University of Wyoming. Phil Oxley suggested I take the course, which was based west of Laramie, Wyoming. In the summer between my junior and senior years, I took the train from New York to Laramie, where I was met by several University of Wyoming students who were working as field assistants in the course.

We drove west thirty-five or forty miles to the geology base camp in the Snowy Range of the Medicine Bow Mountains. The base camp consisted of a series of log cabins and a lodge for dining. Even though it was late May, snowdrifts covered much of the area, including parts of some of the cabins. It was a spectacularly beautiful setting, but I couldn't see the mountains or indeed anything much because of the huge snowdrifts. Each cabin had several bunks and a wood stove for heat. It was cold when we awoke in the morning, but in minutes we had a roaring fire started by igniting kerosene-soaked sawdust.

The course was taught by faculty from the University of Wyoming and Columbia University. Professor Sam Knight, a legendary geologist and chairman of the geology department at Wyoming, was in charge. After spending the first week in base camp, we spent the next five weeks mapping geology in different locations in Wyoming.

Early Monday morning, tents, sleeping bags, and our personal gear were loaded into trucks, and we headed for that week's location. A team of University of Wyoming student assistants went with us to cook and maintain camp while we were out studying and mapping. We returned to the base camp in the Snowy Range on Friday in time to prepare reports on the geology we had just mapped.

Weekends were times for lectures and special events of a social nature. During the week, we sat around a campfire after dinner, often listening to Carl Yost, a student, sing western ballads. It was here that we heard for the first time "The Tennessee Waltz." It was a favorite for all of us, particularly when sung under moonlight in the vicinity of a campfire in Wyoming. I have often wondered if Carl Yost followed music or geology as a career. I thought he was a talented musician.

A weekend highlight was Sam Knight's review of the geologic history of the Rocky Mountains. He lectured with colored chalk in one hand and an eraser in the other and gave action to the history of the region. This was 1950, before computers and PowerPoint slides. After the field course, three of us toured national parks in the Wyoming-Colorado area from Mesa Verde National Park to the Grand Tetons. I was very much taken by the mountain west of the United States.

During my senior year at Hamilton, I was employed as a "trusty" of the geology department to help with the physical and historical geology laboratory sessions. I set up the labs, distributed materials, and collected and graded student papers. Partly as a result of this experience, I realized that sometime in the future I would like to teach geology at a college or university. Phil Oxley and Cecil Schneer told me I would need a doctorate and urged me to get ready. One of the requirements for the PhD would be a reading knowledge of two languages, traditionally French and German. I figured I could get by with my high school French, but I needed to learn some German. I enrolled in freshman German and discovered I enjoyed it.

With the help of professors Oxley and Schneer, I applied to geology graduate schools at Yale, Columbia, Penn State, and Caltech. I was accepted by all four. Caltech indicated I would need to take an undergraduate course in physical chemistry, but I was accepted anyway. Caltech's reputation as a science-oriented university was impressive, so I accepted that offer and was mentally preparing to head across the continent to Pasadena.

But another opportunity appeared. In February 1951, after one of the elementary geology labs, Phil Oxley asked to see me. He had received a letter from Norman Newell, a professor of paleontology at Columbia and the curator of invertebrate paleontology at the American Museum of Natural History in New York City. Newell noted that I had been accepted for graduate studies at Columbia and in his letter to Oxley asked if I might be interested in being a part of his project in the Bahamas and West Texas. The project entailed mapping the coral reef along the east coast of Andros Island in the Bahamas and comparing it to an ancient geologic reef in West Texas. Newell indicated that the newly created Office of Naval Research was interested in the part of the project involving the mapping of the coral reef based on aerial photographs. The ability to define reef conditions from aerial photos was important to the navy.

This was an enticing possibility. During spring break, I met Dr. Newell at the museum. He explained the project in some detail, the underwater work in the Bahamas and then the geologic mapping and collection of fossils in West Texas. Then he offered me a position on the project. I'd join the group in the Bahamas in June, shortly after graduating from Hamilton—if I accepted his offer.

Was I ready to trade the graduate program at highly regarded Caltech, to which I had already committed, for graduate school at Columbia with a trip to the Bahamas that might include a graduate thesis topic? I had to make a choice, one that could influence the rest of my career and, indeed, my life. I was torn.

CHAPTER 3

Columbia University (1951–1953)

"The present is the key to the past."
—Charles Lyell

THE MODEST HOTEL IN MIAMI was not far from a sportfishing pier. I was booked for one night on my way to the Bahamas.

The Bahamas are a group of seven hundred low-lying limestone islands east and southeast of Florida, separated from Florida by a deep channel through which the Gulf Stream flows. Andros Island, the largest of the Bahama islands, lies to the east of the channel and west of a deep area called the Tongue of the Ocean. I would be part of a team studying the coral reef between Andros Island and the Tongue of the Ocean.

On the west, Andros Island is separated from the channel off Florida by the Great Bahama Bank, a vast shallow-water area of fine-grained sediment. I planned to write my master's thesis about the sediments of the Great Bahama Bank, but for the next six weeks, my concentration would be on the reef along the eastern shore of Andros Island. It was the beginning of a new adventure.

As soon as I was registered at the hotel, I headed for the sportfishing pier. Knowing that much of the work in the Bahamas involved spending time underwater, mapping the distribution of corals where sharks and barracudas were present, I was eager to learn about sharks and barracudas. I was impressed by what I saw at the sportfishing pier. Sharks had taken large chunks of flesh out of the marlins that had been hooked; the barracuda had slashed the fish as if with a straight razor. My imagination took over. I would be in the water with those two predators much of the time we mapped the reef. Too late to retreat now; I had committed myself to Dr. Newell and Columbia University.

When I got off the plane in Nassau before noon the next day, I was greeted by Keith Rigby, one of Dr. Newell's senior graduate students and the leader of the second phase of the Bahamas–West Texas project. Dr. Newell had already spent six weeks in the Bahamas mapping the reef and had then gone on to West Texas, leaving Rigby in charge. Rigby was a competent, affable leader who never seemed to get flustered. He had a good sense of humor and laughed a lot, which helped to relieve tension when matters were not working the way they were intended.

Bob Adlington, Newell's assistant at the museum, had been a member of the first group in the Bahamas and stayed after Newell left in order to help the second group get started. We laughed at his account of the first group's initial entrance into shark-infested waters. Unfortunately, he provided no tips on how to survive, something that might have helped us psychologically.

Logistic support in the Bahamas was provided by the Pyfrom family. Ted Pyfrom operated two stores on Bay Street in Nassau. One store was geared to the tastes of tourists, the other to the needs of working-class Bahamians, mainly from the outer islands.[1]

Ted's forty-foot motor launch, *Half Crown*, served as our field home for six weeks, with Ted's seventeen-year-old son, Gene, as skipper. Our guide was a fifty-year-old Andros Bahamian named Bane. With intimate knowledge of the near-shore waters, Bane sat at the prow of the vessel and guided us away from coral heads and patch reefs. Bane was a descendant of slaves brought to the Bahamas during the seventeenth and eighteenth centuries. He had been a sponge fisherman until a disease eliminated the commercially valuable sponges in the area. Highly religious, he feared the creatures of legend, mermaids and chickcharnies.[2] He told us the chick-charnies, local mythical creatures that dwelled in the tops of trees, could take the form of small men about three feet tall or of white birds the same size. Both had burning eyes capable of paralyzing a mere mortal by making eye contact. Chickcharnies were believed to occupy the coastal area of Andros and were different in character north to south, mostly little men to the north and birds to the south. Mermaids were evil in Bane's imagination because they could lure the unwary into the deep waters of the "blue holes" and "ocean holes," never to be seen again.

Blue holes and ocean holes are real and are common in the Bahamas. They are deep caverns formed by erosion of the limestone during the last glacial age, when the sea level was lower. At depth, the holes are connected to the open ocean and respond to the rise and fall of the tide, acting as a fountain with water boiling out of them or as a drain with water sucked down into them. Both the draining and boiling actions are slightly out of phase with the tide at the surface. Ocean holes are similar to blue holes but occur as ponds on land.

Bane was also fearful of being in the water, lest he be attacked by barracuda. Before the six weeks elapsed, we managed to get Bane to wade in waters two or three feet deep. Another great accomplishment involved enticing Bane to row with me in our small dinghy over a blue hole at a time the water was boiling out of the hole. The boiling action created a dome of water four to six inches higher than the surrounding surface water, which made it difficult to row the dinghy directly over the hole. Our dinghy had a glass-bottomed box built into the floor of the boat for viewing the area underneath. With Bane on one oar and me on the other, we managed to row the dinghy over the blue hole, but Bane refused to look down into the depths where mermaids might be lurking. We saved our blue hole excursion for a Sunday, a religious day; Bane prayed and sang hymns continuously during the adventure. For Bane, the blue-hole trip was a major event, a display of his courage.

Once the *Half Crown* was provisioned, we motored across the Tongue of the Ocean to Andros Island and worked our way south along the eastern shore, mapping the reef as we went. We plotted the distribution of coral species on aerial photographs supplied by the navy. This entailed diving in the shallow water of the reef using a Browne diving system with air compressor, drawing sketches of the reef underwater, and taking underwater photographs with a 35-millimeter Leica camera in a heavy brass waterproof housing, mounted on a tripod. Two of us worked together on the bottom, one doing the sketching or photography, the other standing guard (or rather swimming guard) with a long spear to ward off curious sharks or barracuda. I always felt sharks were lurking just beyond the range of my vision.

Barracuda often followed us as we rowed our small dinghy to mapping sites; they never attacked. We were advised, if we saw a shark, to make a big fuss, blow bubbles out of our face masks, wave our arms, and move toward the beast—BUT not to do any of those things if we think the critter is a barracuda. We never had to do those things.

We tried to be precise in our observations, but our field operations were clumsy at best. We took samples of sediments and organisms to supplement our visual observations, and eventually, after refining the maps and analyzing the samples, we came to a reasonable understanding of the nature of this coral reef.

In 1951, the reef was healthy, with massive colonies of corals, sea fans, sea urchins, and other organisms. It was beautiful, and it inspired me to learn what I could about coral reefs, corals, coralline algae, and the relationships of individual organisms on the reef. I saw the same area again in 2003, fifty-two years later. The reef then consisted mainly of dead corals, few sea fans, and no sea urchins at all. If that had been my first view of the reef, I doubt I would have felt much enthusiasm for studying coral reefs. Could the activities of man be so destructive of nature in only half a century? Or was it a combination of man and a downturn in natural cycles that caused such a change? We were not thinking such thoughts in 1951.

After three weeks, we returned to Nassau for a few days' rest, then returned to the reef for the final three weeks of mapping. Every week, a Bahamian mail boat brought the *Half Crown* a standard list of groceries, mostly canned. The groceries were supplemented with coconuts, vegetables, and fruit when locally available and with fresh fish caught by Gene Pyfrom. As we neared the end of our six weeks along the reef, we felt obliged to consume the canned foods that had accumulated during the two phases of the project. We discovered that the first crew had not come close to consuming their weekly delivery of lima beans, leaving us with a more than ample supply. Because we were trying to finish off the leftovers, we received no groceries during our last week. Consequently, our sixth-week diet was almost exclusively lima beans and the fish that Gene caught. Growing up, I had detested lima beans, but somehow I managed to down them during that last week aboard the *Half Crown*. I still don't like them much.

The six weeks in the Bahamas was my first international trip. It was a learning experience beyond my expectations. I was introduced to two cultures, those of the British colonials and of the poor, uneducated descendants of the black slaves. I was learning to observe and appreciate the daily problems, situations, opportunities, and challenges facing people of other cultures. Within a year, I had the opportunity to compare the Bahamian culture, represented by people such as Bane, with another culture strongly related to the sea, the Polynesians of the central Pacific Ocean. My appreciation of the international world was beginning.

THE PERMIAN REEF OF WEST TEXAS[3]

By August, we had completed our research on the living reef off Andros and were ready to examine the Permian reefs in West Texas, reefs 250 million years older than the one we had just studied. We thanked the Pyfroms, said goodbye, our group disbanded, and Keith Rigby and I headed west to the Permian basin.

Our first stop was Houston, where we met with Dr. Harold N. Fisk of the Humble Oil and Refining Company. Dr. Newell had obtained partial funding for the project from Humble Oil, and Dr. Fisk, who headed Humble's geologic research section, was Newell's primary contact. We spent a day with Dr. Fisk, briefed him on the results of our Bahamas reef study, and then caught the train to Marfa, Texas, close to the Permian El Capitan reef. In Marfa, we rented a car and drove to Pine Springs, in the shadow of the Permian El Capitan reef, where we met Dr. Newell and other members of his team. We were here to examine the fossil structure of the reef and related features of the Permian basin. Unlike in the Bahamas, where coral formed the main structure of the reef, the Permian reef was an accumulation of various fossilized calcareous organisms cemented together to form a massive limestone structure.

Dr. Newell stayed with us a few days, then left for New York, and Rigby took over team leadership. We mapped small patch reefs of Permian limestone and collected fossils, the calcium of which had been replaced by silica. We collected blocks of limestone and shipped them back to Columbia University. There they were immersed in a bath of hydrochloric acid, which dissolved the limestone, leaving a residue of siliceous fossils. Our job in Texas was to identify and transport the blocks of fossiliferous limestone from their location in the field to a place where they could be shipped to Columbia. It must have been amusing to see us wrestling large blocks of limestone into backpacks, positioning ourselves into the straps of the backpack, rolling over to all fours, and then, with help, struggling to a standing position and staggering downhill to where our jeep waited. On one occasion, we found an old rubber tire and for fun managed to squeeze a large boulder of limestone into the tire and then send it downhill. We laughed at how the tire with enclosed rock bounced and rolled ever faster downhill. It was last seen on its way to Mexico.

The desert landscape in this part of Texas has its own beauty and its own brand of heat. At midday, the temperature climbed to well above a hundred degrees Fahrenheit. At noon on one occasion, we realized it was dangerous to be out in the heat, so we adjourned to a small roadside general store. When we entered the store, we felt cool and retrieved our jackets from the jeep. The proprietor stood behind the counter perspiring profusely. The thermometer behind him indicated the temperature inside was ninety-eight degrees.

The motel at Pine Springs had little to offer in the way of entertainment, but usually we were so exhausted that we went to bed shortly after dinner. This was not the case on Saturday evenings. Each Saturday evening, a different rancher in the area hosted a barbecue with live music, dancing, and other diversions. The other diversions were usually a bottle of bourbon being passed around to the men in the parking lot while the women talked or danced with each other in the ranch house room that served as a dance hall. We joined the men in the parking lot and made every attempt to be part of the action. Here was another culture to observe. The food at these affairs was always outstanding, with more beef than could possibly be consumed. The band played a unique form of music, and the dancers followed the beat, dancing the West Texas one-step. After about six weeks in West Texas, we headed northeast to New York City.

ON CAMPUS IN NEW YORK

I STARTED GRADUATE SCHOOL at Columbia in late September 1951. My summer work on the Bahamas and West Texas research project gave me a head start on my graduate student career. Dr. Newell had 250 sediment samples from the Great Bahama Bank and suggested I study them for my master's thesis. He was my major professor, so naturally, I agreed.

The Great Bahama Bank consists primarily of carbonate mud. I had seen the area but had never explored it. With Dr. Newell's samples, and knowing something of the geology of the Bahamas, I began my master's research a couple of weeks before classes started. I spent most of my time at the lab, where I cataloged sediment samples, but I managed to squeeze in a game at the Polo Grounds, home of the New York Giants. It was Giants against the Chicago Cubs as the Giants caught up with the Brooklyn Dodgers in the quest for the National League pennant. This was the year of Bobby Thompson's "shot heard 'round the world," the ninth-inning home run on October 3 that gave the Giants the pennant in the third playoff game with the Dodgers—an event I heard on the radio in the lab as I worked on the Bahamas sediments.

I knew I was studying at one of the outstanding geology departments in the United States. Walter Bucher, a structural geologist, was chairman of a department that included such notable geologists and geophysicists as Marshall Kay, Norman Newell, Arthur Strahler, Charles Behre Jr., Arie Poldervaart, Maurice Ewing, Joe Worzel, Larry Kulp, and Frank Press. I took graduate classes from all except Behre and Ewing.[4]

As graduate students in New York in the 1950s, we wore coats and ties to class. I had a room in John Jay Hall, the primary graduate student residence. John Jay Hall was conveniently located; it had its own cafeteria (for breakfast) and it was connected to Schermerhorn Hall, the headquarters of geology, by means of a series of heating tunnels and connecting rooms; you could walk from one to the other without going outside. That connection was important on a cold winter day.

My typical day started around six thirty in the morning. After showering, I had breakfast in the John Jay cafeteria, read the *New York Times* for about half an hour, and then headed to Schermerhorn Hall, where I shared an office with three other graduate students: John Ostrom, who later established himself as a leading vertebrate paleontologist at Yale, and Walter and Don Eckelmann, both Larry Kulp's geochemistry graduate students. The remainder of the day until dinner was taken up with classes, lab research, or writing.

Walter Bucher's structural geology course was offered at one o'clock, immediately after lunch. During his presentations, Bucher used lantern slides, and with the classroom lights turned off, sleep was a temptation, one to which a number of my colleagues succumbed. Somehow I managed to stay awake.

Arie Poldervaart's Friday-afternoon lectures in petrography were followed by a three-hour lab. By this time in the week, most of us were close to exhaustion and occasionally drifted off to sleep, either at the end of the lab session or after one or two beers in the Lion's Den afterward. Poldervaart also led memorable Sunday morning field trips down Fifth Avenue to see the various rocks used as facings on many of the storefronts: labradorite, anorthosite, orbicular diorite, gabbro, greenschist, and many more.

On Friday nights, after we had recovered from Poldervaart's lecture-labs, we could often be found in the West End Grill, a Runyonesque[5] bar on Broadway near Columbia. There we watched the Friday night fights on television, drank a beer or two, and munched on a boiled egg or a hamburger. A tomato on the burger cost extra—this was New York City in the 1950s.

At first, I didn't like New York. It was expensive, noisy, fast-paced, dirty, and confining. Yet as the year proceeded and a group of friends evolved among the geology graduate student population, several of us began to take advantage of the city's offerings. Hockey games at Madison Square Garden stand out, but perhaps the greatest thrill and eye-opener for me came at the old Metropolitan Opera House. I had never been to an opera until a fellow student suggested that we put together a triple date to see *La Boheme* by Puccini. Our seats were toward one side in the fourth or fifth balcony. The building was impressive, but the opera, starring Patrice Munsel, was magnificent. A couple of us were so taken by it that the next night we attended *Madame Butterfly* and stood in the standing-room area for the entire opera. *Madame Butterfly* is a long opera! Later that year, Bizet's *Carmen* with Risë Stevens was added to our portfolio. In addition, there were the Polo Grounds and Yankee Stadium, and Brooklyn's Ebbets Field was not far away. New York City wasn't such a bad place after all.

Sometime in late winter or early spring, Dr. Newell asked me to see him at the museum. He told me that the other graduate students who had been on his project in the Bahamas and West Texas were completing their degrees. Keith Rigby had almost finished and would be heading to a teaching position at Brigham Young University. Frank Stehli was also finishing his doctoral dissertation and wanted to devote full time to that. The same was true of Don Boyd, who would soon be heading to a teaching position at the University of Wyoming, where he ended up completing a distinguished career in geology.

I wondered what he was leading up to. Then he told me he had been asked to lead a multidisciplinary team to study the atoll Raroia, in the South Pacific, the atoll against which Thor Heyerdahl's balsa raft *Kon-Tiki* had been wrecked. The study would take two and a half to three months. Would I like to go with him as his assistant? Wow! Yes, of course I would like to go with him. I was honored to be considered for the position.

As Dr. Newell explained it, the team would include Max Doty, a botanist, and his assistant, Jan Newhouse, from the University of Hawaii; Bob Harry, an ichthyologist from the California Academy of Sciences; Joe Morrison, a zoologist from the Smithsonian; and Bengt Danielsson, an anthropologist from Sweden. Danielsson was the Swede who had sailed with Thor Heyerdahl and four other Norwegians on the *Kon-Tiki*[6] and then had spent a year and a half living on Raroia with his wife. Raroia was selected for the study because Danielsson was available to be part of the team.

I would be responsible for developing a bathymetric chart[7] of the lagoon, studying the sediments and helping Dr. Newell with a study of the reef. We would be out of contact with the outside world for up to ten weeks, except for minimal contact via a small, World War II–vintage radio transmitter. Any mail would be picked up and (possibly) delivered by a French administrative schooner three or four times while we were on Raroia. All of our scientific equipment and a supply of food were to be shipped from New York to Papeete, Tahiti.

For the next several weeks, I traveled frequently from Columbia to the American Museum of Natural History to help Bob Adlington pack the equipment we would need on Raroia. While at the museum, I viewed the sharks mounted in exhibits and was impressed by the size of their mouths and the profusion of teeth within those mouths. The sharks seemed much larger than the ones we saw in the Bahamas. In fact, the great white sharks in the museum were huge. I thought, Oh well, I might as well be prepared, at least mentally.

Shortly before we were scheduled to leave for Raroia, we learned that a shipping strike on the West Coast had tied up our equipment and supplies. Unless we could replace the equipment in Hawaii, we would be without much of what we needed at Raroia.

OFF TO THE SOUTH PACIFIC

THE TRIP FROM NEW YORK to Raroia was a long one, taking several days. We flew commercially, by Military Air Transport, and by Tasman Empire Airways Limited. After several days in Papeete, making final preparations for our stay on Raroia, we took a French administrative schooner to Raroia, a three-day voyage.

Valerie Newell, Dr. Newell's wife, served as our advance party, traveling alone and taking care of necessary administrative clearances in Tahiti. At the time, 1952, Tahiti was open only to visitors from France. Our National Research Council, which sponsored our research, had obtained permission from the French government for us to be there. In Fiji, we took a taxi along the coast from Nadi to Suva, stayed overnight in Suva, and then met the New Zealand airline that took us to Papeete with a refueling stop at Aitutaki in the Cook Islands. As we approached the Society Islands, the plane let down to a lower altitude so that a new co-pilot could be shown each of the islands on the way. The weather was clear and the opportunity to take photographs of Bora Bora, Moorea, and Tahiti was unsurpassed. After we landed in the lagoon at Papeete, small boats took us ashore. Mrs. Newell met us, and a taxi took us to Les Tropiques Hotel, a mile or so out of Papeete.

Unbelievable! We were in Tahiti, preceded by Paul Gauguin, the crew of the *Bounty*, and a relatively small number of others.

During our stop in Hawaii, we had managed to obtain some of the simple equipment we would need at Raroia, but not all of it. Once in Papeete, my high school French served us well. I was able to have a pipe dredge fabricated at a local machine shop by using my limited French to describe what we needed. After using it in the local shops during the day, I practiced my French in the evening—at the bar of Les Tropiques.

Soon after we arrived in Papeete, the senior members of our team— Newell, Doty, and Danielsson—flew by amphibian aircraft to Raroia, 450 miles from Tahiti, and took a series of photographs, from which they constructed a map of the atoll. Using identical cameras belonging to Jan Newhouse and me (Argus C3s), Doty and Danielsson took more than one hundred aerial photographs of the coral reef that formed the atoll, with sand-and-gravel islands atop the reef. We were told that while Danielsson was taking photos, Doty loaded the second camera with film, thereby making it possible to take continuously overlapping photos. Back in Papeete, the photos were developed, printed, and fastened to a large board in the overlapping order in which they were taken. A tracing on vellum of the overlapped photos served as a large master map of the atoll. We made multiple paper copies, which we used after we arrived at Raroia. It was the first map of Raroia ever made, and it was reasonably accurate.

Bengt Danielsson did not return to Tahiti with Newell and Doty but stayed in the village of Ngarumoa with its 125 Raroians to prepare for our arrival by schooner several days later. After his *Kon-Tiki* adventure, Danielsson had returned to Raroia with his wife to study the cultural anthropology of its people and to prepare his doctoral dissertation. He and his wife had lived on Raroia a year earlier and had been adopted by one of the Raroian families. The Raroians considered Danielsson to be part of their community family. While he awaited our arrival, he explained to the Raroians the purpose of our visit and arranged for their exceptional hospitality. The Raroians made several of their houses available to us, dug a new well to provide potable water, created an outhouse for us, and built a thatched building of palm fronds that would serve as our laboratory and office.

Meanwhile, in Papeete, we were winding up preparations for the trip to Raroia and seeing the sights. Moorea, a high island eleven miles northwest of Tahiti, was magnificent when viewed at sunset from Tahiti. We sampled the nightlife at Au Col Bleu and Quinn's Tahitian Hut in downtown Papeete. As our guide to Tahitian nightlife, we used James Michener's chapter on Tahiti in his book *Return to Paradise*, a sequel to his *Tales of the South Pacific*. During our nightly excursions, we were accepted by the locals and taught to do the Tahitian version of the hula, which we did with great enthusiasm. (These lessons served us well after we arrived at Raroia; to their delight, we were able to demonstrate to the young Raroians our knowledge of Tahitian culture.)

After a couple of days of preparation, we boarded the French administrative schooner for the three-day cruise to Raroia. We ate and slept on the open deck—at least originally. For our first meal, all were present, but as time passed and the roll of the ship took over, our team disappeared one by one to the comfort of bunks below deck. On our last evening out, I was the only remaining passenger above deck and the only member of the team not to succumb to the continual roll and pitch of the ship.

We sailed through the pass into Raroia's lagoon, and as we approached the Ngarumoa town wharf in rowboats, we were delighted to see Bengt Danielsson beaming at us as he doffed his straw hat, saying "*Iaorana*," the Polynesian word of greeting. We had arrived at what would be our home for the next two months.

Raroia is one of about seventy-five atolls and low islands that constitute the Tuamotu Archipelago. Elliptical in shape, Raroia is an atoll twenty-six miles long and eight miles wide. Unlike most of the other atolls of the archipelago, it is oriented northeast–southwest, essentially at a right angle to the trend of the archipelago. The surface expression (rim) of the coral reef that forms the atoll averages less than half a mile wide; several hundred sand and coral gravel islands atop the reef make up the land area, accounting for about a third of the rim area. The maximum height of the land surface is eighteen feet above sea level, although most of the small islands do not exceed ten or twelve feet in elevation. The lagoon, which has a maximum depth of slightly over 150 feet, is the location of about two thousand patch reefs, small reefs that rise from the floor of the lagoon. In 1952, most Raroians living on the atoll were in the village of Ngarumoa, and most of them had never been more than a quarter mile from the ocean or eighteen feet above sea level, unless they climbed a coconut palm.

After we unloaded our gear, Bengt gave us a short tour of the village, introduced us to the mayor, and showed us to our quarters. He had arranged for all of our meals to be served by three teenaged girls in a small building adjacent to the kitchen building. There were two radios in town on which one could occasionally (rarely) receive news from Tahiti. The owners of the radios were in competition for the prestige associated with radio ownership; each had a different means of generating the electricity necessary to operate the radios, one from a gasoline-motor generator, the other from a wind-driven generator. We never heard either radio make an understandable sound.

Each day our team gathered for breakfast and then met to lay out the scientific program for the day. Travel to other parts of the atoll was by outrigger canoes propelled by outboard motors. Projects included mapping the coral and the algal distributions of the reef flat and the patch reefs in the lagoon; collecting, identifying, and mapping the distributions of plants and animals in the water and on land; collecting fish and other organisms; measuring water depths along traverses in the lagoon in order to create a bathymetric chart; and studying the family lines and histories of the people living on Raroia.

We spent considerable time fabricating and testing crude measuring devices to serve in place of the equipment that had been held up by the shipping strike. Fortunately, the copies of the chart made from the aerial survey conducted prior to our arrival at Raroia made it possible to plot fairly accurately the locations of samples and observations and to create a chart of the lagoon.

I was assigned the task of developing the first-ever bathymetric chart—map of water depth—of the Raroia lagoon. As with many of our studies, this would not have been possible without the base map of the atoll developed before we arrived at Raroia. I needed two things to do the job: a device for measuring the water depth, and a navigational system by which I could determine with reasonable accuracy the location of my measurements. For the measuring instrument, I created a flat reel-like device out of wood that held one hundred or more meters of fishing line, to which a several-pound fishing weight was attached. The reel was carefully sized so that one complete rotation of the reel equaled one meter of line.

My navigational system relied on the chart that had been put together in Tahiti, a stopwatch for measuring the time under way between measurements, and an intelligent boat operator who knew the names of every small sand island on each side of the lagoon. All of the necessary requirements were available.

Before we set out, I laid out a penciled grid on the chart from known islands on one side of the lagoon to known islands on the opposite side. With my knowledgeable Raroian operating the outrigger canoe, we followed the grid back and forth across the lagoon. My boatman knew about how long it would take to cross without stopping. I divided that total time for each trip by the number of soundings I wanted to make, plus one travel segment to reach the shore after making the last sounding. This crude method permitted me to make a reasonably accurate bathymetric chart.

The maximum depths of the lagoon were fifty to fifty-five meters slightly downwind of the center of the lagoon. The map of Raroia made from the aerial survey prior to our arrival and my bathymetric chart of the lagoon were the first accurate descriptions of Raroia ever made. Several years after our study, measurements made by the US Fish and Wildlife Service using an echo-sounder corroborated the general accuracy of my chart. We had done reasonably well with our makeshift system.

I helped Dr. Newell map the distribution of coral species on the reef flat on the leeward side of the atoll, noting the underwater ridges and surge channels at the seaward extremities of the reef, the ridge of calcareous algae at the outer edge of the reef flat, the diminishing abundance of coral, and the change in coral species toward the beach. We saw blocks of coral the size of large automobiles that had been tossed up on the reef flat by storms. We noted the distribution of sea urchins on the reef flat and the changes in the form of *Porites porites,* a common reef-flat coral, as we approached shore. We saw the narrow grooves in the corals and clouds of coral dust made by parrotfish as they fed. The parrotfish contributed to the erosion of the reef flat as they fed, and so, too, did small snails as they scraped at the blue-green algae that covered the flat in some places. The corals of the reef flat were extremely sharp; over the course of a month or so, those sharp corals completely destroyed the rubber-soled shoes (sneakers) we wore. We were amazed by the ability of the Raroians to walk, even run, on the reef flat with no apparent pain or damage to the calluses on their bare feet.

On several occasions, we attempted to snorkel or dive in the surge channels at the ocean edge of the reef flat. One diver always remained at the surface to watch for sharks. In general, the sharks of the open ocean were much larger than those we encountered in the lagoon. Normally, the wave action in the surge channels was strong and our dives were tiring and of short duration. The bottoms of the surge channels were usually smooth and often had rounded boulders of coral that were rolled back and forth by wave action. Coral growth on the spurs or ridges between the surge channels was robust and healthy. Most of the diving we did, however, was at the abundant patch reefs in the lagoon. The best coral development on these patch reefs was generally on the windward side, where an overhang of coral was common, caused by the aggressive growth of corals in the direction from which waves were advancing. Coral gravel and sand were shed toward the back or leeward side of the patch reefs.

Unlike the rest of the atoll, more than two miles of reef at the south end of the atoll was devoid of sand-and-gravel islands. Dr. Newell and I examined that part of the reef flat, walking in water only two or three feet deep for a mile or so. We were a considerable distance from land when we realized that we were the objects of curiosity of twenty to thirty sand sharks, each between two and three feet long. The sharks, with the black tips of their dorsal fins showing, swam up to us and came within a couple of feet of where we stood on the flat. It was uncomfortable (understatement) to be among so many sharks so far from land. Fortunately, their curiosity was limited, and we were able to walk back to the nearest islet.

Breakfast and dinner were our primary relaxation times at which we shared with each other what we were learning about Raroia. The younger members of the team, Newhouse and Byrne, teased or flirted with the Polynesian girls who waited on us, complimenting or complaining about the meals. The coffee they served had little resemblance to the coffee we were used to in the States, probably because the beans were roasted in a frying pan. The young ladies came up with names for us—I was Tihoni. I don't know whether this was their version of Johnny or whether it was a name made up because I always addressed the girls as "honey." As the summer wore on, our team became more and more compatible, both with each other and with the Raroians.

On Sundays, we often played games with the Raroians, usually gringos versus natives. We taught them to play volleyball and our version of capture the flag. They were good at both, but sometimes susceptible to subterfuge. There was much laughter in spite of language differences. We learned a few Polynesian words; they, a few English words. In addition to *ioarana*, an all-purpose greeting, we learned other words and had short conversations using *maitai* (good) or *aita maitai* (no good). Inflections could turn a declarative use of *maitai* into a question and vice versa.

It was on Raroia that I had the best piece of fruit I've ever eaten. Outside our laboratory hut was a slender papaya tree with a single papaya on it, about eleven or twelve feet off the ground. When Dr. Newell and I first noticed it, it was a uniform green. As the summer wore on, it changed color to a yellow and then to a vibrant golden orange. We watched it ripen day by day. Finally, one day toward the middle of August, we looked at each other and knew our thoughts were the same. *This* was the day to harvest the papaya. Dr. Newell hoisted me on his shoulders. I reached up for the papaya and as I barely touched it, it nestled into my hand. It could not have been riper. We enjoyed it minutes later. Since that day in August 1952, the Raroia papaya has been my gold standard for all papayas.

I was probably the favorite of the Raroian kids. After my chores were complete, I played catch and other games with them. This bothered Dr. Newell, and he chided me for it, which took me aback; I wasn't accustomed to being criticized. He felt I should be looking for other tasks to do once my own duties had been satisfied. He was correct, I guess, but I felt that improving relations with our Raroian hosts was important, too. Besides, it was fun. But I took his chiding seriously, and I tried to make up for it the remainder of the time we were on Raroia.

I was twenty-four years old; I thought it would be interesting to fall in love with a Polynesian maiden, but there weren't any suitable young ladies available. The closest seemed to be one of the girls who served our meals. Terava, at sixteen, was the oldest of three sisters. Her younger sister, Tehie, was fourteen and truly pretty, and the youngest, Tahia, was twelve. Both Terava and Tahia looked like their mother, a handsome Polynesian woman of some substance. The mother was protective of all three girls and appeared concerned on occasion that those strangers from America might be mischievous with her daughters. Not to worry. Bengt Danielsson spoke their language and reported their concerns to us. We were careful not to erode the good feelings we and the Raroians had for each other. I never did fall in love with a Polynesian girl.

The economy of Raroia was based on copra, dried coconut meat. The Raroians had several copra stations around the atoll, where they gathered fallen coconuts, split them, and spread them out on a tarpaulin to dry. As the coconut meat dried, it shrank and separated from the hard shell. The shells were discarded and the coconut meat was turned over to dry more thoroughly. When it was dried to their satisfaction, the Raroians shoveled it into burlap sacks and stacked the sacks until the next copra schooner arrived. To me, the curing copra had an aroma similar to that of blue cheese. Toward the end of our stay, we had the opportunity to accompany the Raroians on a trip to a copra station at the southwest part of the atoll. We worked with the Raroians, ate together, and, following dinner, relaxed together. One of the Raroians had brought a guitar, and we sat around a campfire and watched the reflection of the setting sun on the lagoon as we listened to Polynesian songs. It was a magical moment. We admitted to each other that if we had seen this in a movie, we would agree that Hollywood had gone too far. It could never happen . . . but it did. We had an interesting conversation that night. One man, Etienne, had spent considerable time in Tahiti and spoke French as well as Tuamotuan. He would ask me a question in French, to which I attempted to reply in French. He then translated my answer into Tuamotuan, then the Raroians would ask him to ask me another question. In this way, we talked about things they wanted to know about: the United States, where we had come from, New York, Hollywood, and did we know Roi Roger (Roy Rogers) and Jayne Autry (Gene Autry)? They were big on cowboy movies. With the use of several languages, some pidgin English, and diagrams drawn in the sand, we had a wonderful exchange involving people of two different cultures with similar interests. It was a memorable evening for us and, we thought, for them.

As the time approached for us to leave Raroia, I shaved off my two-month-old beard and prepared our samples and equipment for shipment back to New York. When I shaved off the beard, my appearance changed significantly, and the girls who worked for us exclaimed, "*Nehi, nehi!*" (pretty). Oh well.

Jan Newhouse went with a few of the Raroians to Takume, the atoll to the north of Raroia, to do a quick study of the botany there. Max Doty tried to convince me to go to Takume as well, pointing out that I could do a quick survey of the geology of that small atoll and write a publishable paper about it. Because of the criticism I had received from Dr. Newell earlier in the summer, I told Max I couldn't go. It was my responsibility to pack the samples and equipment to be sent back to the American Museum in New York City. I devoted most of the following week to packing the equipment, glassware, and samples, using whatever packing materials I could find, including coconut husks. Later, I felt satisfied, very satisfied, when I learned that everything arrived back at the museum in good condition, without a single piece of broken glassware or damaged equipment. During our stop in Honolulu on our return, Ernestine Akers, an administrator of the Pacific Science Board that arranged for the project, told me that Dr. Newell held me in the highest esteem and was very proud of my performance. For me, that was worth missing the trip to Takume.

After several days of preparation, we were ready to leave Raroia and return to the United States. We were told that the giving of personal gifts at a time of separation was a Polynesian custom. All summer I had worn a blue polo shirt, so much so that I was identified closely with that shirt. I laundered and neatly folded the shirt and presented it to Terava. Her sisters were ecstatic; she was probably embarrassed.

As they did on most important occasions, the Raroians dressed up for our departure. The men wore their best clothes; the women made new dresses for the event, as they did for the Easter church service. Terava looked nice in the new dress she had made for the occasion. We said our goodbyes and made the usual promises of keeping in touch and someday coming back to Raroia. The Raroians looked sad as we climbed into the launches that took us to the administrative schooner waiting at anchor a short distance from the town wharf. They crowded onto the wharf and waved as we approached the schooner. We took our final pictures of them, then turned our backs and headed for Tahiti.

Mont Orohena loomed large as we approached Tahiti and sailed along the reef that separated the lagoon at Papeete from the open ocean. The Tahitians had long known how to identify the pass through the reef from the sea, day or night. Following their guides, we passed through the reef and proceeded to the municipal dock where the administrative schooner tied up.

After a few days in Tahiti tying up loose ends, we were off for home via Tasman Empire Airways Limited to Suva, Fiji, with an overnight emergency stop in Aitutaki for aircraft repairs. We took a few extra days in Nadi, Fiji, awaiting a Pan-American aircraft that had been diverted by a storm in the southwest Pacific. In Honolulu, we reported the results of our stay at Raroia to the management of the Pacific Science Board, said goodbye to Max Doty and Jan Newhouse, and boarded the flying boat of the Military Air Transport Service for the mainland. In San Francisco, Dr. Newell and I said goodbye to Bengt, Bob, and Joe. We made the usual promises of staying in touch, but other than Max Doty and Norman Newell, I have never been in touch with any of them since that wonderful summer at Raroia. Bengt Danielsson later sent me *The Happy*

Island, the published account of his and his wife's eighteen months on Raroia, translated from the Swedish. It is inscribed, "To John, from his Raroian friend, Bengt." I treasure that volume.

BACK AT COLUMBIA

BACK ON CAMPUS, Raroia was very much with me. My room in John Jay Hall was decorated with memorabilia collected in Tahiti. Nautical charts of the South Pacific adorned the walls, and books about Polynesia and other stories of island life were neatly arranged. My attitudes on a number of things had been expanded. After that trip, I ate in Japanese restaurants, practicing my newly acquired skill with chopsticks. I had purchased records of authentic Polynesian music while in Tahiti and listened to them often. I daydreamed about my summer in the South Seas, but I was at peace with my life in New York City as I settled in to complete my master's thesis on the sediments of the Great Bahamas Bank.

The summer with Dr. Newell and the traveling and mixing with other cultures had helped me to feel more confident about myself, more seasoned. He and I talked about my geological interests and discussed the possibilities for me at Columbia and elsewhere. Columbia's Lamont Geological Observatory, on the Hudson River north of New York City, was coming into its own as a major oceanographic institution under Maurice Ewing's leadership; an affiliation with it would certainly be a possibility for me. On the other hand, Lamont was essentially a deep-water, blue-water operation, and my interests were focused on shallow water and the sediments deposited therein. Dr. Newell suggested I might benefit from studying with a geologist named K. O. Emery at the University of Southern California. I said, let's explore that possibility. Newell called Emery, and Emery said he would be pleased to have any student recommended by Dr. Newell. The plan Dr. Newell and I developed was for me to head to Los Angeles at the end of the fall semester, assuming I had completed my master's thesis by then.

There was still much research to be done on the sediment samples from the Bahamas. Fortunately, Keith Rigby was still around and was particularly helpful, not only in providing general guidance concerning the ways of writing graduate theses, but also in the actual analysis of the sediments. During the Christmas break, Keith and I worked with Karl

Turekian, a geochemistry graduate student, making spectrographic analyses of a number of the sediment samples—both of us learning about spectrographic analyses and also about Armenian food. Karl always brought a lunch from home, which he occasionally shared with us. Karl went on to a successful extended career on the geology faculty at Yale, and Keith had a long and successful paleontological and geologic career at Brigham Young University.

The Bahamas project was still on the front burner as Dr. Newell, Keith, and I continued our research. The financial supporters of that project maintained an active interest in the Bahamas part of the study and also in the Permian Basin part. As it turned out, my contact with Dr. Fisk of the Humble Oil and Refining Company's Geologic Research Section would prove very important to me later.

During the fall semester at Columbia, I presented a successful seminar on the geology of Raroia to the geology students and faculty. I also came to an agreement with Dr. Newell that I would study the Raroia sediment samples and write a short report on them after I arrived at USC. Dr. Newell included my report in his overall review of the geology of Raroia, later published by the American Museum of Natural History.[8] I completed my master's thesis, "The Sediments of the Great Bahamas Bank," by the end of the semester, in time to drive west with my father before the beginning of the spring semester at the University of Southern California. My goals were to obtain the PhD and find a wife—but possibly not in that order.

CHAPTER 4

The University of Southern California (1953–1957)

A wife and a PhD

THE DRIVE TO LOS ANGELES was a windows-down excursion through much of the southern United States, and my left arm was a healthy tan by the time my father and I arrived. We were compatible, we saw a part of the country that neither of us had seen before, and we generally felt good about our trip together.

Once I was settled in a dormitory at the University of Southern California and my father had returned to New York, I paid a courtesy call to Dr. Emery in preparation for the usual signing in for classes. He invited me to join him and Professor Richard Merriam on a short coastal field trip to Palos Verdes on the following Sunday morning. I found both Emery and Merriam to be congenial. It was a good introduction to my time at USC.

Dick Merriam specialized in petrography and mineralogy. I didn't take any of the courses he offered, so the field trip was one of the few opportunities I had to become acquainted with him. Kenneth Orris Emery had studied at the University of Illinois with Francis Shepard and subsequently followed Shepard to the Scripps Institution of Oceanography. At Scripps, Shepard developed one of the first programs in marine geology in the United States and is generally considered to be the father of American marine geology. After obtaining his doctorate under Shepard, Emery took a professorial position at USC, where he developed a lengthy bibliography of papers in marine geology and sedimentation and became well known for his studies of the marine geology off southern California. He once admitted to me that his major form of recreation was writing scientific papers. He preferred to be called K.O. and was pleased when one of his colleagues said, "K.O., you're OK!" He was a significant member of the world's first generation of marine geologists.

Possibly as a result of growing up during the Depression, K.O. was thrifty. To save water at his Palos Verdes home, he landscaped his yard with xerophytes, desert plants. It was reported that, to wash dishes, he and his wife, Kay, drew hot water in the bathroom and carried it into the kitchen because the bathroom was closer to the water heater than the kitchen tap. After the dishes were washed, the water was used to irrigate the plants outside the house. But he was generous with his students. He occasionally invited students to his home for a poker party at which he served expensive snacks—fried or chocolate-covered grasshoppers. He was generous with his time also, sharing visiting scientists with his students, and he was easy to be with.

The first semester at USC was a learning experience for me in many ways. Los Angeles smog made an impression, but the first clear day made an even greater one. On that day, I discovered the striking view of the mountains that border L.A. The city's relaxed culture was very different from that of New York City, and it took me a while to adjust. Based on my New York/Columbia background, I wore a sport coat and tie to the first afternoon social event I attended, only to discover that sport shirts were the dress code. The next time I wore my new sport shirt, only to discover that sport coats and ties were the standard for that gathering. I never did figure out the dress code, so I wore a conservative sport shirt and kept a sport coat in the car. By surreptitiously surveying early arrivals, I could determine the dress expected for the occasion and adjust accordingly.

Dr. Emery's marine geology and sedimentation classes and lab were held in the Allan Hancock Foundation building, the locus for virtually all marine sciences on the USC campus. Captain G. Allan Hancock, owner of the Rancho La Brea Oil Company, was one of Los Angeles's prominent civic leaders and philanthropists. He maintained an unlimited commercial airplane pilot's license and unlimited master's papers for serving as captain of any ship. At one time he owned much of Wilshire Boulevard west of downtown L.A., including the famed La Brea Tar Pits. In addition to the building, Captain Hancock provided USC with the research vessel *Velero IV*. He was an accomplished musician, often playing cello with the Los Angeles Symphony Orchestra or chamber music with friends, whom he often took with him aboard the *Velero IV* when he captained the vessel on research cruises.

I took my first cruise aboard Captain Hancock's *Velero IV* during the spring of my first year at USC. We cruised to the Santa Barbara basin off southern California, where we were introduced to standard oceanographic techniques. We established hydrographic stations, collected water samples, measured temperatures at various depths, collected sediment samples, and made biological collections by plankton net and bottom trawl. The research techniques were similar to those of any oceanographic research vessel of that time. What happened after the ship anchored at five o'clock was, I'm sure, not standard, especially when Captain Hancock was in command. We showered, dressed for dinner (coats and ties), and assembled in the lounge for a glass of sherry and chamber music by the captain and his small group of musicians. Then we were served a gourmet dinner that culminated with baked Alaska, the first I had ever had. Captain Hancock was seventy-eight years old when he commanded that cruise.

Dr. Emery served as major professor for a half-dozen graduate students, most working on a doctorate. Emery's graduate students developed into a particularly compatible group that remained in contact long after leaving USC. Several of his students played significant roles in my professional and personal life.

I shared an office in the Hancock building with Donn S. Gorsline, another of Emery's students. Gorse, as we called him, was a graduate of the Montana School of Mines and a former naval officer. Gorse became a lifelong friend whom my wife, Shirley, and I later regarded as a member of the Byrne family. He had grown up in Los Angeles and still lived in his family's nineteenth-century home not far from the USC campus. He had a mischievous sense of humor and engaged with me in wild conversations. Bonnie Smith, the geology department secretary, said talking with Gorsline and Byrne was like walking through a field of mush. We probably rose to the occasion when we talked with her.

After I had been at USC several months, I was fortunate to acquire an assistantship as a lab instructor for the beginning undergraduate course in general geology. There were several of us, and we reported to Dick Stone, the senior graduate student in the department. "Stoner" was older, a World War II veteran, about six feet tall and slightly portly. He almost always had a cigarette dangling from his mouth. He was affable and a favorite of undergraduate students, particularly the young ladies. His small office in the temporary World War II building that served as the teaching lab for the introductory courses became the off-hours gathering place for a number of graduate students, notably Gorsline, Don Fissell, Bruce Fleury, and me as a core, with others drifting in from time to time.

Don Fissell was a teaching assistant we called "the Big Bear," an appellation he achieved as a result of referring to the students in his labs as "little bears." He and his wife, Rose, were part of our social group. Bruce Fleury became part of the group first as an undergraduate and then as a graduate student. He took particular delight in engaging Stone in arguments about the relative strengths of West Coast and Big Ten football. He knew his way around Los Angeles and spent much of his free time at one or another of the race tracks. To complete the group, I must add Elazar Uchupi and Joanna Resig. Uchupi, whom we called Al, was a short, pudgy, sweatshirt-wearing Basque from Brooklyn. We never understood what attracted him to USC, so far from his folks and their Basque restaurant in Brooklyn. He was well liked by all. After obtaining his degree, he accompanied Dr. Emery to the Woods Hole Oceanographic Institution, where he built an eminent career and was a favorite of the students there. Although Joanna Resig didn't hang out with the rest of us in Stone's office, she was a favorite of the group. One of Professor Orville Bandy's micropaleontology graduate students, she obtained her doctorate at the German oceanography center at Kiel and completed a long career in oceanography at the University of Hawaii.

For my dissertation, Dr. Emery, whom we all came to call K.O., suggested I study the sediments of the Gulf of California, which at the time was thought to be developing as a modern geosyncline. Geosynclines were defined as linear troughs of subsidence of the earth's crust in which huge amounts of sediment accumulated, turned into rock, then were uplifted to form mountains. The geosynclinal theory was used during the nineteenth and first half of the twentieth centuries to explain linear mountain chains of sedimentary rocks.

K.O. recommended I analyze sediment samples collected by the Scripps Institution, and he arranged for me to have access to the samples. The topic was acceptable to me, in part because at Columbia I had taken courses from Marshall Kay, the acknowledged world expert on geosynclines. It was mid-1953, more than a decade before the development of the theory of plate tectonics, which replaced the concept of geosynclines in the 1960s and 1970s.

I was under way on my quest for the doctorate, but I still felt socially deprived. As compensation for the lack of female companionship, I frequently attended athletic events in Los Angeles, prizefighting at

Hollywood Legion Hall, Hollywood Stars and Los Angeles Angels minor-league baseball, track and field in the Los Angeles Coliseum, and USC basketball and baseball games. In a chemistry course I was auditing, I met an undergraduate who became a friend and introduced me to the sorority system at USC. I was not impressed by her sorority sisters. No help there.

At the end of the spring semester, I moved out of the dormitory and into a small apartment several blocks north of the USC campus. Early every weekday morning, I drove to campus and parked my 1949 Chevrolet close to the Hancock Building. There I sat and read a newspaper until the student union cafeteria opened for breakfast. As I waited, I was able to observe the young women walking from the Town and Gown women's dormitory to the cafeteria. For several days in a row, I noted an attractive, slim, blonde girl wearing a tight brown skirt, white buck shoes, and bobby socks. Her hair was cut short in a style often referred to as a "duck butt," or perhaps more graciously as a "duck tail." Subsequently I noticed her in the cafeteria and other places around campus. On one occasion, I pointed her out to a couple of my friends, including Bruce Fleury.

Several days later, Gorsline, Fissell, Fleury, and I were eating lunch in the Grill, a lunch spot in the student union, sitting in a booth near the entrance. The young lady I just mentioned walked past the booth. Fleury, who was seated next to me, nudged me and asked if that was her, the girl I had pointed out earlier. I said it was. He said, "I dare you to meet her." By this time, she had ordered her meal and had picked a table farther into the dining room.

Well, a dare is a dare, so I got up and walked to her table. Standing in front of her, I said, "I can't think of any subtle way of meeting you. Do you mind if I try a direct approach?" She offered me a seat, and as is often said, "The rest is history." Her name was Shirley O'Connor; she had just graduated from Whittier College and was at USC to work on a graduate degree in music; she was staying at Town and Gown; she planned to teach fourth grade at a school in Long Beach in the fall. I told her about me. I drew geologic diagrams on napkins. We talked for more than an hour.

Shirley O'Connor, an only child, had grown up in Bell, California, now part of Los Angeles. She was adventurous, interested in doing different things, as sassy as I was, and smart, too. She was a petite, attractive, blue-eyed blonde. I tumbled hard.

Shirley continued to teach fourth grade and work on her master's degree. I taught Geology 101 labs. I studied for and took my doctoral preliminary exams and prepared for a summer assistantship at geology field camp. During all of this, Shirley and I dated. We went to the beach together, listened to West Coast Dixieland jazz, and enjoyed getting to know each other. She introduced me to her cousin Pat and Pat's husband, Jerry, and their kids, Terrie and Mike. The kids and I had a lot of fun together, playing croquet and softball and generally horsing around. I used to kid Pat and Jerry that someday they would be stopped at a railroad crossing while a long train of tank cars went by proclaiming "Byrne Oil," "Byrne Oil," "Byrne Oil." It never happened.

Shirley and I dated for the better part of a year. In May 1954, we agreed we wanted to spend our lives together and set a wedding date for Thanksgiving weekend of 1954.

GEOLOGY FIELD CAMP

SOMETIME EARLY IN 1954, Tom Clements, chairman of the geology department, asked if I would be interested in helping Professor John Mann conduct the summer USC geology field camp near Ely, Nevada. The job entailed trips into the field helping students with their mapping and then evaluating their geology reports at the end of the season. I told Dr. Clements I would be very interested. John Mann was a young professor whose specialty was groundwater geology. I hadn't taken any of his courses, but it was an opportunity to get to know him, and there was a modest, but important, stipend that came with the assistantship.

The six-week camp was headquartered in a farmhouse west of Ely, which was noted for the Ruth Pit, a large open-pit mine from which low-grade copper ore was extracted. Some students brought tents, others elected to sleep under the stars. The students were paired up for the geologic mapping of assigned areas and writing of a report. Dr. Mann and I accompanied students into the field each day to advise on the mapping and answer any questions. Rotating pairs of students were assigned camp duty each day: preparing breakfast, making sandwiches, cleaning camp, filling the shower tank with water, and preparing the evening meal. Field trips to the Ruth Pit and the smelter where the ore was reduced to pure copper were also part of the educational agenda.

On Saturday evenings, the students had free time to visit Ely for Saturday night dinner, movies, or gambling. On Sundays, we visited ghost towns in the area and toured the nineteenth-century beehive ovens in which charcoal had been made to fire the original smelter.

During the last couple of days of camp, Dr. Mann and I retired to a motel in Ely to evaluate and grade the students' geology reports. Over dinner in an Ely restaurant, Mann asked me about my career goals. I told him I wanted to teach, eventually become a college president, and receive an honorary degree from some institution. He quizzed me further. I told him I truly enjoyed teaching the Geology 101 labs and thought I was reasonably good at it. I thought by being a college president I could help others become more effective as teachers, and I could help set the direction of higher education. The honorary degree would be evidence that others thought I had achieved something worthwhile during my career. The answers seemed to satisfy him. He raised his wine glass and said, "Worthy goals, Byrne. Let's drink to them." We became good friends and remained so for the rest of his life.

A day or so later, we returned to camp, distributed the reports with comments, packed up the camp, and headed back to Los Angeles. I was longing to see Shirley, so I drove all night.

NEWLYWEDS

SHIRLEY AND I WERE MARRIED in a small Presbyterian church in Montebello, California, on the day after Thanksgiving, November 26, 1954. Our guests were family, friends, Shirley's colleagues, some of her fourth-grade students, and my graduate-student friends. Dick Stone was my best man, and Donn Gorsline and Don Fissell were ushers. I had bought matching neckties for the three men and asked them to wear blue suits, if they had them, or blue blazers. The neckties were the "uniform" for the occasion. As I recall, they were conservative blue-striped ties. Gorsline showed up wearing a garish spotted necktie. It was his idea of a joke. He got the reaction from me that he was after and then changed to the tie I had given him. It was vintage Gorsline. The reception was a home-done affair at Shirley's cousin Pat's home. Afterward Shirley and I headed to the Miramar Resort in Santa Barbara, stopping at a nice inn in Hollywood on the way. We had a pleasant two-day honeymoon in Santa Barbara, visited the Scandinavian village of Solvang, and headed back home on Monday so that Shirley could teach on Tuesday.

We rented a small furnished apartment in Southgate, a suburb of Los Angeles halfway between Long Beach, where Shirley taught, and USC. Our bedroom was on an alley, and when the garbage collectors came by

The bride and groom, November 26, 1954. (Byrne collection)

on their rounds, it sounded as if they were in the bedroom with us. We had two cars at the time: a 1949 Chevy and a 1951 Chevy, total value about $200. After breakfast each day, we each left about the same time, headed in opposite directions.

We added to the furnishings in our apartment, but not too much, with a piano, a so-called portable (it was very heavy) black-and-white television set, and a high-fidelity phonograph player. The hi-fi speakers were first class; the amplifier-tuner was a Heathkit that I built in the evenings after returning from USC. The piano was an early 1900 Steinway upright owned by Shirley's mother; it must have weighed at least seven hundred pounds. We had one pet, a small parakeet that someone at Shirley's school had given to her. After hours of lessons from Shirley, Tweety-bird (yes, that's what we called it) became bilingual, with a vocabulary that included *"Buenos días,"* "Happy Birthday, John," "I love you," and a few other words. When we tried to show off the bird's vocabulary to friends, the bird remained silent. If we had a party with lots of people conversing, the bird sat in the corner jabbering to itself and running through its entire vocabulary.

As newlyweds and not very accomplished cooks, we had a lot to learn: how to read a recipe, how long to cook a roast, how big a rib roast should be if you want it to be a "standing" roast, how to make gravy. Our first attempt at a standing rib roast involved a slab of beef that was too thin to stand on its own, so we created a leaning rib roast by impaling the beef with a corkscrew so that it could be cooked on all sides. Our first attempt at gravy also revealed how little we knew. The gravy was very tasty but had the consistency of well-cooked oatmeal. And we learned that when the recipe calls for so many minutes for roasting chicken or turkey, it means minutes per pound, not the length of time for the entire bird.

One night we hosted a dinner and invited Donn Gorsline and Professor Hiroshi Niino of the Tokyo School of Fisheries, who had come to USC to learn from K. O. Emery. Over dinner, our conversation turned to a comparison of American universities and Japanese colleges, including some of the cultural aspects of each. We talked about athletic teams, mascots, cheers, and fight songs.

Niino asked if he could demonstrate a Japanese tradition. Of course. He went back into the bedroom; we waited. Without warning, Niino came flying into the living room, fists clenched, with a shout of "hayaaaa!" He was stripped to the waist and barefoot, pants rolled up to his knees, and his necktie tied around his forehead. He burst into a song/shout in Japanese while gesturing vigorously with his entire body. Without understanding what we were witnessing, we applauded. He explained that we had just seen the fight song and dance of the Tokyo School of Fisheries. The evening was a small and wonderful example of how people of two cultures could share with each other, without pretense, when they were comfortable with each other. Sometime later, Niino reciprocated our hospitality by hosting a number of the graduate students to an authentic Japanese meal in a restaurant in Los Angeles, followed by a Japanese movie.

I enjoyed teaching the geology laboratories and frequently did extra preparation for them, making models of geologic structures from children's modeling clay, looking up interesting history and facts about the areas selected for topographical map studies, and preparing exercises that demonstrated the principles of contouring or drawing geologic cross-sections from which simple geologic histories could be worked out. I loved the teaching and the students. However, I didn't forget that my remaining primary objective at USC was to get the PhD. I had already found a wife.

I passed the preliminary exams for my doctorate, along with the two required language exams in French and German, and focused on my dissertation research on the marine geology of the Gulf of California, also known as the Sea of Cortez. I had already done most of the analyses on the Gulf sediments. When I was ready to start writing, I disappeared for two weeks. My folks wanted to see Bryce and Zion parks and the Grand Canyon with me and their new daughter-in-law. I told Dr. Emery I would be away for a couple of weeks on family business, which it was, sort of. We saw the parks, rode mules down into Grand Canyon, and Shirley hit a jackpot on a "one-armed bandit" in Las Vegas. The trip strengthened family ties and provided me with a valuable break before diving into the final preparation of *The Marine Geology of the Gulf of California*.

I had a general idea of what I wanted to include: a detailed description of the sediments, the nature of the trough in which they were deposited, and the oceanographic conditions in the Gulf. I still needed background information about the geology of the surrounding area, including the kinds of rocks, the geologic structure, the drainage into the Gulf—all the things that affected the geology of the Gulf and the marine sediments. I wanted to relate the Gulf to similar features in the geologic record and make a few predictions about what would happen to the Gulf as it filled with sediments some millions of years into the future. I calculated it would take me three to four months to write the dissertation, including preparing the illustrations critical to telling the geologic story.

As I wrote, I encountered a few gaps that needed to be filled and new questions that needed to be addressed, including earthquakes in and around the Gulf. There was no better place to obtain answers to earthquake questions than the California Institute of Technology in Pasadena. The two recognized world experts on earthquakes, Charles Richter and Beno Gutenberg,[1] were there. They were the scientists who, in 1935, developed a scale for measuring the magnitude or strength of earthquakes—the Richter scale.

I made an appointment and drove to Caltech. Richter, tall with a bushy head of hair, received me affably, and we had the conversation I had hoped we would have; I could now fill in the gap in the earthquake part of my dissertation. To me, just being with Richter was impressive.

But there was more. As we were finishing our conversation, I heard a loud ringing of a bell, like a fire alarm. Richter jumped up and said, "Come on. We have an earthquake." He led me to a large globe, perhaps three feet in diameter, to which was attached a long measuring tape divided into seconds. The tape was attached to the globe at the location of Pasadena. Next to the globe was the recorder for the Cal Tech seismometer. The area around the globe was filling up rapidly with staff, graduate students, and scientists, including a short, bald man who proved to be Beno Gutenberg. Wow! I thought: Gutenberg and Richter together responding to an earthquake.

All eyes were fixed on the seismic recorder. The original alarm had gone off when the primary push-pull (P) wave from an earthquake had arrived at the seismometer. We were now waiting for the secondary or surface (S) wave to arrive. From the time between the arrival of the primary wave and the arrival of the secondary wave, the distance from the earthquake to the seismometer can be determined. The globe's tape had been laid out to measure the distance to any earthquake in seconds.

After several seconds, the secondary wave arrived. Richter grabbed the tape and began swinging it in an arc around the spot where it was attached to the globe, Pasadena. The arc intersected the deep-sea trenches along South America, the trench off Japan, and the trench near the Tonga Islands—three locations where significant earthquakes were common. Gutenberg and Richter began guessing where the earthquake had most likely occurred. They couldn't say for sure until they received information from two other seismic stations because measurements from three stations are needed to pinpoint a quake's precise location. Later I learned that this earthquake had occurred under the Tonga Trench and that it had a magnitude of more than six on the Richter scale. I had indeed been fortunate to be in Richter's office at that very moment. I got the information I needed for my dissertation, and I witnessed two giants of seismology in action—a memory for a lifetime.

I was ready to start writing when Dr. Clements called me to his office. He said he was going on a sabbatical leave and wondered if I would like to use his office in the Hancock building while he was away. I readily accepted. It seemed I was living a charmed life.

My plan was to write sections of the dissertation on weekdays and prepare the final illustrations on Saturdays. Some weeks I altered the plan and prepared the maps or graphs first, in order to write about what the graph or map showed. My plan, which I followed closely, included typing the first draft, then editing and retyping. I always took the latest draft home with me and guarded it carefully. There were no copies.

The writing and drafting of illustrations each day was intense, so in the evenings I tried to do something different as a diversion. It was always relaxing to get home to Shirley. After dinner, she would practice the piano, and I would put together models of ships and airplanes. I felt refreshed when I started the next day, and I managed to stay on schedule. But the intensity of activity finally got to me, and as I approached the end of the dissertation draft, I suffered severe stomach pains. I turned to Owner Barker, the only doctor I knew, who put me on a rigorous low-cholesterol diet. That did the trick, and I finished writing in good health.

In its final form, the dissertation was 298 pages long, with fifteen tables, forty-six figures, and 104 references. I delivered the final draft to my committee for comment, and it was well received by all. I was particularly pleased by the response of Dr. Clements, who had a reputation for holding dissertations and theses for prolonged periods. He returned mine with substantive comments in less than a week. A scientific paper on the sediments of the Gulf, coauthored by K. O. Emery and me, was published in the *Bulletin of the Geological Society of America* a few years later.

For most of this time, I was receiving financial support from the Humble Oil and Refining Company. My connection with Humble had started while I was in the Bahamas. Dr. Newell had gained financial support from Humble, possibly through Harold N. Fisk. I'd met Dr. Fisk briefly while in the field in the Bahamas and then again when Keith Rigby and I stopped in Houston to brief him on the results of our work. Because of this support, I hoped I might work for Humble after I completed the degree. It turned out that Dr. Fisk had assumed so, too. I made a trip to Houston to confirm employment with Humble. At that time, I reviewed my dissertation results with Dr. Fisk and showed him my illustrations. I told him I thought I would like to work for him and Humble for three to five years, and then I would like to find a teaching job, that I had my heart set on being a teacher at some time in the future. He said that was fine. He had been a teacher, and he understood why I wanted to do that. He seemed pleased and indicated he and his associates were looking forward to my joining them. It was a pleasure and a relief to have a job waiting for me after I got my degree. I really did have a charmed life.

In early 1957, Shirley told me she was pregnant. We anticipated the baby would be born shortly after we arrived in Houston. I stood for the final defense of the dissertation. Then Shirley and I were ready to pack up and leave for our next adventure in Houston. It was May 1957, and we were starting a new life. I had my degree, I had a job, and we would soon have a family. Houston was new to us, but we thought we were ready, taking one challenge at a time. I loved my wife, I looked forward to my new career, and I felt enormously fortunate.

CHAPTER 5

The Humble Oil and Refining Company (1957–1960)

The oil patch

WHEN WE ARRIVED IN HOUSTON, because of Shirley's pregnancy, we felt pressure to find a place to live and buy a car. We had sold our two Chevrolets in Los Angeles for a total of $200 and had in mind buying a small sedan. An MG Magnette (sedan) used by a dealer as a demonstrator was a great find. It had a stick-shift transmission and a mahogany dashboard, and it was affordable.

The apartment we found looked great in the late afternoon, but in the next day's morning light it didn't look so good. In fact, it looked terrible. It was on the ground floor, and cockroaches found it easy to enter. Window-unit air conditioners in the bedroom made it barely livable, and having no furniture to speak of, we had breakfast on TV trays in the bedroom.

Signing the lease on this apartment had been a mistake. Fortunately, the landlord was an understanding person and allowed us to rent the apartment by the week. We searched for and found another place to live, a nice unfurnished upstairs apartment close to the River Oaks section of Houston one-half block from the bus stop on Westheimer Boulevard. It was too expensive, but my folks said they would back us up both on the rent and in purchasing furniture. We took the plunge, signed a lease, and lived in that apartment all of the time we were in Houston.

My office was in the Humble building downtown, where Dr. Fisk and a few other old hands of the geologic research section were located. I boarded a bus on Westheimer and in thirty minutes got off a block from my office. African Americans sat in the back of the bus, and even when there were empty seats in back, many white people stood in the front. Racial separation existed in Houston in 1957.

Most of the people in the research section were assigned to the new Humble Laboratory Building on Buffalo Speedway and, except for me, the other new hires were located there. The downtown contingent I worked with included Dr. Fisk and his deputy, Ray Wood; Ted McFarlan, a longtime associate and my supervisor; and Howard Gould, who had also completed his PhD under Emery at USC. The other new hires were Chuck Riley, a mineralogist/petrologist; Duane Le Roy, a micropaleontologist; and Jack Jordan, a general geologist. We were hired to do basic research or research addressing practical company problems: finding oil and gas. Our basic research was fundamental to an understanding of sedimentary processes and deposits and their geologic environment. It was similar to research we might be doing at a university. The two types of research were closely related: what we learned doing one type of research could often be applied to the other research.

A short time after the new hires arrived, a seminar for all the geologists and geochemists in the research section was held. Ray Wood presented a summary of the schist ridge project. The schist ridge was a linear structure of metamorphic rocks buried beneath the sedimentary rocks of the Appalachian Mountains and underlying a number of sedimentary basins having oil potential. Understanding the geologic nature of the ridge was important to future petroleum exploration in that region.

Ray explained the project clearly in an informative way. I thought the seminar went well until we reached the question-and-answer period just before the coffee break. At that point, one of the geochemists asked a number of questions that would have been appropriate in an elementary geology course. The Q and A with the geochemist went from one elementary question to another and lasted ten minutes or more (it seemed longer). Then we recessed for coffee.

A day or so later, Dr. Fisk gathered the new hires, plus Ray Wood and Howard Gould, in his office to indoctrinate us to the geologic research section. At times, Harold Fisk could be brusque in the extreme, particularly with those who might not agree with him. He questioned the group of new employees: "What did you think of the seminar we had yesterday?"

Chuck Riley: "I thought it was excellent, sir. I learned a lot about the schist ridge project."

Jack Jordan: "Yes, sir. It was very good, sir. It is an interesting project I didn't know about. I was pleased to attend, sir."

Their answers impressed me as the kind of answers Riley and Jordan thought Fisk wanted to hear, not necessarily what they may have thought themselves.

Fisk: "John, what did you think?"

I said, "Well, I thought it was good, but I thought it could have been improved."

And just then, as if on cue, Fisk's phone rang, and he answered it. The looks I got from Ray Wood and Howard Gould, and to a lesser extent from Riley and Jordan, if translated into words, would have said, "Boy, you just cut your own throat."

In the seconds before I responded, I thought, Humble hired me for what I think, not what might be politic to say.

Dr. Fisk put the phone down. "What do you mean, John?"

I responded, "I thought the presentation by Ray was excellent, but the question-and-answer period went on too long. The questions asked by the geochemist were really elementary geology questions, and rather than waste the time of the rest of us, those questions could have been handled one-on-one with the geochemist during the coffee break."

All heads turned toward Dr. Fisk to see how he would respond to the answer from this brash newcomer. He looked thoughtfully at me for what seemed a long moment. Then he said, "I think so, too. We should have handled it that way. We'll do it that way next time."

That was my first one-on-one encounter with Dr. Fisk. I quickly learned that he loved to debate. He once told me that he would rather argue than eat. I think he liked me because I didn't back down in debates with him, although I don't recall that he ever changed his opinions as a result of what I said.

One evening, after returning from my office in downtown Houston, Shirley said it was time to go to the hospital for the birth of our first child. She had selected a doctor for the delivery, and arrangements had been made with the Methodist hospital. While she was in labor, I was assigned to the delivery waiting room; husbands didn't participate in or observe deliveries in those days. I waited there all night, concerned and trying very hard to be patient.

Toward five in the morning, the doctor came to the waiting room to inform me that Shirley had delivered a baby boy, but he regretted to tell me he was a stillbirth, at full term. He said the baby had a congenital heart defect and there was nothing he could have done to deliver a healthy child to us.

The news was devastating. When Shirley asked the nurse, "How is my baby?" the nurse could only shake her head. Shirley said that when I came into her room I had tears in my eyes. I said to her, "I'm sorry, Toots. We'll manage." I told her I loved her.

After a few days, we went back to talk with the doctor. He pointed out that Shirley was healthy, and there was no reason she couldn't deliver a healthy baby. We realized that what had been destroyed was our expectation that we would have a new son or daughter at that time.

In short order, Shirl came to terms with our loss and sought and obtained a position as a music teacher in the Houston elementary school system. She did a fantastic job and was asked to have her students perform at the annual state meeting of teachers held in Galveston. I was so proud of her.

Before the year was out, we made a special trip to New Orleans at Easter, and in August, Shirley delivered a healthy eight-pound, three-ounce baby girl, Donna Marie. About ten months after Donna was born, Shirley informed me she was pregnant again. Four months after that, she shocked me with the news that we were going to be the parents of twins. At about the eighth month, we made a rushed trip to Methodist Hospital again, but her labor was intentionally delayed to bring the babies to full term, and we went back home. Six weeks later, on December 20, we welcomed Lisa Kay and Karen Lynn as new members of the Byrne family. We had three little girls in a period of sixteen months—three little girls my father called "the Texas trio."

After about a year, the company moved me from the downtown building to the Humble lab on Buffalo Speedway, only about a half mile from our apartment—close enough to walk or ride a bicycle to work. I often worked in my new office on Saturday mornings. Frequently, Dr. Fisk came in on Saturday and saw me in my office when others were not in their offices. I think this may have impressed him.

Although I had already met most of the scientists in the geologic research section, being with them at the Buffalo Speedway laboratory was an opportunity to know them well. Stu Levinson chaired the paleontology section, which included Duane Le Roy and Russell Jeffords. Pete Masson was responsible for structural geology, together with Ron Wilcox. I had two assistants who worked with me on cores of sediments and sedimentary rocks and accompanied me on field excursions to the

Mississippi Delta. Jay Smith was more than six feet tall and weighed well over 200 pounds. Arleigh Reynolds was just the opposite, barely exceeding five feet four inches tall and weighing perhaps 130 pounds soaking wet. The three of us got along very well.

I was fortunate. I liked the folks I worked with, and I think they liked me. In addition to the geologists, I worked well with Bill Rankin, the photographer for the group. Bill was particularly helpful when I was given the assignment of setting up geologic displays in the conference room at the laboratory. The displays were educational tools to inform viewers about recent sedimentary deposits representative of oil-bearing rocks.

In setting up those displays, Bill and I went first class: cost was no obstacle. Cores of recent sediments were preserved in slabs of Lucite. They were important elements in three-dimensional displays that related the cored sediments to the environments in which the sediments occurred. Photographs and carefully drafted diagrams helped to convey educational messages. Bill had good design ideas and the ability to turn them into photographs that enhanced the displays. Dr. Fisk knew what he wanted, but left the design of the displays to me. I was honored by his confidence in me.

Most of my interactions at the lab were with the sedimentation/stratigraphy group, the structural geologists, the micropaleontologist, Duane Le Roy, and to a lesser extent with the invertebrate paleontologist, Russell Jeffords. Stu Levinson, the head of the paleontologists, demonstrated his leadership by leading the charge to the lunchroom for coffee. It was on these occasions that we all really became acquainted.

I didn't find everyone equally compatible, at least not at first. Russell Jeffords presented a challenge. He seemed to regard the research that we did, other than his brand of paleontology, to be of little consequence. He made demeaning remarks about sedimentology, the kind of research I was engaged in. Frequently he aimed those comments directly at me, perhaps hoping I would react. I recognized this almost immediately and consciously decided I would not react negatively. Rather than allowing Russ to get to me, I would turn him off graciously. When he made a derogatory remark, I responded by pointing out that I could see why he thought as he did, and then I said something complimentary about the work he was doing. This went on for the three years I was at Humble. It worked. After I left Humble, whenever I saw Russ at a scientific meeting, he sought me out to share something that had happened in the research section or to admit something to me he wouldn't share with others. I had become his friend, even his confidant. It was a wonderful lesson for me, one I have tried to use since.

In many ways, my daily activities at Humble were similar to what I had done as a graduate student. With the help of my assistants, we collected sediment samples, often in the form of vertical cores. We described the cores and the sediment characteristics and related what we learned about the samples to the larger environment in which the sediment occurred. Then I wrote reports describing what we had learned.

Sedimentary rock cores sent to us from the operational part of the company were studied in a similar fashion in order to interpret (guess) the environment of deposition of the sediments forming the rocks. Our job was to help the exploration or production geologists use knowledge of the environment in which the sedimentary rock had formed to predict where the next exploratory well might be drilled. Responding to requests from company geologists was our highest priority, but that took only about 25 percent of our time.

On occasion, the research on company problems taught us new ways to approach our fundamental research. Obtaining cores of rocks from great distances below the earth's surface is expensive. It was important to be accurate in determining how the sediments forming the layers of rock had been deposited so that if the cores were from a hole that did not produce petroleum, the geologist would have some clue as to which way to offset the next exploratory hole. For example, if it were determined that a sandstone had been originally deposited as a beach or near-shore sand, the next hole might best be drilled along the margin of the depositional basin. If that same section of sandstone were determined to have been a river deposit, the next hole might be drilled at a right angle to the margin of the basin, based on the assumption that most rivers flow more or less at right angles to the basin. In both cases, it is important to know the orientation of the depositional basin, which is often determined from geophysical measurements.

When we weren't working on a company problem, we spent our time on basic research, usually designated by Dr. Fisk. Because of his interests, much of our work was on the sand deposits of the Mississippi Delta or of southern Louisiana. Occasionally a company problem and our basic research overlapped and we learned important lessons that applied to both.

Such a learning experience occurred when one of Humble's operating divisions collected a long sequence of rock cores from an exploratory hole drilled in Mississippi. Obviously, the hope was that this hole would turn into an oil well, but if it didn't, they wanted some indication of which way to turn to drill the next hole. In order to learn as much as possible about the geology of the area, the geologist on the drilling rig had requested that the driller obtain a long section of sandstone cores. He asked for help from the research section. Ted McFarlan, Howard Gould, Duane Le Roy, and I traveled from Houston to a warehouse in Mississippi where the cores were being held.

Ted had worked with Dr. Fisk on the Mississippi Delta and was familiar with the types of sand deposits common to the delta. Duane, our micropaleontologist, had knowledge of benthic Foraminifera, microscopic animals that once lived on the ocean floor. The depth of the water when these fossils were deposited is unknown, but that depth can be inferred by comparing the fossils to their modern living counterparts, which live at a known water depth. All of us worked collaboratively to determine the original environment of deposition of the rocks represented by the cores we looked at. I wrote the report.

On the floor of the warehouse, the cores were neatly laid out in wooden boxes arranged in the order in which they had been retrieved from the drill hole. The sandstones seemed fairly uniform in texture, top to bottom, and were separated by sections of shale that had originally been deposited as fine-grained mud. Ted was convinced he had seen similar cross-sections of sand and fine-grained mud on the Mississippi Delta. He convinced Howard and me that we were looking at a normal sequence of shallow-water river sands and river-mouth bar sands lying on top of shallow-water silts, a sequence typical of a delta building out into the depositional basin. Ted, Howard, and I were comfortable with the idea that the sandstones in the cores had been originally deposited in shallow water, perhaps less than a hundred feet deep.

Duane said nothing while he took samples of the shale above and below each of the sandstone sections. Later, back in his lab, he separated the microfossils from the shale, identified them, and compared them with their living Foraminiferal counterparts, for which the water depth they live in is known.

About a week after we were back from Mississippi, Duane called. His analyses showed that the fossils were typical deep-water organisms and indicated that our "shallow-water delta" had been deposited in six thousand to ten thousand feet of water. We were shocked. How could we have been so far off the mark? When all the evidence was in, we surmised that we had been looking at sandstones originally deposited from turbidity currents[1] well down in the depositional basin—not from along the basin's shoreline at all.

Perhaps because of the bias created by familiarity with one environment of deposition, and because we had not looked carefully enough at all of the sedimentary characteristics, we had failed to consider alternatives. With the evidence of the microfossils, our minds had been alerted to consider alternatives to what initially seemed obvious—a lesson that applies to many dimensions of life. Things are not always what they first seem to be.

FIELDWORK ON THE DELTA

The Mississippi Delta and its deltaic plain are among the most interesting flat places anywhere in the world. They serve as a valuable natural laboratory for the study of modern sediments and sedimentary processes. The deltaic plain is the result of two geologic processes: deposition of sediments, and subsidence (sinking) of the region. As the Mississippi River extended its main channel by depositing sediments at the river mouth, the gradient (slope) of the river flattened, and the river, seeking steeper outlets to the Gulf of Mexico, formed the distinctive bird-foot delta pattern. At the same time, regional subsidence caused the areas where sediment was not being deposited to sink lower. This sinking created a steeper route to the Gulf, and eventually the river changed its course and flowed in the new direction, depositing sediment at its river mouth and forming a new delta. As regional subsidence continued, the Mississippi changed course repeatedly, forming subdeltas each time. Over time, these subdeltas overlapped to form the large deltaic plain that comprises much of southern Louisiana.

Today the delta is disappearing at an alarming rate. In recent years, human efforts to control flooding through the construction of artificial levees and other flood-control devices have caused the river to maintain a single main channel without shifting its course. These human efforts have had unintended consequences. Sediment carried by the Mississippi is all deposited directly into the Gulf of Mexico; none is deposited on the existing deltaic plain. While this is happening, the subsidence continues, and without new sediment, the deltaic plain sinks below sea level. The balance between deposition and subsidence has been lost. Land areas are disappearing, leaving little room for human habitation. People who had their homes on the delta are forced to leave, and the human cultures historically typical of the delta continue to be lost.

Fisk, always a teacher, used the delta as one of his classrooms. He took pleasure in sharing his knowledge of sedimentary environments, taking us on field trips on the ground and by air to see the environments of the delta, the Chandeleur Islands to the east (now wiped out by hurricane Katrina), and the salt flats of Laguna Madre, which separate Padre Island from the mainland of south Texas.

Dr. Fisk inserted himself into the sediment research more than he did in the paleontological or structural geology research. Those of us interested in sediments became Fisk's students and his personal field crew, collecting samples and conducting basic analyses for him. We studied the peat deposits of the delta because Fisk was asked to write a scientific paper on coal and its possible origin as a delta deposit. The peat deposits of the delta, he speculated, could be interpreted to be the original organic deposits from which coal developed.

I was frequently assigned the job of collecting samples and drill-hole information from the delta. This involved digging shallow holes to obtain sediment samples, logging sediment with depth using a water-activated hand-held drilling rig, or obtaining cores with a simple tubular hand-held coring device. When the trip involved drilling, I took my two assistants, Jay Smith and Arleigh Reynolds, both "good ol' Texas boys." We drilled, or attempted to drill, in the swamps bordering the levees and in the more distant marshes.

We learned to be courteous about asking permission to obtain samples on private property. Usually we explained the nature of our research and how it could be meaningful to the people on the delta. We often operated in remote areas of the delta where the people spoke only Cajun French. Fortunately, my high school French was good enough to communicate with those local folks. Even if my diction was awkward, they seemed to appreciate my effort to speak their language.

If we happened to be anywhere close to New Orleans, we found a motel on the side of the city nearest our sampling area. We tried to have dinner in a different New Orleans restaurant each evening, and if there was time, we'd take in a show afterward. Fieldwork wasn't so bad, even though it was physically demanding—and we became familiar with New Orleans.

The country we worked in belonged to the mosquitoes and chiggers. We were often in water up to our knees, so we watched out for water snakes, but fortunately never saw any. Samples from beneath the marshes were relatively easy to obtain. This was not the case in the swamps, where tree roots were prevalent. Our drilling device, muscled by hand, frequently encountered logs or other wood debris that prohibited sampling at any depth below the surface. Sometimes it took five or ten attempts to find a suitable spot. In order to get the sample we wanted, we frequently had to venture well into the swamp and some distance from our overnight accommodations. Once we were achieving success, we stayed in the swamp until we had our samples. Only then did we pack up and make the long drive back to our motel. This often involved a sixteen-hour workday for the three of us.

Reimbursed on an hourly basis, Smith and Reynolds were appropriately paid time and a half for working more than eight hours a day. Because I was not paid by the hour, this meant that while we were in the field, they often earned more money than I did. That didn't bother me one bit. They worked hard and made it possible for us to complete our tasks. We were getting our job done. Apparently the differential in our pay bothered some folks in the main office in Houston. I was given orders never, never to exceed an eight-hour workday, even if it meant leaving the drilling rig in the middle of the swamp overnight. That order came down from Howard Gould, my supervisor, a middle manager. I tried to convince Howard that the order didn't make sense if you were out in the field. But he was firm: an order was an order. It was infuriating to me, and to Smith and Reynolds.

On the next field excursion, it happened that Howard temporarily substituted for me. Interestingly, the "eight-hour limit" order was rescinded soon afterward. Field reality can be a meaningful alternative to management imagination. The person closest to the action frequently has the best knowledge of what makes sense. I have never forgotten that.

We had a similar problem in convincing the machinists who constructed our coring devices that we needed large tolerances in the way the pieces of the coring device fit together. The machinists took pride in being precise; they made tooled instruments for us that worked well in the clean environment of the machine shop. Unfortunately, one or two medium-size grains of sand in the field could turn a precisely crafted instrument into an inoperable piece of junk. It was another example of how the person close to the action, with knowledge of local working conditions, often knows best.

The tip of Southeast Pass, an extremity of the Mississippi, was an excellent place to obtain cores of the riverfront bar sands that prograded into the Gulf to form a sand body called a bar finger. As the Mississippi flows into the Gulf of Mexico, its speed is slowed and it drops the heavier sand it carries, forming a sandbar. As more sand is dropped, the sandbar extends farther into the Gulf, forming a finger of sand surrounded by the finer-grained silts and clays that settle more slowly and take longer to be deposited. If preserved in the geologic record, the bar finger of sandstone could form a reservoir rock for the accumulation of petroleum.

Humble Oil contracted a drilling firm to obtain a series of cores of these recent bar-finger sediments at Southeast Pass. For the drilling crew, experienced in drilling holes in consolidated rocks, it was difficult to obtain cores of the unconsolidated, recently deposited sediments. In normal oil-well drilling, the drillers push a large-diameter pipe, called a casing, through the recent sediments until they reach hard rock. They don't care about the soft sediments; their objective is to drill into the rock beneath the recently deposited sediments. Obtaining cores of the recent sediments was a new challenge for them. The drilling crew was up to the challenge, and after about a week and a half of setting up and then coring the sediments, a number of bar-finger sand cores were obtained and the project was considered a success.

Ted McFarlan and I had been sent to the drill site as the geologists on the project. When the Cajun drilling boss signaled that they had obtained a core, Ted and I took it and preserved it in melted paraffin for shipment back to the lab in Houston. One of the Cajun drillers had heard that a good way to remove feathers from a goose or other game bird was to dip the bird in melted paraffin. When the paraffin had cooled, you could pull it off the bird and the feathers would come with it. Having a barrel of melted paraffin at hand was too much for the Cajun; he had to try it, and he did. He got his shotgun out, shot a goose and, using the paraffin technique, stripped the feathers from it in short order. It soon became obvious to me that in such a remote place on the delta, the drillers had little regard for Louisiana Fish and Game Department regulations. Food was food, and state and federal agency people weren't around anyway.

It was interesting and enjoyable to live on the site with the Cajun drilling crew, to eat their kind of food and drink their strong Cajun coffee. Being a black-coffee drinker, I managed to swallow the stuff, but I noticed that the Cajuns drank theirs with an equal volume of milk. The trip was another learning experience about differences in culture.

Another memorable field experience occurred shortly before I left Humble. It was a trip to the construction site of a flood-control lock for ships at Old River, a distributary of the Mississippi. Here, if left to nature, the Mississippi would divert into the Atchafalaya River. The lock at Old River was part of the flood-control system that kept the Mississippi in its course and permitted the passage of ships to and from the Mississippi and the Atchafalaya.

The Old River lock provided an opportunity to examine, in three dimensions, the depositional features of sands deposited at meander points of the river. A meandering river erodes one bank and deposits sand at the opposite bank, or point. As the river continues to shift, the deposits of sand are laid down in different attitudes, and an accumulation of sand is formed in which the beds cross over one another, a result called cross-bedding. The accumulation of these cross-bedded river sands is termed a point-bar, a type of deltaic sand accumulation different from the bar fingers described earlier.

A major project at the lab was the preparation of facies sheets for various sand deposits. The word *facies* refers to a body of rock or a sedimentary unit with distinctive features that differentiate it from adjacent rock or sedimentary units. The facies sheets summarized in simple form the characteristics of recent sand deposits that might ultimately become reservoir rocks for oil. Our goal was to develop a portfolio of facies sheets that could be useful to a geologist in an exploration or production office in identifying the relevant environment of deposition of the sedimentary rock. On each sheet, we described everything we knew about a specific sand deposit: grain sizes and their distribution; paleontology; bedding; minor structures such as cross-bedding, ripple marks, and burrow; and relationship to other types of sedimentary deposits. We included diagrams showing lateral and vertical distribution of the sands. Each facies sheet bore the name of the person who had developed it, and my name was on several of them. When I returned to the Humble lab a year or so after I left the company, I was not permitted to see the facies sheets—even the ones I had created. Finding oil is a highly competitive activity.

As time progressed, I worked more and more directly with Dr. Fisk. Shortly before I had been with Humble three years, he asked me to work with him on his paper on the organic sediments of the Mississippi Delta and how they can turn into coal. He had a unique method of preparing the paper. I sat in his office next to his desk and went over the geology I had been working on for him. When we agreed on the geology, he called his secretary into the office and dictated the paper to her. He articulated a sentence, looked to me for approval, and then indicated to the secretary to keep those words in the text. Occasionally I suggested a word change, and he usually accepted it. My position in the research section was maturing.

In early 1960, I received a note from Bob Stevenson, with whom I had worked as a graduate student at USC, informing me that a new oceanography department had been created at Oregon State College, and they were looking for a marine geologist. He thought I might be interested in looking into such a position.

In fact, I had been reviewing the geologic literature for possible positions, so I added Oregon State to my list. I wrote to a Dr. Wayne Burt, who was establishing the department. With my letter, I included my resume and a reprint of the recently published paper Dr. Emery and I had prepared on the sediments of the Gulf of California.

Dr. Burt wrote back. He had checked my references and decided he wanted me to join the new oceanography department. He was offering me a job, sight unseen. I suspected Dr. Burt was aware there were not many marine geologists available at that time. I replied that I couldn't make such a career decision without visiting Oregon State. He understood, indicated that he was interested in talking with me, and invited me to come to Corvallis at the college's expense.

As I made arrangements to visit Oregon State College, I reminded Dr. Fisk of my original intent to work for Humble for three to five years. I told him I had this invitation from Oregon State and that I planned to visit the college. Dr. Fisk, who had his undergraduate degree in geology from the University of Oregon, commented that he didn't think Oregon State would ever amount to much, but said I should go ahead and visit. I think he thought nothing would come of my visit. He added that he hoped I realized I was making my mark in the research section at Humble.

I knew I was. I felt good about my increasing experience and stature in the research section. I also realized that changes were taking place with all the New Jersey affiliates of the Standard Oil Company of New Jersey, of which Humble was the major domestic producer of oil and gas. Efforts were under way to consolidate the research sections of the various affiliates, and if I stayed at Humble, I might have a role in that consolidation. I had already participated in one meeting with research geologists from one of the affiliate research groups and knew they were impressed by the papers I had written while at Humble.

I flew to Corvallis. Wayne Burt met me at the Corvallis airport. I noted three things when I arrived: the air was clear; you could see Marys Peak;

and Wayne's blue Simca automobile had the aroma of mildew. I met the dean of the School of Science, who had been instrumental in the creation of the oceanography department, and Wayne had arranged for his one graduate student in geological oceanography, Vern Kulm, to show me around and to take me down to the geology department to meet the faculty there.

There wasn't much to see—no building, no ship, just an attractive campus. Wayne did indicate that the Office of Naval Research had promised funds for a new research vessel. I don't remember much else about the visit. It was obvious that oceanography did not have much to show in the way of programs or facilities, but with an energetic visionary like Wayne Burt at the helm, Oregon State oceanography seemed to be off to a reasonable start.

Before I returned to Houston, Wayne offered me the position as the geological oceanographer. I would be an assistant professor on a twelve-month appointment at a starting salary of about $9,000, half from the state of Oregon and half from the Office of Naval Research. I would be expected to teach during two quarters of the year and would be free to do research for the remaining two quarters. The salary was about the same as I was making at Humble. As Wayne delivered me back to the airport for my flight home to Houston, I told him I would think about it and let him know my response within a week.

During my return to Houston, I had ample time to consider the Oregon State offer and what I would be giving up if I left Humble. Oregon State had little to offer other than an opportunity to help develop a brand-new department, both in terms of preparing students to be oceanographers and doing some research in an area where little had been done—and I would have the opportunity to teach.

I didn't know any of the people at Oregon State, although they seemed like nice folks. On the other hand, my position at Humble seemed solid, I was being given more and more responsibility, and if there were changes in the nature of the company, I had a good chance of being involved. I knew the people at Humble and liked them. The salaries were about the same. On the face of it, I'd probably be crazy to give up a solid position at Humble for the thin potential of the infant program at Oregon State, where, judging from the aroma of Wayne's automobile, it rained a lot of the time.

By the time I arrived home and explained all of this to Shirley, I had made my decision. Shirley gave me confidence when she told me that whatever I decided would be perfect with her. I wrote a short note to

Wayne, explained I could not have made my decision without the visit to Oregon State, thanked him, and indicated I would remain with the Humble Oil and Refining Company. Dr. Fisk seemed pleased when I told him I intended to stay with the company. I had closed the door on Oregon State, or so I thought.

Before the week was out, I regretted my decision. I was convinced I had made a mistake. Since high school, I had wanted to teach. I had enjoyed teaching immensely as a graduate student at USC, and I had just turned down the first opportunity presented to me to teach at a university level. So be it. I was unhappy with myself . . . but, I reminded myself, the Humble Company's research section was a good place to be.

About six weeks later, I received another letter from Oregon State College. Wayne Burt had searched extensively for a marine geologist; he had talked with K. O. Emery, my major professor; he couldn't find anyone else who met the qualifications he had in mind. Wayne asked me candidly what it would take to attract me to Oregon State. He had bumped the salary up a bit and promoted the position from assistant to associate professor. He was offering more. He wanted me. He didn't know I would have come for less. I telephoned him and told him I would be delighted to join the new department of oceanography and should be there by July 1.

It isn't often a person has two opportunities for something he really wants, even if he doesn't realize it at the time.

I knew Dr. Fisk well enough to know he would not take kindly to my news. Rather than spoil life for the people close to him, I decided to wait until late Friday afternoon to tell him of the reversal of my decision. I went in to see him at just about closing time. I told him I'd had another offer from Oregon State, that I had given it a lot of thought, that teaching was something I felt I had to do, and that I had accepted the offer.

Dr. Fisk reacted about the way I had expected. He hit the ceiling, called me immature and other things I have forgotten, and while I was there, he picked up the phone and called the vice president and chief geologist of Humble to share the news about my decision. Fisk was asked if I had been working on the cores of the highly confidential Champion-Klepak well. Fisk indicated that I had, and the vice president responded by ordering Fisk to get my resignation from the company immediately. I was essentially fired from the Humble Oil and Refining Company.

I told Dr. Fisk I was sorry to cause him any grief and left his office. It took me about twenty minutes to walk home. When I opened the door, Shirley said Dr. Fisk had called and wanted me to call him as soon as

I got home. I called him immediately. He told me not to do "anything rash" and to meet with him at ten o'clock Saturday morning in his office. I didn't know what he meant by "rash," and I would certainly be in his office at ten on Saturday.

When I arrived, Ray Wood and Howard Gould were already there. Apparently, Dr. Fisk had not told them the purpose of our meeting. With the door closed, Dr. Fisk said, "John has told me he will be leaving us to take a teaching position at Oregon State College, in their new oceanography department. I have talked with the vice president of Humble, and he has requested John's immediate resignation."

Ray Wood burst out, "I think John Byrne is crazy." Howard seconded that opinion.

Dr. Fisk said, "Well, I don't. Some of the happiest days of my life have been teaching. I wish John well, and I want him to leave here on good terms with all of us. John has made a real contribution here, and he has lots of friends at Humble. I think we should arrange a coffee reception for him Monday or Tuesday morning so that everyone will know what's going on." And that's what they did.

At the coffee reception, I was presented with a beautiful pair of agate cuff links. I still have them and wear them with pride and fond memories. For the next several days, as I was cleaning out my office, I continued to work with Dr. Fisk on the Mississippi Delta coal deposit paper. I signed the letter of resignation that had been prepared for me on that Saturday morning, and after that I worked with Dr. Fisk as a friend, not an employee.

I would not have traded my time with the Humble Oil and Refining Company for anything. It was more than the equivalent of today's postdoctoral fellowship. I gained respect for an industry that is often maligned. The men and women I worked with at Humble were among the finest I have known—intelligent, honest, and hardworking. My time at Humble could easily have expanded into a lifetime career. It didn't turn out that way, but it was a major period of learning for me as a scientist, as a leader, and as a person. It was there that I developed values and principles that have served me well ever since. I was part of the Humble Company; it was part of me; and I supposed to some extent it still is. I learned a lot, not the least of which is how important it is to identify with the organization you are part of. That organization had been the Humble Oil and Refining Company; it was about to become Oregon State College. I was ready for a new life, I thought.

CHAPTER 6

Corvallis and Oregon State (1960-1966)

"Within a vale of western mountains"
—Oregon State University alma mater

THE BENTON COUNTY COURTHOUSE was among the first things my father and I saw after we drove over the bridge across the Willamette River into Corvallis. I realized that a significant part of my life was behind me. I was about to begin the journey I had been preparing for since I took my first geology course at Hamilton College twelve years earlier. It was late Saturday morning in mid-July 1960. My father and I had driven to Corvallis from Dallas, Texas. Shirley and our three daughters were visiting her folks in Southern California after a visit with my folks in New York while I moved us from Houston, found a house, and moved in.

Corvallis[1] was the home of Oregon State College. The sign as we entered town advertised a population of 21,253. At the time, no one could tell me if that number included the eight-thousand-plus students who attended OSC nine months of the year. There was no question that this was a college town; there didn't seem to be much beside OSC and the businesses that supported the college.

I was eager to learn what I could about our new hometown at the confluence of the Marys and Willamette Rivers. When I arrived in 1960, the town had three motion picture houses, two restaurants (Wagner's, a coffee shop in the center of town, and the Chinese Tea Room, regarded as the best eatery in town), and three drive-in fast-food restaurants. A railroad to the coast ran through the center of town, as it does today, but, as now, there was no passenger service. There was no diaper service, only one shoe-repair shop, and if you wanted to purchase something upscale, you might get it in Salem, Eugene, or Portland, but probably not in Corvallis. Nevertheless, the store clerks were friendly, wanted to help, and almost always informed you they could order whatever you needed and have it for you in one or two weeks.

Vestiges of the past existed on Second Street in the form of Gerding's grocery store and Robnett's hardware store. At Gerding's, you could get cheddar cheese sliced off a huge wheel or choose your eggs from a barrel. Robnett's still has an oiled hardwood floor, and you can still buy bolts, nuts, or screws by the piece rather than in a plastic package with more units than you need. Outside the store, the metal rings embedded in the curb so you could tie up your horse and wagon are also still there. The town had a central park across the street from the public library.

Originally called Marysville, Corvallis had been platted in the mid-nineteenth century by its original settlers, the Averys and the Dixons. Both families donated the land on which the Benton County Courthouse was built, with the provision that the land would remain in the public domain as long as the courthouse remained a courthouse. Partly for that reason, the Benton County Courthouse is the oldest courthouse in Oregon to be in continuous service. There was one newspaper, the family-owned *Gazette-Times*, and only a few professional and manufacturing businesses. In 1960, there could be little question that the main economic reason for the existence of the town was Oregon State College.

Our first stop after lunch was a real estate office. I told the agent that I would be a new faculty member in the Department of Oceanography and that I was looking for a place to rent until we could get settled, and then I would want to buy a home. The first place he showed us, on Twelfth Street, was clearly acceptable. After seeing it and before seeing two other places, my father couldn't understand why I didn't tell the agent right away that I'd take it. I wanted to have a choice, so we looked at the other two, but there was no comparison; the first was clearly the best. The agent said that the folks who owned the house wanted to sell it, but he thought they might be willing to lease it for a year. It was a small three-bedroom house located in the middle of a two-block street that dead-ended at the elementary school on Garfield Avenue.

The owner was available to meet with us that afternoon. After we met and discussed our mutual situations, we came to an agreement, and it couldn't have been better for the Byrnes. The owner agreed to lease the house to us for a year. If at the end of the year we wanted to buy it, 85 percent of what we'd paid on the lease would count as our down payment on the house. What a deal! It was a comfortable house, and with three infant girls, we couldn't beat the location: half a block from an elementary school, a block and a half from a middle school, and three or four blocks from Corvallis High School. We lived in that house for twenty-one years.

I called Wayne Burt to tell him I had arrived and was looking forward to getting started. Wayne invited me to dinner at his home on Sunday evening. I talked to Shirley every day by phone and kept her informed of the decisions I was making, hoping for her approval, which I always received. Our furniture arrived Saturday, the day before my dinner with the Burts. By the end of Saturday, the furniture was in place. All that remained was to put the sheets, blankets, towels, and kitchen utensils in their proper places before Shirley and the girls arrived early the following week.

That Sunday was one of the most exhausting days I can remember. Every kitchen utensil required a decision on where it should go, since I wanted the location of each to be as similar as possible to its location in the Houston kitchen we had recently left. I wanted Shirley to feel comfortable about this move to Oregon, which even at best would be a big disruption in her life. By the time I had to leave for the Burt home, I was tired, really tired, yet the evening with the Burts was a success, and I felt truly welcomed.

Shirley, Donna, and the twins, Karen and Lisa, arrived the following week. I picked them up at the Portland airport. The last half hour of the two-hour trip from Portland was a period of constant screaming by three very tired little girls. I marveled then and still marvel at how Shirley managed to travel with three youngsters, all in diapers, from visiting my folks in New York to seeing hers in Los Angeles and then from Los Angeles to Portland, Oregon. She was and is an amazing woman. Shirley says, "You do what you have to do."

The following week added to her challenges as a mother and homemaker when the temperature rose to above one hundred degrees and held at that level for several days. We had sold our four window-unit air conditioners in Houston before moving. It was obvious to me that Shirley would need help as she set up a new home and cared for three infants. Fortunately, a high school student, the daughter of a Corvallis High School math teacher, was available and wanted to help us. She was a gem and helped us get the family settled. Then it was time for me to learn about my role as a new faculty member at Oregon State College.[2]

STARTING AN OCEANOGRAPHY DEPARTMENT

WAYNE BURT came to Oregon State College in 1954. After receiving his doctorate from the Scripps Institution of Oceanography, Wayne served as the associate director of the Chesapeake Bay Institute in Maryland and then spent a year in the oceanography program at the University of Washington. But Oregon was home, and it was in Oregon that he wanted to establish an oceanography program.

After the University of Oregon turned him down, he contacted the dean of the School of Science at Oregon State with a proposal: if he could get funding from the Office of Naval Research (ONR)[3] to support his salary at OSC, would Oregon State create a position for him? The dean told Burt that if he could get the money, and if the president and board agreed, the college would fund a position for him on a year-by-year appointment.

Oregon State College had nothing to lose and, as it turned out, everything to gain. The proposal was approved, ONR provided the grant money, and in September 1954, Wayne Burt started a project on the coastal oceanography of Oregon waters. He was given an annual appointment in the Department of General Science in the School of Science at OSC and was paid $7,000 for a twelve-month position.

During the fall of 1958, the geophysics branch of the ONR proposed Project TENOC, a program for expanding navy-sponsored oceanographic research. It called for navy support of at least ten institutions of oceanography throughout the United States over a ten-year period. The primary objective was to fund basic research relevant to naval operations. Wayne Burt was excited by the opportunity Project TENOC might provide for starting an oceanography institution at OSC.

Wayne's wife, Louise, in her history of the first two decades of the School of Oceanography,[4] recalls:

> On the evening after learning of the TENOC proposal, Wayne came home and told me about its possibilities. Perhaps even Oregon State would be one of the institutions selected. He had a restless night and the next morning at breakfast he asked me to look up a quote from Shakespeare's Julius Caesar:
>
> "There is a tide in the affairs of men, which taken at the flood, leads on to fortune. Omitted, all the voyage of their life is bound in the shallows and in miseries. On such a full sea are we now afloat and we must take the current when it serves or lose our ventures." (Brutus to Cassius, Scene 3, Act IV, of *Julius Caesar* by William Shakespeare)

Wayne was intent on catching the rising tide, on taking the current when it served.

By September 1958, Wayne had been at OSC for four years, teaching courses in oceanography and carrying on ONR-funded research along the Oregon coast and in its estuaries. The total oceanography budget that year was approximately $25,000, most of it coming from the ONR. Wayne had convinced Gordon Lill and Art Maxwell at ONR that with their support, an oceanography department at Oregon State College was feasible. With the announcement of the TENOC program, he was ready to move forward. He submitted a detailed proposal for TENOC support and at the same time indicated to the OSC administration that he was confident the navy would support a "department of oceanography at a significantly higher level."

Wayne engineered an oral agreement with Lill and Maxwell that ONR would provide funds both for operating and for capital improvement—$250,000 in fiscal 1960 for a research vessel and $200,000 for an oceanography laboratory—and Oregon State College would create an oceanography department. Wayne then persuaded the administration at OSC to create the academic department, the administration persuaded the State Board of Higher Education, and the Department of Oceanography at Oregon State College came into existence July 1, 1959.

The ONR funds also made possible the construction of the first new oceanographic research vessel built in the United States since the end of World War II. Later, on a cold, drizzly day in February 1961, I watched the eighty-foot *Acona* slide down the ways into the Willamette River in Portland. We would soon have the ability to conduct research in the near-shore waters of the Pacific from our own vessel.

On my first day on campus, with directions from Wayne, I found the Department of Oceanography office on the second floor of OSC's Food Science and Technology building and started my new career. My desk was in one of the department's two large rooms; the other was devoted to the secretary's desk, department files, and access to the small office occupied by Wayne Burt. We were just down the hall from a food-tasting lab.

I was the first of the new faculty to arrive. Bill Pearcy, June Pattullo, and Beth Strong arrived a week or so later. Bill had recently received his doctorate in fisheries from Yale University, and June and Beth were coming from the Scripps Institution of Oceanography, June as the physical oceanographer and Beth as the financial assistant to Wayne. I met Herb Frolander and Bruce McAllister, both of whom had joined the department a year earlier from the University of Washington. Bruce was an instructor working on his PhD in physical oceanography at Oregon State. Herb was an associate professor specializing in marine zooplankton. We were all pioneers, either foolish or prescient.

Wayne explained to me that my appointment was for twelve months at the rank of associate professor. I was expected to devote two academic quarters to research, funded by the ONR, and two quarters to teaching, funded by the state of Oregon.

The oceanography department was almost exclusively a graduate department. At the time it offered only one undergraduate oceanography course. Students who aspired to become oceanographers were expected to come to the department with an undergraduate degree in one of the sciences or mathematics.

After getting settled, I made my way across campus to introduce myself to the faculty in the geology department. Being the new kids on the block, we oceanographers were given a certain amount of slack by some and viewed with suspicion by others. Don Wilkinson, who had just succeeded Ira Allison as chairman of the geology department, was my first stop. Wilkinson, a crusty field-geologist type, was wary of having a geologist in another department on campus, and he didn't hold back in expressing his belief that I really should be in the geology department. I visited with Don frequently and we became good friends. I often served as his sounding board for thoughts he could not or did not want to express to members of his own department. Other members of the geology department I came to know well included Jon Cummings, Keith Oles, and Bill Taubeneck. In many ways I had more in common with them than I did with my new associates in oceanography. I liked them and enjoyed a professional relationship with them.

Jon Cummings taught the sediment-related courses in geology. He had worked with Wayne Burt to obtain support from National Science Foundation (NSF) for a summer oceanography experience for undergraduates. Jon invited me to come along as the "real oceanographer" in the NSF-sponsored experience. With an oceanographic technician, we took a group of undergraduates to sea off Coos Bay, Oregon, in a forty-foot fishing vessel. We demonstrated the sampling of water, sediment, and ocean bottom organisms using standard oceanographic equipment, noted turbidity with a Secchi disc, and measured temperature with a bathythermograph.[5] It was my first experience at sea off Oregon, and it enhanced my relationship with the geology department.

Keith Oles had recently been hired away from the Union Oil Company. He was a stratigrapher and, with Don Wilkinson, taught the OSC summer field course near Mitchell, Oregon. Keith and I were compatible as two ex-oil patch faculty new to Oregon State. Bill Taubeneck and I had little in common geologically, but both of us had graduate degrees from Columbia University and were roughly the same age, so we hit it off. Bill, a hard-rock geologist, spent much of his time doing fieldwork in the Wallowa Mountains of northeastern Oregon. Later, when he left the United States on sabbatical, I filled in for him with one of his doctoral students.

I was fortunate to have two graduate students awaiting my arrival, Vern Kulm and Neil Maloney. Vern had come to Oregon State as a graduate student in geology and had transferred to oceanography the year before I arrived. Neil was finishing his master's thesis in geology and would join oceanography in the fall. They were both helpful to me in starting a sediment laboratory, setting up exhibits for open houses for the public, and other activities that moved the new department along.

That first year was a year of beginnings, adjustments, getting acquainted with colleagues, and coming to know my new home. It was also a time for making the community and the state aware of what oceanography was all about—how important the oceans are to humans who live on the land surfaces of this planet. I began to learn what a land-grant college was, what was meant by Extension Service, the pecking order among schools and departments at Oregon State, and the power structure in the system of higher education. It was a challenging, exciting time.

SOCIAL LIFE

BECAUSE OUR DEPARTMENT was small and most of us were new to Corvallis, we served as our own social community. The Burts treated us as their extended family, inviting us for Thanksgiving and Christmas dinners. Parties and picnics together were common. We got together for morning and afternoon coffee breaks. These coffee times were important for sharing research discoveries, the problems we faced, opportunities for multi- or interdisciplinary research. These were times that brought us closer together.

Toward the end of our first year in Corvallis, Shirley and I looked for another house, but couldn't improve on the Twelfth-Street location. So we bought the house we were in, added a utility room for a new washer and dryer, and put cupboards in the carport. To a great extent, Shirley had been confined to home with three infant girls, all in diapers. With no diaper service, as there had been in Houston, the combination washer-dryer in the kitchen was running virtually all the time. It had come with a one-year guarantee, and shortly after the year was up, the machine stopped, completely worn out. We had only one car, which I used during the rainy season, further confining Shirley to the house. Fortunately, bakery goods were sold and delivered to the door, as were dairy products. A market on Van Buren Avenue took grocery orders over the phone and delivered those orders the same day. Their prices were higher than elsewhere, but the convenience of home delivery was essential.

Finances were tight. We watched our budget and, whenever possible, bought groceries in a number of different stores, chasing lower prices: one store for bread, another for meat. After a few years, I bought a bicycle and rode it to work as often as possible. We had a piano that Shirley had a passion to use, but I doubt she had time to play it very often. Our son, Steven, was born in December 1962. I tried to be home as much as possible while the girls and Steven were awake, timing my trips to the office at the times of their naps. Thinking back, it must have been a stressful time for all of us. I do remember it was stressful for me when I was preparing three courses simultaneously. It must have been equally stressful, or more so, for Shirley, all of the time. Somehow, we managed, and we thrived because we loved each other.

EARLY GROWTH

THE EARLY 1960S was a time of growth and associated turbulence for all of us in the oceanography department. In the line of public heroes, oceanographers were one step behind astronauts. We thought we could handle that. The department was getting bigger, and we were on the move, literally. For about a year, I shared office space with a taxonomist. Within a year, I was moved to the "pickle lab" on the first floor of the Food Science building. Kulm, Maloney, and a new student and I shared the room that served as both office and laboratory, and Joe Berg joined us in order to initiate a geophysics program. Geophysics developed into a major component attached to, but not integrated completely with, oceanography. It was only a short time before we were all moved to the third floor of the Physics-Chemistry building. Then, in 1964, we moved into the first permanent oceanography building, built with NSF funds.

In most universities, faculty members are expected to teach, create new knowledge, and provide service to their department, university, and society. The mix of these activities differs from one faculty member to another, but most are expected to be engaged in all three. I came to Oregon State because I wanted to teach, and I did, probably more than anyone else in the department. I enjoyed teaching Introduction to Oceanography to undergraduates, mainly through fifty-minute lectures three times a week.

My graduate courses were at two levels: intensive courses for those who aspired to careers in oceanography or geology and less-intensive ones for nongeologist oceanographers who were preparing to be physical, biological, or chemical oceanographers. For me, the most challenging courses were those offered for the potential geologists. They were taught partly as lectures and partly as discussions. Because I didn't always know what direction the discussions would take, preparation for these courses was broad and took a considerable amount of time. Occasionally I discovered shortly before class was to begin that I wasn't prepared. On those occasions, I often made up a series of questions for the class and then let the discussion develop around those questions. I truly enjoyed the free give-and-take with the students.

The geological oceanography course for the nongeologist oceanographers was satisfying in a different way. Usually there were more students in this course than in those for geologists, so I lectured more, but still used questions to stimulate discussion. Because marine sediments are affected by physical, biological, and chemical factors of the ocean, I could relate what I was covering to the full spectrum of what was known about the ocean. It was an opportunity to summarize the nature of the ocean in its many aspects. This course was the final required course for all oceanographers.

Shortly after I arrived, I teamed up with the chairman of the General Science Department to offer an honors colloquium on the philosophy and ethics of science. Honors students read articles on some aspect of the subject and then discussed the thoughts behind the articles for an hour or so. It was a pass-fail course. No one ever failed.

Another extra teaching activity I offered was a brown-bag seminar on terrestrial sediments. Several geology graduate students were aware that I had worked with Harold Fisk at Humble Oil and, because Fisk was a noted expert on the Mississippi River, these students must have figured that I knew something about river deposits. I was flattered and pleased to hold this seminar, even though it was done on free time for all of us. It also fit into my portfolio, inasmuch as I was helping a geology department graduate student with his dissertation on the sediments in the Willamette Valley. It was through this student that I first learned details about the Spokane or Missoula floods, which had back flushed into the Willamette Valley during post-glacial times, repeatedly forming a huge lake from which the rich Willamette silts were deposited.

Apparently I did a reasonably good job as a teacher because in 1964, the students awarded me the School of Science's Carter Award for Outstanding and Inspirational Teaching. At that time, the award was given for teaching at both the undergraduate and the graduate level. It is an award I am very proud of.

COASTAL OCEANOGRAPHY

NOT MUCH WAS KNOWN about the ocean off Oregon in 1960. Wayne Burt thought that coastal oceanography out to a depth of one thousand fathoms had been neglected off the entire West Coast, and he had used that lack of knowledge as a strong argument for establishing an oceanography department at Oregon State. Consequently, much of our pioneering research was on this section of the ocean.

My research goals and Wayne's meshed well. Little was known of the morphology of the continental margin, the distribution and sources of continental shelf sediments, the subsurface geologic structure of the shelf and slope, the nature of the abyssal area beyond the continental slope, or the relationship of continental shelf and slope geology to that of the Oregon landmass. I don't recall that I ever committed my overall research plan to paper, but in my mind it was obvious. It included a study of the geomorphology of the continental margin and, when equipment became available, the subsurface geology of the shelf and slope. Sediment studies started with the sources of sediment, then the distribution of sediment offshore from beach to shelf, slope, and abyssal areas. I intended to follow the plan as new graduate students and faculty were added to the Department of Oceanography.

With the help of my two marine geology graduate students, Vern Kulm and Neil Maloney, we immediately began to implement the plan. Vern had already initiated his study of the sediments in Yaquina Bay and was addressing the question of where the sediments were coming from. Were they coming from the drainage basin of the Yaquina River or from the ocean? Vern, Neil and I drove the length of the Oregon coast and sampled river sediments above the tidal influence on the major streams and rivers that discharged into the Pacific Ocean. Once we had the *Acona*, our research efforts shifted to the continental shelf. Bottom sampling and mapping of the bottom topography were our initial focus. About the time of those initial studies, a number of oil companies expressed an interest in the oil and gas potential off Oregon's shore. From their geologists, we attempted to obtain information about the structure of the rocks beneath the continental shelf, with little success, but we did learn some things from the geomorphology of the shelf, and we inferred something about the geologic structure.[6]

The *Acona* made it possible for Neil to begin his studies of the morphology and bottom materials on the continental shelf off Newport. In those days, navigating by Long-Range Navigation (LORAN)[7] was not nearly as accurate as it would become when satellites were used for accurately determining location at sea. Nevertheless, the navy imposed severe restrictions on the publication of precise data; Neil's research was just short of the precision required for security clearance. During the Cold War, security clearance was a price paid for doing oceanographic research. With the possibility of missile attacks from submarines, anti-submarine warfare was a major concern of the United States and the Soviet Union. Many of the OSU oceanography department faculty and I had top-secret security clearances.

As additional geology graduate students were added to the department, the research program expanded to studies of continental shelf sediments from the Columbia River to Cape Blanco; the nature and sedimentary deposits of Astoria Canyon, a submarine canyon off the mouth of the Columbia River; the Astoria Fan at the base of Astoria Canyon; and the Cascadia Channel on the Cascadia abyssal plain.

Two of my early graduate students, Bill North and Charlie Hollister, were interested in interactions between the ocean and the neighboring land geology. Bill worked on landslides of the northern Oregon coast, relating the land geology to ocean wave–induced landslides. Charlie was mapping the geology of a coastal area on land together with a study of the geology and ocean processes immediately offshore. Both students went on to successful careers in areas related to their oceanographic studies.

The faculty in geological oceanography expanded in 1963 with the addition of Gerald Fowler, a micropaleontologist from the University of Southern California and one of Orville Bandy's students. With his help, we were able to show that the rocks exposed on the continental shelf had been formed from sediments deposited at continental slope depths and then accreted to the continent.

Vern Kulm completed his PhD and joined the faculty in 1964. Vern became an outstanding researcher and served as an OSU oceanography professor for his entire career.

In search of information on the geology of coastal Oregon from other sources, I visited the Department of Oregon Geology and Mineral Industries (DOGAMI) in Portland shortly after I joined the OSC faculty. A number of my research papers on Oregon's offshore marine geology were published in the *Ore Bin*, DOGAMI's monthly newsletter. As a result, I came to know Hollis Dole, the head of DOGAMI and Oregon's state geologist. Hollis became a close friend and later played a major role in my appointment as administrator of National Oceanic and Atmospheric Administration (NOAA) in 1981 and in my becoming a member of the Burlington Resources board of directors in 1987.[8]

It was common for a major professor to publish scientific papers jointly with his or her graduate students. I frequently gave my students responsibility for submitting the paper and following up with the journal until it was published. Often, the paper was largely a result of the student's thesis research; in this case, the student would be the primary author. If I had made a major contribution, I might be the lead author.

Occasionally, a paper submitted to a journal is rejected for reasons other than its quality. This happened to me twice. When my paper "An Erosional Classification for the Northern Oregon Coast" was turned down by a regional geological journal, I recognized it as a geographic rather than geologic study and submitted it to a national geography publication, the *Journal of the Association of American Geographers*. It was published almost immediately.

Another paper, "Uplift of the continental margin and possible continental accretion off Oregon," was submitted by Jerry Fowler, Neil Maloney, and me to *Science*, the journal of the American Association for the Advancement of Science. The paper was based on Jerry's discovery that the benthonic foraminifera microfossils in Stonewall Bank, an exposure of rocks in less than six hundred feet of water on the outer continental shelf, had lived in deep water, comparable to the water depths five to ten miles farther offshore, where the modern counterparts of the fossils were living today. We inferred from this that the sediments that ultimately became the rocks of Stonewall Bank had been deposited with contained foraminifera in deep water, then consolidated to form rocks and subsequently uplifted and exposed. The rocks between those exposed at Stonewall Bank and the location of similar foraminifera today had been added, or accreted, to the continent.

In the past, igneous rock petrographers used the term *continental accretion* to explain the evolution of the granitic continental crust, as contrasted to the basaltic rocks of the oceanic crust. After our rejection by *Science*, we surmised that the editor may have sent the paper to be reviewed by "old school" petrologists, who rejected it because of our use of the term *continental accretion*. I appealed the editor's decision, explaining in simple terms what we thought had happened in the geologic past—that the continent had been accreted to. The editor deferred to us, and the paper was published in 1966 in *Science*, volume 154.

Oceanography was new not only to Oregon State College but to the state of Oregon as well. Spreading the word about the new Department of Oceanography and educating the public about the ocean through public talks was one way of making the department known. Herb Frolander and I gave more of these talks than anyone else in the department, probably because we enjoyed doing it and we did it fairly well. I usually used the title, "The Water's Cold Off Oregon." The talks varied, but the title never did. Anyone who has visited the coast of Oregon knows the water is cold, particularly during the summer, but some may not know why. My talk provided an opportunity to explain ocean processes such as coastal upwelling, the fundamental reason the water is so cold during the summer—and also to sell the Department of Oceanography.[9]

We also felt we needed to inform professional colleagues at other institutions of the development of oceanography at Oregon State. Each year the department collected reprints of our scientific papers and sent a volume of them to other oceanographic institutions—this was before the advent of the Internet. Additionally, when each of us attended scientific meetings of our own disciplines, we made it known that we were from a new department at Oregon State. I always tried to be a speaker at the professional meetings I attended. When I wasn't giving a talk, I usually asked a question of the presenter, making sure to identify myself, my department, and that I was from Oregon State.

The word must have gotten out that I gave a reasonably good talk because I was invited to become a member of a cadre of oceanographers who visited nonoceanographic universities to enlighten their students to the ways of the oceanographer. This program was sponsored by the American Geophysical Union as its visiting geophysicist program. I enjoyed doing this and became acquainted with a variety of colleges and universities.

FUNDING THE RESEARCH

AN IMPORTANT ASPECT of our service to the department was to support Wayne as he worked to raise money for OSU oceanography. Wayne was constantly preparing grant proposals to the NSF, ONR, and private foundations. These proposals often resulted in a site visit by a panel of experts. My students and I helped prepare for these visits and created displays for open-houses on campus.

Every year, the ONR, which funded much of our basic research and supported ship operations, sent a team to evaluate our program. It was at the time of the Cold War, so our presentations emphasized how our basic research applied to antisubmarine warfare. Support for ship operations was particularly important. ONR shared block-funding of our ship operations with the NSF. We had only to justify our overall research efforts to ONR in order to guarantee about half of the money needed to operate our vessels. NSF supported the other half with a single grant for ship operations. Eventually block funding of ship support disappeared, and it became necessary to justify funding for ship operations project by project.

The visits of the ONR panel normally lasted two and a half days. The first two were devoted to scientific presentations, discussions, and requests for funds. On the morning of the third day, following their evening of deliberation, the site team briefed us on their decision. This was done in a fairly relaxed environment over a continental breakfast. We always took care to arrive before the site visitors showed up.

On one memorable ONR site visit, we entered the meeting room to discover a blackboard still covered with calculations—apparently left by the review team. The numbers led us to believe our funding was about to be reduced substantially.

Wayne Burt was a hard-charging person at any time, and all the more serious and intense when ONR came to visit. When he saw the numbers on the blackboard, he was fit to be tied, became red in the face, and used salty language about the ONR team. We did what we could to calm him down, but it didn't work. Fortunately, the first ONR team member who came into the room erased the blackboard and said, "We're sorry, Wayne. This was meant to be a joke. You folks came out very well." Even though most of the agency visitors were personal friends of ours—oceanography being a small, tight-knit community in those days—Wayne found it difficult to exhibit a sense of humor at these times.

Under Wayne's leadership, we continued to prosper and to grow in size and in quality. We usually did well financially, often coming out ahead of other oceanographic institutions in our funding.

THE MARINE SCIENCE CENTER

ANOTHER SITE VISIT, this time by an NSF team to Newport in 1962, was in response to a proposal for funds for a building on the Corvallis campus and a dock and ship-support facility in Newport. At the time, we were mooring the *Acona* at the Newport municipal dock, paying a monthly fee. After scouting a number of locations for a new ship-support facility, Wayne selected the sandy area on the south side of the bay, the site of an old ferry slip. Vern Kulm, Neil Maloney, and I mapped the sand area using standard geologic mapping techniques. Newport civic leaders of Newport were willing to lease the site to OSU if NSF funded the facility. An NSF panel of oceanographers came to evaluate our proposal and have a look at the site.

The Newport city leaders hosted a dinner for us and the NSF team at a local restaurant. At the dinner, each panelist was presented with a framed aerial photograph of the entrance to Yaquina Bay, with the inscription "One Bell from Bar to Berth," implying it was only a short distance from the ocean to the mooring places for ships in the Newport harbor. One of the team members suggested the framed photograph would make a nice cocktail tray if an *E* were added to the word *Bell*. Whether this was a factor in Wayne's hiring the man a few years later is undetermined. In any case, NSF provided funds for a building on campus, but not for the ship-support facility. Funds for that facility and for an adjacent laboratory building came from a different source a few years later.

In 1963–1964, the Georgia-Pacific paper and lumber mill in Toledo, just up the Yaquina River from Newport, laid off a significant number of its employees. This led to a local economic depression. Lincoln County, where Toledo and Newport are both located, was declared the most economically depressed county in Oregon. At that time, the federal Area Redevelopment Administration (ARA)[10] provided funds for the economic recovery of depressed areas.

Governor Mark Hatfield asked the higher education chancellor, Roy Lieuallen, if there was anything higher education could do in Lincoln County to assist in its economic recovery. He informed Lieuallen of the possibility of funding from the ARA, and this information was passed down the line to OSU president James Jensen. Subsequently, Wayne Burt and others at Oregon State prepared a proposal to the ARA requesting funds to develop a facility on the site of the old ferry terminal on the south side of Yaquina Bay—the same site where the NSF had earlier declined to fund a dock for our research vessel. The proposed new facility would include a museum and aquarium to attract visitors, offices and laboratories for researchers—and a dock for berthing research vessels.

The ARA accepted the proposal and provided a grant of almost $960,000 for the buildings and dock. The state provided funds for the ship-support building, and the NSF funded the scientific equipment. In 1964, construction began on the OSU Marine Science Center. The building had a central public wing that included a museum, aquaria, auditorium, and book/gift shop, as well as wings for research laboratories and offices.

Faculty from the OSU art department, notably art history professor Mark Sponenburgh, collaborated on the museum's design. I represented the oceanography department and provided the scientific ideas for the museum. Sponenburgh and I hit it off and were close friends from those days until his death in 2013. He had considerable experience in designing museums, and by working closely with him, I learned much about creating public art—knowledge that proved useful later when I was the administrator of NOAA.

My undergraduate course in oceanography was excellent preparation for designing this marine museum. The displays represented a short course in oceanography, covering the geology of the ocean basins, shoreline features, the physical and chemical nature of seawater, currents, tides, and marine biology. Each display could stand alone or be an element in the unity of design for the entire museum. My students and I provided the grunt work as Sponenburgh built the displays.

President Jensen appointed Wayne Burt as director of the Marine Science Center and Tom Scott, chairman of the OSU fisheries and wildlife department, as co-director. Since both Wayne and Tom were located on campus in Corvallis, they each appointed a resident director for a portion of the center. William McNeil directed the center's west wing, the Pacific Fisheries Laboratory, and Joel Hedgpeth directed the east wing, the Yaquina Biological Laboratory. These appointments may have made political sense, but they certainly did not make management sense. Animosities developed; Tom Scott didn't trust Wayne Burt, and Joel Hedgpeth and Bill McNeil didn't get along. The tensions that developed on campus and within the Marine Science Center were palpable.

As plans were made for the public opening in the spring of 1965, Wayne asked me to serve as the master of ceremonies for the celebratory banquet. Naturally, I said yes. In 1990, at the twenty-fifth anniversary of the center, I again served as the banquet master of ceremonies. I'd kept my notes for the initial banquet, and I'd discovered that, of the twelve or so jokes I used in 1965, in 1990, because of political correctness, I could use only three. Societal awareness had progressed significantly in twenty-five years.

In honor of Senator Mark Hatfield, the OSU Marine Science Center was renamed the Hatfield Marine Science Center in 1983. The senator had been largely responsible for funding the creation of several federal agency facilities at the center, thereby creating a marine science campus.

Seatauqua

In spite of the management problems, many good things were happening at the Marine Science Center. Shortly after the center opened to the public, a number of us reasoned that if we could keep tourists busy at the center until two in the afternoon, it would be virtually impossible for them to leave Oregon that day, and the town and the state would benefit economically. This realization caused the leaders of the public programs at the center to schedule attractive lectures and other programs for the afternoon. Those lectures represented the center's first outreach efforts.

A short time later, President Jensen requested that the university's summer-term director develop a summer program to increase OSU's visibility at the coast. The result: a program of classic movies of the sea, two-day short courses, one-day field trips, and afternoon and evening lectures of intriguing topics related to the ocean—all open to the public. Because the offerings were similar to the Chautauqua lectures of old,

Don Giles, an Extension agent at the center, proposed that we name the program "Seatauqua." Personally, I thought the name was incredibly corny, but we went with it, and it caught on.

I enjoyed leading the Seatauqua bus trips with Don Giles.
Here, I explain a geological feature near Newport on a 1966 tour.
(OSU Special Collections and Archives Research Center)

TAKING NOTICE

AS FACULTY MEMBERS in a fast-growing department, we oceanographers exemplified the modern developments going on at Oregon State. The public was taking notice, and so were state leaders. We were surprised and gratified when Governor Hatfield, who was finishing his last term as governor before becoming a US senator, wanted to document the exciting events and accomplishments that had happened during his tenure as governor, including the development of oceanography at Oregon State. The governor asked President Jensen for a history and status report on our department.

The president told Wayne he wanted the report on his desk by five o'clock on a Friday afternoon. Wayne was pleased to oblige. I have no idea how much time he was given to complete this task, but I do know that with only a week to go, Wayne called me to tell me about it and to inform me that he was leaving for Washington, DC, on Monday morning. He said he would like me to complete the report and have it on President Jensen's desk by five o'clock the following Friday afternoon.

Wayne had already pulled together the necessary financial information and other data on the number of faculty, staff, students, but he had not prepared narratives about the teaching or the research programs, nor had he assembled the final report. It was left to me to complete the report, produce the requested ten copies, and deliver the package to President Jensen's office before the five o'clock deadline. Since I was teaching half a dozen classes at that time, I knew this would be a tall order.

Wayne alerted the faculty and staff to help me as much as they could. I followed up by requesting short narrative reports from the senior faculty of their respective research activities. By late Wednesday and early Thursday, reports from the faculty began to be delivered to the central office for typing on mimeograph masters—we had no word processors or copy machines in those days. Some of the reports were typed, others were handwritten. They all needed to be edited for consistency, prepared on mimeograph masters, copied, proofread, corrected if necessary, and multiple copies printed, collated, and stapled together with report covers.

All hands turned to, and when all the material was in, the clerical staff took over, organized themselves, and completed the job. We all glanced at the clock from time to time on Friday afternoon. Five o'clock came, but we were not quite done. By ten minutes after five, I had a bundle of ten completed reports in my possession and was hurrying across campus to the president's office. At five fifteen, I handed the package to the president's secretary and learned that President Jensen had already left for the weekend.

Disappointed? Yes. Proud? You bet! The oceanographers—faculty and staff—had worked together to accomplish an almost impossible task. What a great group of people! I felt good that Wayne had entrusted me with this task, and I certainly felt good about the support I had from faculty and staff. I realized how important the staff are to any operation.

SABBATICAL PLANS

THE TEXTBOOK I used, or didn't use, for my undergraduate oceanography survey course was badly out of date. Textbook publishers learned that I taught the large-enrollment undergraduate course and sent their sales personnel to visit me frequently. "Dr. Byrne, why don't you write an oceanography textbook for your course?" was a common question from those sales reps. I gave this idea some thought, a lot of thought, and prepared an outline that I shared with some of them.

The textbook idea occupied my thoughts more and more as my eligibility for a sabbatical leave in 1966–1967 approached. Where should I go to write the book? The University of New Hampshire was my first choice. It was a relatively small university, and Cecil Schneer, one of my geology professors at Hamilton College, was in the geology department there. They had a new marine program in early stages of development, and New Hampshire was an attractive state, unknown to the Byrne family.

Early one morning in 1966, my office phone rang. It was Joe Creager calling from Washington, DC. Joe was my counterpart in the oceanography program at the University of Washington. I had known Joe since graduate-student days at Columbia. He was a good friend. At the time of his call, he was serving a one-year assignment as program manager for oceanography at the National Science Foundation in Washington, DC. He was approaching the end of his tenure, and he wanted to know if I would consider succeeding him at NSF.

The timing was right—a year at NSF would be in lieu of a sabbatical leave. I told him I would certainly consider it. I made the trip to Washington for an interview and was offered the position. Shirley and I considered what a move to DC would entail. It would mean leaving Corvallis, renting our house, and attending to all the other logistics of a move from one coast to another. Our kids would be exposed to a different part of the United States. Living in the nation's capital would be a great learning experience for them, and for Shirley and me, as well.

Professionally, I would be on leave without pay from OSU and would forgo my sabbatical leave. The move would have an impact on the geology group in the Department of Oceanography. Vern Kulm could serve as major professor for my newer students, and he could provide guidance to my students who were writing their dissertations. I would provide some long-distance support from Washington.

The key question from Shirley: "John, do *you* want to do it?"

Until my interview trip, I hadn't been to Washington, DC, since I'd vacationed there with my folks when I was in third grade. Of course, at the time I didn't realize that in future years I would live there on two occasions and would make the round trip from Corvallis, Oregon, to DC very, very frequently. Washington is a city I would come to know well, but at that time it was new to us, impressive, and unknown.

CHAPTER 7

The National Science Foundation and Life in Washington, DC (1966–1967)

A year in Foggy Bottom

In October 1966, the Byrne family moved into the Grosvenor Park Apartments in Maryland, just outside the Beltway around the District of Columbia—three high-rise buildings with outdoor swimming pools, tennis courts, and a fish pond. A free shuttle bus was available in the morning and evening for transportation to and from the District. Our apartment was large and accommodated our family of six with room to spare.

My workday started at seven-thirty in the morning when I boarded the shuttle bus for the trip to the District and ended a little after six when I returned to our apartment. I managed to read and edit sections of my students' dissertations on my commute, which left evenings at home free for the family and me. On weekends, we were tourists, seeing things Washington, DC, had to offer. We kept a scrapbook of our visits to historic sights, federal buildings, museums, and art galleries. After we returned to Corvallis, the scrapbook served our daughters well in school: they became the de facto experts on United States history and on Washington, DC.

The National Science Foundation[1] (NSF) had been created in 1950 to support and stimulate basic research at US universities and colleges. The NSF offices were located at 1800 G Street Northwest, one block from the Old Executive Office Building and two blocks from the White House. I was one of the crew of managers in the Earth Sciences Section, responsible for managing the funding requests for nonbiological ocean research: geological, geophysical, chemical, and physical oceanography. A different part of NSF funded biological oceanography and construction of new facilities.

Bill Benson headed the earth science section. Dick Ray handled proposals for funding geology projects. Alvin Van Valkenburg was responsible for requests involving petrology and mineralogy, and Roy E. Hanson took care of geophysics requests. They were regular employees of the NSF; I was the only temporary employee, a so-called rotator.

Research funds were distributed on the basis of competitive proposals reviewed by scientific peers. My job was to manage proposal evaluation and distribute funds to successful applicants. I selected the peer reviewers, managed the panels of scientists who came to Washington to discuss and recommend funding (or not), and then informed applicants of the results. Proposals recommended for funding were often ranked and funds distributed accordingly. Most were not funded at the requested level. I spent almost fifteen months with the NSF managing this review and grant process.

The peer-review system provides a threshold of scientific competence, but it also tends to discourage ideas outside the mainstream. Revolutionary ideas are frequently dismissed by peers and were almost never funded by the NSF. However, major advances in science are often made by scientists who think outside the box. Fortunately, for oceanographic research, the Office of Naval Research did not use a peer-review process but relied on the expertise of ONR program managers, who were free to fund the scientist with the far-out idea. This didn't happen often, but occasionally ONR did take such a chance, frequently to the benefit of oceanography.

My time at NSF overlapped for a month or so with Joe Creager's, and Joe served as an excellent mentor. Together we traveled to a number of oceanographic laboratories. On these trips and the subsequent trips I made by myself, I met many of the oceanographers at the major oceanographic institutions throughout the United States.

OCEANOGRAPHY IN THE 1960S

IN THE UNITED STATES, the 1960s were marked by unprecedented attention to the ocean. The National Sea Grant College Program Act was passed in 1966 "to provide for the understanding and wise use of coastal, ocean, and Great Lakes resources to create a sustainable economy and environment." That same year saw passage of the Marine Resources and Engineering Development Act, which created the National Council on Marine

Resources and Engineering Development, with Vice President Hubert H. Humphrey as its chair. That act called for a fifteen-member advisory commission on marine science, engineering, and resources, which was chaired by Julius Stratton. In 1969, that panel, known as the Stratton Commission, issued its report, "Our Nation and the Sea." This report strongly shaped the future of ocean research at the nation's universities.

In 1967, the United Nations convened the Law of the Sea Convention, which met until 1982. Also, during 1966 and 1967, the Deep Sea Drilling Project was getting under way. A test hole was drilled in the Gulf of Mexico, and although care was taken to avoid drilling into an oil reservoir, the early cores did reveal hydrocarbons. Nevertheless, this early test was a scientific success, and with it the Deep Sea Drilling Project, funded largely by NSF, began and achieved remarkable scientific results for more than four decades.

In March 1968, President Lyndon Johnson endorsed an International Decade of Ocean Exploration for the 1970s, and in December the United Nations General Assembly formally welcomed the proposed decade focus. The national posture regarding the oceans was changing rapidly. It was an exciting time for an oceanographer to be at the National Science Foundation.

After the Sea Grant College Act was passed, the national office for the program was assigned to the NSF. Although I was not responsible for any of its activities, its location within NSF gave me the opportunity to become acquainted with the program's leaders. In 1970, Sea Grant was moved to the newly created National Oceanic and Atmospheric Administration (NOAA).

In March 1967, an Oceanography Section was created within NSF when the Ocean Research Program of the Earth Science Section was combined with the Oceanographic Facilities Program, managed by Mary Johrde. It was a pleasure working with Mary. I had first met her in the early 1960s when she visited Oregon State as the leader of the site-review team to evaluate Wayne Burt's proposal for a new building on campus and a ship-support facility in Newport. Mary's adept management of oceanography facilities money was important to the future of university ocean research.

Occasionally I received requests for information from the NSF congressional liaison office. Because the request may have been in response to a direct query from a congressman or senator, the need for the information was always "urgent." NSF had strict rules about program managers contacting members of Congress; only members of NSF's congressional liaison staff were permitted to make such contacts. Sometimes we ignored the NSF prohibition and contacted the legislator anyway. For example, in early 1967, I received a request from the NSF liaison, forwarded from a New Jersey congressman, for a list of institutions at which a student could obtain a college degree in oceanography and a short statement of the oceanography research under way at America's universities. My secretary and I calculated it would take several days, possibly weeks, to provide the information on the research. We appealed to the NSF liaison, but, no, the congressman must have it, and soon.

After anguishing over this for some time, my secretary and I decided to do the unthinkable: a call to the congressman's office was in order, even if it was verboten. Further, we decided it would be better if my secretary called the congressman's assistant rather than my calling the congressman directly. She could inquire exactly what was wanted, explaining that we wished to be responsive and give them precisely what they needed, even though it would take us some time.

She made the call. The response: "Oh, heavens, no! We just want to respond to this postcard we received from a high school sophomore asking where he might go to college to study oceanography and what sorts of new and exciting things scientists are learning about the ocean." A previously prepared thick manila envelope, including a letter from me, was on its way to the student in the next mail. We ignored the request from the NSF congressional liaison people and never heard from them again on this matter.

What a shock it was when my secretary decided to leave NSF, and without much notice. Before she left, she put in a request for another secretary for me. The personnel office did not respond in a timely manner. For about a month or more, I operated without a secretary.

During that month, however, I learned more about how the foundation operated in making grants than I did in all of the rest of my time at NSF. I also became acquainted with many of the nonscientific staff, particularly in the grants, finances, and personnel offices. After I returned to Oregon State, I prepared a paper for the earth science publication *Geotimes* explaining the funding process in more detail.[2]

I must have done a reasonable job as program manager, because as the end of my term at NSF approached, the director of the Division of Environmental Sciences offered me the opportunity to stay on permanently. The offer was flattering, but change was taking place at Oregon State, and I wanted to be part of it. I enjoyed teaching and doing research, and I was looking forward to helping the OSU oceanography program grow.

The NSF experience was a good one for me professionally. It opened doors to the ocean research community nationwide. It broadened my interest in the many dimensions, political and academic, of a national program of ocean research important to the United States and the rest of the world. It also raised my visibility as an academic oceanographer throughout the country and provided me with administrative experience that would be important to me and to my university.

A MEMORABLE VACATION

WHILE AT NSF during the summer of 1967, we took a family vacation to the Outer Banks of North Carolina, long sand islands separated from the mainland by Pamlico Sound. The main attractions for Shirley and me were the many historical sites, but for the kids, it was the history of pirates who plied the waters around Hatteras and Ocracoke Islands.

Finding "pirate treasure" might be an exciting adventure for our kids, so before we left DC, I bought a metal box from an army-navy store and painted it black with a white skull and crossbones. Shirley and I put junk jewelry and English copper pennies in the box and, when these didn't quite fill it, added poker chips and round pebbles painted gold. We smuggled the treasure chest into the car and headed south to pirate country.

At a rest stop in Nags Head, we learned that the town may have been named after the plunderers in the eighteenth century who hung lighted lanterns over the necks of mules, or nags, and paraded them along the tops of the dunes at night. To ships at sea, the lights looked like ships, thus indicating it was safe to sail closer to the shore. When those ships ran aground, the plunderers boarded them and relieved the ships of their cargo.

Our next stop was Kitty Hawk, where, on the morning of December 17, 1903, Wilbur and Orville Wright made history. The way they scientifically engineered their Wright Flyer was particularly impressive to me because they did it on their own, without any financial assistance from the United States government. What would life today be like without airplanes?

Finally, we reached the small community of Rodanthe on Hatteras Island, the site of the first Life-Saving Service station. The Chicamacomico Station, the first of its kind on North Carolina's Outer Banks, operated from 1874 until 1954. The men of the service pushed longboats through the surf to rescue people from foundering vessels that had run aground. The house we rented was isolated, about a quarter mile north of the remains of that lifesaving station and about one-half mile south of the nearest house on the beach. We were struck by the beauty of the banks, the isolation of the house, and the impressive number of mosquitoes.

At breakfast the day after we arrived, I noted a folded-up paper, oil-stained and obviously old, protruding from the bottom of a picture on the wall. Nine-year-old Donna brought it to the breakfast table. We opened it up and saw that it was a crude map of the shore of the Outer Banks. It had a large *X* on it with the notation, "Buried under the bowsprit of the sloop *Pearl*." It was signed by Captain Timothy Payne. I pointed out to the girls and Steven that from the shape of the shoreline and the fact that there was the wreck of a boat buried out in front of the house we were in, quite possibly that wreck was what was left of the sloop *Pearl* and there might be treasure buried there. Should we look for the treasure? Absolutely! But we would have to search when there was no one around if we wanted to keep any treasure for ourselves. There was a family picnicking on the beach not far from where we were located. We would have to wait until they were gone.

Later that day, the beach was empty. We could see no one to the north or the south. It was time to see if the wrecked boat half buried in the sand was the sloop *Pearl* and if it was, to see if Captain Payne had in fact buried his treasure there. With shovel and camera in hand, we all went out to the wreck. Tension and excitement gripped us. I dug into the sand as the kids crowded around. I seemed to know where to dig into the loose sand under what must have been the bowsprit of this unfortunate vessel. One shovelful of sand, two, three, perhaps we should look elsewhere, or possibly this was not the *Pearl* after all.

"Let's dig a little deeper," said Donna. So I did. My shovel hit something hard. Quickly, I shoveled more sand out of the hole. There was something there. "Girls, see if you can clean the sand off whatever it is." Imagine the thrill that ran through all of us as the sand was swept away to reveal a black box, a box with a white skull and bones painted on top, there in the bottom of the hole. With a great strain, I lifted the box out of the hole and set it on the sand. I forced it open. Jewels, pearls, and coins gleamed in the bright sunlight. The girls and Steven danced for joy. (Shirley filmed the entire episode.) We had found buried treasure. Let's tell the newspapers. No, because then we'll have to share the treasure with the state of North Carolina. We'll have to keep it to ourselves. Let's take the chest into the house to see the treasure more closely.

At the breakfast table, the kids emptied the chest of its jewelry, coins, and gold nuggets. Donna was the first to bring doubt to our discovery of treasure. Looking closely at one of the coins, she said, "This coin is dated 1965. They're all dated 1965." Lisa chimed in next with, "Hey, these look like our poker chips painted gold."

This wasn't pirate treasure at all; it was a hoax! But who could have done it? Those people on the beach? No. The people who own this house? Maybe. Finally, Mom and Dad admitted they had wanted the kids to have the fun and excitement of finding pirate treasure where pirate treasure might actually be buried. Should they have done this? What lasting effect would it have on the kids? Would they forever be suspicious of good fortune? Would they never trust their parents again? Would it make the vacation of August 1967 one of their favorite memories? Who knows?

We kept the chest and some of the treasure for a while after we moved back to Corvallis. If anything, that adventure is something we all remember. It was done because we love our kids. In many ways, it was the high point of that summer and perhaps even our time on the East Coast, at least for our kids.

The Byrne family in 1966, just before leaving for Washington, DC, and the National Science Foundation. Shirley and John are standing behind (left to right) Karen, Steven, Donna, and Lisa. (Byrne collection)

CHAPTER 8

Chairman, Department of Oceanography (1968–1972)

"... full speed ahead!"
—Captain David Farragut

WE ARRIVED BACK IN CORVALLIS in mid-December 1967. Our home on Twelfth Street had survived as a rental house, a bit beat up, but presentable after a coat of paint. It was good to be back, with new knowledge about our country and memories to last a lifetime.

While we were away, there had been changes at Oregon State and within the oceanography department. Shortly before we left for Washington, DC, in 1966, Jack Ward had been appointed dean of the School of Science, which was the home of oceanography. Dean Ward had come to Washington in 1967 to participate on an NSF panel, and I'd made it a point to meet him. That same year, Wayne Burt became ill and resigned as Department of Oceanography chairman. Herb Frolander, a senior member of the department, had been named interim chairman. Dean Ward appointed an advisory committee to choose a chairman from among the oceanography faculty. I was their choice, and I became chairman early in 1968. Later, Jack Ward told me he would have picked me even if his committee had given him a different name. I liked Jack and counted him as one of my friends. I think my time at NSF was a strong factor in my selection.

The appointment of a leader from within can pose problems. Will your former colleagues recognize and respect your new authority? Will their behavior toward you be the same as before, or will it show a new level of formality? Does the change in authority generate changes of attitude in them, or in you, or is it something only you are sensitive to? These were questions I pondered as I took on my new position. I thought I sensed changes on the part of some members of our faculty or their spouses. I didn't want those changes, if in fact they existed. I thought my attitudes toward my colleagues hadn't changed and hoped their attitudes toward me hadn't, either. But how could they not change if I did my job and exercised my new responsibilities for the health and progress of the department? Over time, the faculty and staff accepted my new role as department chair, and so did I.

I think Shirley was also affected by my new assignment and may have had the same concerns about the possible separation of friendships. Fortunately, she had a professional life of her own: she had her own piano students and was also employed as an accompanist in OSU's music department and developed musical colleagues there.

My relationship with Wayne Burt continued to be comfortable and mutually respectful. I moved into the office that had been his. Wayne had recovered from his medical situation and had come back to university administration as associate dean of research for oceanography. Wayne and I shared a secretary, and we worked well as a team.

I had been part of the evolution of oceanography at OSU from its earliest days. I understood and accepted the structure of the department, the informal divisions of the traditional disciplinary groups of physical, chemical, biological, and geological oceanography. Later, when the department became a school, that structure was continued: no departments, only disciplinary groups. I accepted the assistants Wayne had selected: Marcia Griffin, secretary; Beth Strong, finances; Vic Neal, academics; Dave Zopf, business affairs. These assistants were in addition to the office clerical staff and the ship operations staff.

The department had grown considerably since its beginning in 1959. We had a total staff of 122, of whom 65 were professional scientists and academic personnel. There were 108 graduate students in all areas of oceanography, and at the commencement exercises in June 1968, twenty oceanography students received PhDs and ten students obtained master's degrees. That year, the department had an annual operating and research budget of $2.7 million, of which 91 percent came from federal sources. Part of the remaining 9 percent that came from the state of Oregon had actually been generated as indirect costs on the federal grants to oceanographers. Oceanography was a good deal for the university and for the state. The Office of Naval Research and the National Science Foundation were the major sources of funds, with the Atomic Energy Commission and other federal agencies making up the remainder of funds from external sources. The cost of operating the ship was split between ONR and NSF block grants.

The *Acona*, launched in 1961, had been replaced by the *Yaquina* in 1964. The *Yaquina* was a converted 180-foot World War II supply ship. Its FS (freighter, small) design lent itself to conversion to a research vessel. Similar vessels had been converted for use by the University of Rhode Island, Texas A&M, and the Scripps Institution of Oceanography. This vessel could operate almost anywhere in the world's oceans except where weather and sea conditions were most severe. The *Yaquina* gave us the capability of becoming a major blue-water oceanographic institution. Other smaller OSU vessels, such as the thirty-three-foot *Paiute*, were available for near-shore and estuarine research.

We managed the department from the four-story Oceanography Building, built with NSF funds in 1964. We all knew this building would eventually be named Burt Hall in honor of Wayne Burt. (It was so named in 1987, four years before Wayne's death.) The building provided offices and laboratories for sixty faculty and staff and seventy-five students. By early 1968, it was severely overcrowded, so the department acquired nearby vacant houses that the university had purchased to make room, eventually, for parking lots. These houses relieved the space pressure, but only temporarily. Oceanography soon developed the reputation as a "building monster." A second oceanography building was scheduled for construction before the end of 1968, with funds again coming from the NSF and the state of Oregon. Oceanography faculty and staff also worked out of the Marine Science Center and ship-support facility in Newport.

Learning the ins and outs of finances and ship operations placed me near the bottom of a steep learning curve, but that wasn't all. I was also responsible for managing an academic department in the School of Science while teaching the introductory undergraduate oceanography course and a course on the geology of the ocean basins during winter quarter and attending to some external commitments. I had a full plate.

I began to realize how different the oceanography department was from all of the other departments in the School of Science. Other than the one undergraduate survey course in oceanography, we did not have an undergraduate instructional program, the mainstay of the other departments. We depended on external funds for our existence, not on state funds as the other departments did. Financially, we lived in a high-risk but exciting environment; the other departments lived in a more modest environment, low in risk and possibly low in excitement. If I worried about anything, it was usually money. Other department chairmen may have worried about student enrollments in their courses because student numbers were part of what determined their budgets, but 90 percent of our budget came from research grants and contracts and a portion of the indirect costs associated with those grants and contracts. For our survival, it was essential that our grant proposals be successful.

Meetings of the department chairs were interesting at first; later they became tedious. For me, the excitement was in all matters related to the ocean. The *Cayuse,* designed for use in near-shore waters and protected areas, such as the Gulf of California and the inland passage of Alaska, was nearing completion. In April 1968, shortly after I became chairman, the eighty-foot *Cayuse* was christened (by Shirley Byrne). Sea Grant activities were something to look forward to, and OSU received one of the first three awards of Sea Grant funds. The addition of scientists to our faculty created space problems, and it also opened new research doors. Overall, our staff continued to increase: 122 in 1968, 142 in 1969, 155 in 1970, and 165 in 1971.

In 1968, the federal oversight of our budget seemed fairly relaxed. Because ONR provided an omnibus grant that included a number of research projects, ship operations, and a certain amount for administration, and because NSF wasn't focused closely on the facilities monies we had received, Beth Strong, our financial manager, was able to transfer funds from one account to another as needed. As long as the funds were being used for oceanography and for the development of the department, the federal program managers seemed to accept her sleight of hand. I wasn't comfortable with her financial maneuvering, but I was learning, and I had decided to stay the course, at least until I knew what I was doing.

Within a few years, new federal Office of Management and Budget policies introduced tight financial controls. Federally funded researchers were expected to account for their time with great precision. One federal examiner told me that she expected researchers to report how they spent their time to the accuracy of one tenth of an hour. I asked her if she really meant that researchers should account for their time on a six-minute-by-six-minute basis. Her response: "Absolutely!" But that's not the way it was in 1968. Beth Strong was honest, she was innovative, and we trusted her to keep us all out of jail.

Ship safety was another area of interest and some concern. There is always a certain element of danger in operating on the high seas, and using heavy equipment during the rolling motion of the ship also presented a risk. We prided ourselves on having one of the most efficient ship operations in the entire academic fleet under the guidance of two retired US Navy officers, Captain Ellis Rittenhouse and Commander Richard Redmond. Rittenhouse was in charge and was stationed with other oceanography administrators on campus. Dick Redmond was in charge of the operation in Newport and had his office at the ship-support facility at the Marine Science Center. They both ran tight ships: our vessels were clean, well kept, efficient—and safe.

In the 1960s, oceanography was a male-dominated field, although that was changing. With OSU's Dr. June Pattullo helping to lead the way, more and more women were attracted to oceanography as a career; consequently, the female population of our graduate student body was increasing. These women had the right to go to sea, and for much of their research, it was essential that they do so. At the time, we required that whenever a woman went to sea, she must be accompanied by another woman, usually another oceanography graduate student. (Yes, I was a male chauvinist!) We thought we had good reasons for this requirement but learned otherwise. The culture was changing, and it was time for us to change our gender-related shipboard requirements. In this, as in finances, ship operations, and other things, I was a new learner. In the beginning, I decided to accommodate the way matters had been handled in the past. I soon learned that this was not always the best policy.

NOT INVITED

COBB SEAMOUNT is a flat-topped volcanic undersea mountain about 270 miles off the southern Washington coast. It rises from a depth of about 9,000 feet to 110 feet below the sea's surface. Because of its shallow summit depth and relatively close proximity to the Washington coast, there was increasing interest among scientists at the University of Washington and one or two Canadian universities to use the summit as a location for an ocean-monitoring instrument array. They recognized the desirability of having an instrumented monitoring station offshore that could provide continuous oceanographic and atmospheric data. Cobb Seamount was the logical site. These researchers banded together under the leadership of retired Admiral Emory Stanley to form an organization called the Sea Use Council, devoted to placing an instrument array atop Cobb Seamount. Oregon State was not invited to join the Sea Use Council.

Unbeknownst to the Sea Use Council, several Oregon State University oceanographers and engineers were pursuing a similar idea. In 1967, several OSU oceanography faculty had fabricated a 184-foot spar buoy for mounting atmospheric and oceanographic monitoring instruments. They planned to tow the spar buoy horizontally to Cobb Seamount and then flood a portion of it so that the buoy would rotate into a vertical position. Then they would anchor it to the top of Cobb Seamount. The buoy, named *Totem*, was tested in the waters off Oregon, and preparations were made to tow it to Cobb Seamount. It was all very hush-hush because one goal was to scoop the Sea Use Council.

When I learned of this undercover project, my immediate reaction was, "This is not the way to do this; we should be cooperating with the folks at the University of Washington." The project was well along, however, and those already involved seemed to want to make it a great coup over the folks in Seattle. I agreed to go along with this "secret project." It was a mistake. Secrecy had never been part of my operating style. I should have followed my instincts.

In June 1968, the *Cayuse* and the *Yaquina* towed *Totem* to Cobb Seamount. There were problems in erecting it and putting it in place atop the seamount. Apparently the buoy had been damaged either en route or in the erection process. According to Peter Kalk, quoted in Louise Burt and Miriam Ludwig's history of the first twenty years of OSU oceanography:

> The weather began to deteriorate. OSU headed home, planning to return in late July to install the weather instruments. Two weeks later scientists aboard the University of Washington research vessel, *Thomas G. Thompson*, reported they had observed *Totem* down in the water. The upper half, apparently held by one of the anchors, was floating nearby.[1]

Later, the *Cayuse* returned to the site of Cobb Seamount, gathered up the *Totem* debris, and returned to Newport. We had egg all over our collective faces. A few weeks later, my phone rang. It was Admiral Emory Stanley of the Sea Use Council, inviting me to come to Seattle to talk about our "adventure at Cobb Seamount."

There was no way I could or would turn down his invitation. I went to Seattle and met with the executive team of Sea Use Council. I was as forthright with them as possible. I explained exactly what had happened.

I admitted it was my mistake not to have spoken up when I first learned what my associates at OSU had intended and the secrecy involved. I told them what I thought I should have done, that keeping it secret was not my way of doing things and that we should have contacted our colleagues at the University of Washington. I probably told them that we were disappointed not to have been invited to be a member of the Sea Use Council.

By the time the session was over, we had cleared the air. If anything positive had come out of the entire affair, I had learned a lesson. I realized that I could manage the oceanography department and its oceanographic affairs effectively if I did it my way, based on my own principles, my own instincts. Subsequently, Admiral Stanley and I became good and longtime friends.

INDUSTRY COOPERATORS

WHEN I ASSUMED THE LEADERSHIP of the oceanography department, I recognized the special value private dollars could have in enabling the department to take on activities outside the normal purview of state government and without the constraints imposed by state regulations. I also quickly learned that all private fund solicitation must take place from the president's office—private fundraising was not a part of the job description for department chairs. But I also realized that some of our research activities were of interest to the oil and gas industry. I saw this as an opportunity to bring in nonstate, nonfederal dollars and at the same time enhance our relationship with a major industry.

It had been less than a decade since I had been active in the petroleum industry. I still felt comfortable with members of that industry, and I noted that a number of other oceanographic institutions had developed relationships there, the main purpose of which was to obtain money. OSU oceanography could do the same. I knew this could be construed as a violation of the president's mandate about fundraising, but it was also a way to enhance relations with an industry that might provide employment for some of our graduates. An advantage I thought we had over the other oceanographic institutions was that the head of our oceanography program, namely me, had spent three years in the industry and approached the relationship in a slightly different manner than the other institutions.

I contacted ten companies and asked for, and subsequently received, annual support of $10,000 each—probably a pittance to them, but significant for us. At the time we really had no other fundraising program. In return for their contributions, the oil companies were invited to send representatives to a two-day meeting at which we shared the latest knowledge we had created through our research, presenting those in attendance with a portfolio of our research papers. The participants were interested in our research generally and specifically in what we were doing in geophysics and geology.

The scientific presentations at the meetings were well integrated, giving those present an organized view of the latest knowledge of the areas in which we had been active. Also, we were prepared to share unpublished data and information in areas in which they might be interested. All of the publications and data were available to the public as publications or as data stored in national data banks. Our contribution was little more than a well-organized presentation. Our scientists were available for presentations at their company sites at cost, with no additional stipend. Thus, the Oceanography-Industrial Cooperation Program (OICP) was created.

We hoped to receive advice and input from the company representatives as to the nature of research they thought we should engage in. We were unsuccessful in obtaining their input on suggested research; their questions in the open sessions were guarded. As one representative put it to me in private discussion, comments and questions in an open session at which your competitors were present could be too revealing; it was better to keep quiet.

The OICP program was successful for a number of years but succumbed to an economic downturn in the petroleum industry, after which most companies abandoned direct support of US oceanography laboratories. At the time, the possible influence of industry on academe was recognized and needed to be guarded against. I was well aware of that possible influence, particularly from the petroleum industry. Even so, possibly as a result of this program, a number of our graduates developed successful careers in that field.

A DECADE OF GROWTH

TWO MAJOR EVENTS during the 1970s affected the way ocean research was done in the United States. OSU oceanography was significantly involved in both. The first was funding for the International Decade of Oceanographic Exploration (IDOE). The second was the creation of the

University National Oceanography Laboratory System (UNOLS), adopted in 1972. OSU oceanographers were about to be part of a revolution in the conduct of ocean research.

On March 8, 1968, President Lyndon Johnson called for "an historic and unprecedented adventure—an international decade of ocean exploration." In a report released in May 1968, the National Council on Marine Resources and Engineering Development described the general concept for such an international undertaking. Special committees under the aegis of the National Academy of Science developed the details, and the National Science Foundation was given responsibility for the IDOE.

The IDOE supported major multidisciplinary, multi-institutional programs. OSU oceanographers participated and provided leadership for a number of them, such as the IDOE Coastal Upwelling Experiment (CUE), conducted off the Oregon coast to address the physical aspects of coastal upwelling. It was led by Bob Smith of Oregon State and James O'Brien of Florida State University and included researchers from OSU, Florida State, Woods Hole, the University of Washington, Pennsylvania State University, and the University of Chicago. CUE was the precursor to the Coastal Upwelling Ecosystem Analysis studies off Oregon, northwest Africa, and Peru, which involved investigators from ten US institutions, including Oregon State, and institutions in twelve other countries.

Oregon State oceanographers were key participants in the IDOE Seabed Assessment Program, which included the Nazca Plate project off South America, with Vern Kulm as a coleader, and the Galapagos Rift study, in which deep-sea hot vents and their unique faunal communities were discovered for the first time—and by OSU scientists. The decision to participate in the Nazca Plate project of the Seabed Assessment Program was not taken lightly. It meant the *Yaquina* would be away from Oregon for up to six months at a time, thereby precluding its use at home. In order to decide whether we would participate in this program, I called an all-faculty meeting to discuss the program's pros and cons. We chose to participate. This decision was instrumental in transforming the OSU oceanography program from a modest near-shore oceanographic laboratory into a major deep-water oceanographic institution.

OSU researchers took part in other IDOE projects, including the Geochemical Ocean Sections program and the Climate Long-Range Investigations Mapping and Prediction program. Big science had arrived at Oregon State. There can be little doubt that participation in IDOE was significant in elevating our program to a major national level.

UNOLS had its origins in the 1969 report by the Stratton Commission, mentioned in the previous chapter, which recommended the establishment of a small number of University National Laboratories, presumably Scripps, Woods Hole, and Lamont at Columbia University. The middle-sized and smaller laboratories, such as those at the universities of Rhode Island, Texas A&M, Miami, Oregon State, and Washington, resisted because they had been left out of the Stratton Commission's recommendation. Following two years of heated debate involving the directors of laboratories both large and small and the leadership at NSF, the UNOLS concept was formulated and adapted to include the smaller institutions as well as the larger ones.

One major effect of UNOLS was to create a national academic ocean research fleet. Prior to the existence of UNOLS, ships were operated by each oceanographic institution for its own scientists. Afterward, all university-operated ships were scheduled jointly in a collaborative manner. The UNOLS accomplished more efficient use of vessels, standardized basic equipment, created uniform safety requirements, and resulted in the cooperative use of the nation's entire academic oceanographic fleet. It meant that OSU's vessels sometimes operated without an OSU researcher aboard, and that OSU oceanographers might conduct their research from a ship assigned to another institution.

UNOLS has operated successfully since 1972. I was chosen by NSF to be one of the five laboratory directors who drafted the original UNOLS proposal. I served as the first chair of the UNOLS council, which monitored the program. Both IDOE and UNOLS fostered cooperation in the conduct of ocean research to the benefit of all US oceanographers, particularly those at laboratories that cooperated fully, as OSU's department did.

My visibility among academic oceanographers, already established during my time at NSF, continued to increase. The community of academic oceanographers was still relatively small, and being the chairman of a rapidly expanding organization added to that visibility. I was asked to serve on committees that added to my national recognition and to Oregon State University's stature as an oceanographic institution. During 1968–1972 I served on a number of advisory committees for the NSF (oceanographic research, ship operations, undergraduate scientific equipment, and others), the US State Department, the National Research Council's Ocean Affairs Board, the Coastal States Organization, the Oregon Governor's Advisory Committee on Oceanography, and the Oregon Environmental Science and Technology Advisory Committee. I chaired the National Research Council's Ocean Science Committee and was one of the vice presidents of the Marine Technology Society. I also became involved with the science advisory group of the US delegation to the United Nations Law of the Seas Conference.

SCHOOL OF OCEANOGRAPHY

IN 1970, the three-person OSU Goals Commission appointed by President Jensen delivered its report to the new president of OSU, Robert MacVicar. Among its recommendations was that the Department of Oceanography become a full-fledged School of Oceanography.[2] The commission recommended that the activities of the school be essentially the same as those of the department; that it offer only graduate degrees; that there was little need for departments within the school; and that those oceanography faculty currently engaged in fisheries research be transferred to the Department of Fisheries and Wildlife or given joint appointments with that department.

Wayne Burt and I drafted a detailed proposal citing the commission's recommendations and our own preparedness for this new status. After approval by the dean of science (at that time acting dean Tom Parsons), the proposal moved through the university bureaucracy and was approved by the OSU Faculty Senate in 1971 and then by the Oregon Board of Higher Education. In March 1972, the Department of Oceanography became the School of Oceanography.

The next question to be answered was, who will be the dean of the School of Oceanography? I think Wayne wanted to be the first dean, probably not so much to be an administrator of the school as to be its visible leader. Some oceanography faculty strongly recommended a wider search, believing that this was an opportunity to attract a high-quality, high-visibility oceanographer from outside Oregon State. President MacVicar, who had taken over in 1970, exercised a pragmatic approach and simply said, "John, you are the dean of the School of Oceanography." I know some oceanography faculty were disappointed.

For me, not much changed other than the reporting structure. I no longer reported to the dean of science; I was now a member of the Council of Deans and reported directly to the president. I suspect the visibility of oceanography at Oregon State changed—and, of course, the letterhead and all the business cards needed to be changed, too.

The meetings of the Council of Deans made more sense to me than the department chair meetings had, but after the initial learning took place, I began to find the meetings dull, although relaxing. I remember taking some pleasure in informing the other deans that, in my opinion, academic deans were the least important academics on campus. Faculty were the most important, I told them, because "faculty *are* the university"—as an older faculty member at Columbia University had once informed the then-president of Columbia, Dwight D. Eisenhower. Next in importance is the university president, because he or she sets the overall image and policy for the university. Then come the department heads—the line officers responsible for translating the policies of the president into action by their faculty. Last in line of importance are the deans, who, admittedly, do have certain communication and leadership roles, but by default are fourth in line of academic importance.

Further, because the School of Oceanography did not have departments, the dean of that school was required to assume the role of the department head in translating policies into action. Thus, the oceanography dean was more important in the scheme of things than any of the other deans by virtue of his department head responsibilities.

When I told them this, the other deans just smiled as if to say, "Byrne, you have a lot to learn." They were right.

CHAPTER 9

A New School and a New Dean (1972–1976)

"A rose by any other name"
— Shakespeare

WHEN THE DEPARTMENT OF OCEANOGRAPHY became a school in 1972, it had a staff of 165, 98 students, and an annual operating budget at the four-million-dollar mark. The size of the staff and budget had increased every year since 1959. The student body had leveled off at about one hundred graduate students, with 25 percent of them receiving graduate degrees annually.

The School of Oceanography operated as it did when it was a department, with no increase in staff and no changes in philosophy or policies. Because we were a growing organization, space continued to be a problem. The vacant houses we acquired near the oceanography building may have been OK for offices, but we still needed more space for storage, shop facilities, and other supporting activities. Rod Mesecar, who had developed a first-class research equipment design and construction group, was the obvious person to take over the construction of support facilities.

Rod learned very quickly that any building valued at more than $50,000 required approval at the legislative level, whereas buildings valued at less than $50,000 could be built without external approval. Prefabricated buildings cost $49,000. Rod knew how to design and build them, and Dave Zopf knew how to obtain approval from the physical plant and university administration. Rod and Dave were a great team. We built five of those buildings on the south edge of campus without the involvement of the Board of Higher Education or the legislature.

Wayne hired Dave to attend to daily management problems that were outside the purview of the oceanography faculty researchers. Dave was a clever fellow. He had an office in the oceanography building but rarely used it. Finding him when I needed him was frustrating at first, until I discovered that he operated out of a metal-covered notebook he always carried with him and that I could probably find him in the university commons drinking coffee with someone from the physical plant, the financial office of the university, or the upper administration. It didn't take long to become aware that his friends would go out of their way to do special favors for oceanography, largely as a result of their trust in Dave.

THE MARINE SCIENCE CENTER—AGAIN

Wayne Burt and Tom Scott, the nominal directors of the Marine Science Center, were both located in Corvallis, but they didn't seem to want to have anything to do with management problems in Newport. The two resident directors at the center, Joel Hedgpeth and Bill McNeil, apparently didn't get along with each other. Captain Dick Redmond, a capable manager of ship operations in Newport, served as the facilities manager for the entire center. Redmond was something of a martinet, and his management style contributed to morale problems in both areas of the center.

Dave Zopf learned about the center's problems and came to me with a proposal: I, John Byrne, would become the single director of the center, relieving Drs. Burt, Scott, Hedgpeth, and McNeil of their facility management responsibilities. Dave would become facility manager for the center, relieving Captain Redmond of that responsibility, and would commute to the center three days a week. I would go there once a week.

I wasn't looking for extra work, but the center was important, and Dave convinced me to try out his proposal on Drs. Burt and Scott. The proposed management structure seemed simple to me, but adoption of the proposal required the approvals of Wayne Burt, Tom Scott, and Fred Burgess, dean of engineering and a member of the center's advisory group. Wayne and Tom seemed delighted with the idea, and Burgess saw no problems. So I presented the idea to President MacVicar. In 1972, I became the acting director of the Marine Science Center, and Dave Zopf was appointed facility/business manager. I had always had a good relationship with Joel Hedgpeth, and that didn't change when I relieved him of some of his management responsibilities for the Yaquina Biological

Laboratory. Tom Scott informed Bill McNeil of the changes. No problem there, either.

My day in Newport became a welcome distraction from the routines and challenges of managing oceanography. I liked the people at the center, and I became familiar with the beautiful scenery of the Coast Range between Corvallis and Newport. I'm not sure I contributed very much to the development of the center, although we did build some student housing during my tenure as acting director. Give Dave Zopf credit for that. It did become obvious to me, however, that if the center was ever to reach its potential, it needed a full-time resident director who could develop programs, serve as its local champion, and develop positive relationships with the people of Newport.

For the next five years, I tried to convince President MacVicar that the center needed a full-time resident director. Finally in 1976, Mac appointed a committee to examine the center's management structure. The following year, he appointed Lavern Weber as resident director. In 1983, the center was named the Hatfield Marine Science Center in honor of Senator Mark O. Hatfield. Under Weber's leadership, the center developed as a major element in the marine programs of Oregon State University and a significant part of the Newport community. Weber continued as director for more than twenty-five years.

MARINE RESOURCE MANAGEMENT PROGRAM

AS COASTAL POPULATIONS and activities increased in the late 1960s and early 1970s, it became clear that there was a national need for well-trained managers of coastal and near-shore businesses, ports, marinas, fisheries companies, and other organizations. We at Oregon State were well positioned to create a cross-disciplinary program combining oceanography, social science, and business courses that could be effective in preparing students to fill the management vacuum. I saw the opportunity to create a program that few if any other oceanographic institutions were pursuing, so I asked Vic Neal, who attended to many of the details of our academic programs, to prepare a plan for such a program. He did an excellent job, and in 1974, we introduced a new master's degree program in Marine Resource Management (MRM). Students took courses in ocean and atmospheric sciences, fisheries, political science, economics, anthropology, sociology, communications, business practices, and

law. Faculty members from other departments were extremely cooperative. The MRM program has been well received and successful for more
than a quarter of a century.

THE WAVE RESEARCH LABORATORY

WITHOUT A NATIONALLY recognized oceanography presence at OSU,
O. Howard Hinsdale might not have turned to OSU to test his company's method of building wave-resistant structures. It all started in the
late 1960s and early 1970s, when the US Atomic Energy Commission
anticipated the construction of artificial islands on the continental shelf
off the east coast of the United States for the siting of nuclear power
plants. Umpqua Navigation Co., a subsidiary of Bohemia Lumber Company, was then the major construction firm that built the jetties protecting the entrances to the bays along the Oregon coast. These jetties were
constructed by carefully placing huge blocks of basalt in an interlocking
fashion.

O. H. Hinsdale was the CEO of the Umpqua Navigation Company, and
he was convinced that Umpqua's method of constructing wave-resistant
structures was superior to any other. He recognized there could be a great
financial gain for his company if it could get the contract for building
the proposed offshore islands. First, however, Hinsdale needed to convince others of the efficacy of the Umpqua method of construction. He
approached the US Army Corps of Engineers to conduct research tests of
the Umpqua method in one of their wave research facilities. The Corps
declined, and there was no other adequate wave research facility in the
United States to do the tests.

Hinsdale knew of our growing oceanography program, and he was
also aware of the high reputation of OSU's school of engineering. Hinsdale asked OSU to construct a wave tank and conduct the impartial
tests that he was convinced would demonstrate the Umpqua way to be
the best. OSU was fortunate to have two engineers, Jack Nath and Larry
Slotta, who were confident they could design and build such a wave tank.

OSU agreed to build the tank and conduct the tests. But we insisted
the tests would be unbiased and might demonstrate that the Umpqua
way was not the best. Hinsdale was willing to take that risk. The result:
a wave research flume 342 feet long, 12 feet wide, and 15 feet deep at its
deepest point, with the capability of generating a five-foot random wave.

The tests were conducted, and the results did validate Hinsdale's claim of superior construction. Unfortunately for Hinsdale, the AEC decided not to build the offshore islands. Fortunately for OSU, it had a new wave research tank, the largest of its kind in North America. The excellence of wave research by OSU engineers brought recognition to OSU as a Center of Excellence for wave research by the US Navy. Later, the NSF designated Oregon State as a center for tsunami research.

O. H. Hinsdale made other contributions to OSU. For some time, the tugboat he had converted into a recreational yacht sat at the dock in Newport, his gift to the oceanography department. Because it was a tax-deferred gift, the law required that OSU keep the vessel for a period of time before turning it into cash. I had hoped to find a use for the tugboat, but unfortunately couldn't, so it sat at the dock for the required period of time before becoming a cash donation.

THE RESEARCH VESSEL *WECOMA*

MAINTAINING A HEALTHY FLEET of research vessels has been a national problem since the rebirth of oceanography following World War II. Since then, the navy and the NSF have been the major sources of funds for the conversion of existing research vessels and the construction of new ones. Replacement of aging vessels has been a concern, and when new vessels are built, the competition for their assignments has been intense.

Sometime around 1973, the NSF made a decision to fund the construction of two new mid-size research vessels ("mid-size" means about 180 feet long), assigning the design and operation of the vessels to the Woods Hole Oceanographic Institution. Woods Hole's design of the mid-sized *Oceanus* created a new class of vessel.

Both the University of Rhode Island and Oregon State University submitted proposals to NSF to be the operator of the second new ship. We wanted to replace the highly regarded *Yaquina*. Wayne Burt had developed a fine proposal, and we felt we had a good chance of winning the competition. Wayne and I traveled to Washington, DC, to make our case to an NSF panel of ocean scientists. I was informed later by one of the panel members that our presentation was the better of the two. In Washington, politics are ever-present, and such was no doubt the case in the selection of the second ship operator. It is quite likely that NSF officials and their advisors realized that, by giving the nod to Oregon State,

Senator Claiborne Pell of Rhode Island, a strong ocean advocate, would see to it that enough federal funds became available to construct a third new vessel, which would be assigned to the University of Rhode Island.

That is exactly what happened: we got the second vessel, and a third was approved for the University of Rhode Island. All three new vessels were built in Sturgeon Bay, Wisconsin: *Oceanus* first, *Wecoma* next, and then the University of Rhode Island's *Endeavor*. The *Wecoma* was launched on May 31, 1975. It was fun to hear the Sturgeon Bay High School band play "On, Wisconsin." It was less amusing when they played the University of Oregon's fight song rather than the Oregon State Beaver fight song, but I was probably the only person at the launching who noted the mistake. Oh well.

The *Wecoma* was finished and equipped for sea duty. Our new research ship made the trip down the St. Lawrence Seaway and then down the east coast and through the Panama Canal, arriving in Newport on January 2, 1976. Final modifications were carried out in Newport, and the *Wecoma* was ready for dedication on July 23. That July, the *Wecoma* began a successful thirty-six years of service as a UNOLS vessel assigned by the NSF to Oregon State University. What the *Yaquina* had been to the first generation of OSU oceanographers, the *Wecoma* was to the next generation. At the end of the *Wecoma's* period of service, the *Oceanus* was reassigned from Woods Hole to Oregon State, and the *Wecoma* was decommissioned on March 23, 2012.

STUDENT RELATIONS

The end of the 1960s and early 1970s was a period of student activism and social change, particularly on university campuses, essentially brought on by the Vietnam war. Students increasingly exercised their voices and their wills in the pursuit of authority, and by so doing changed the relationship they had with faculty and university administrators. I felt it was wise to listen to them. I began to receive reports from faculty and staff that some of our students were upset about a variety of things in oceanography.

I asked the students to meet with me, just me and the students. I set the meeting for late afternoon on a weekday in a room in Cordley Hall, outside the environs of oceanography but near the oceanography building. At the appointed hour, the room was packed with close to ninety students, standing room only. After opening the meeting, I told the students I was there to listen to them. There would be no attribution of comments; I would take notes on what they said and I promised action on their recommendations when and where it was possible. The meeting lasted close to two hours, and, as I recall, I took about three pages of closely spaced notes. Basically, the students wanted better communication with the department. They wanted more information concerning the operation of the department, and they wanted a means to communicate their feelings on issues of all types. Further, they requested improved access to oceanography facilities at all times, twenty-four hours per day, seven days a week.

Among their many requests were some that could be implemented overnight, which we did. We issued building keys to every student, posted ship operation schedules, put out news information as appropriate with copies in every student mailbox, and so on. If their requests were impossible to implement, I explained to them the reasons why. I felt it was extremely important that we be as responsive as possible.

I judged the meeting a success and decided to make it an annual event. The second year about forty students showed up for the meeting, and the third year the number was down to fewer than twenty. After that the meetings seemed no longer necessary; we were communicating in an improved manner.

It had also been my practice to hold department, and later school, meetings to which all staff and students were invited. It was my belief that everyone was important to the success of the oceanographic enterprise. I stressed this in the special meetings with the students. The students still wanted a closer relationship with the administration, so I established a student advisory group of about eight students who would meet with me on a regular schedule. The members of that group were selected by the students, recognizing that each of the subdisciplines of oceanography must be represented. These special meetings with students and the advisory group seemed to work; students were not reticent to bring up matters of concern, nor was I.

One particular meeting stands out in memory. This meeting did not address matters of student concern, but rather was an opportunity for the student group to sit at the table with one of the world leaders of ocean engineering, Robert F. Bauer, the CEO of Global Marine, Inc., the company that built the drilling vessels for the Deep Sea Drilling Project. It was June 1974, and Bauer was in Corvallis to attend his daughter's graduation from OSU.

Global Marine had completed the construction of the *Glomar Explorer*, a drill ship more than six hundred feet long, and was preparing to use it to recover manganese nodules from the deep sea.[1] The students engaged Mr. Bauer in a detailed discussion of manganese nodule recovery, and he was forthcoming in his discussion of the details.

Within weeks it was revealed that there had been no intention of using the *Glomar Explorer* to recover manganese nodules. The ship had been built under secret contract with the Central Intelligence Agency with the sole intent of recovering a Soviet ballistic missile submarine that had sunk in the North Pacific Ocean in 1968. In fact, the *Glomar Explorer* had been on its way to the submarine recovery site as the discussion in my office was taking place. A portion of the Soviet submarine was recovered a short time after the discussion with Bauer. It was possibly as close to the Cold War as most of those students would ever come.

ADMINISTRATION GROWTH

By the mid-1970s, I began to feel the School of Oceanography was thin administratively. With no separate departments within the school, I was operating simultaneously as a dean, the chairman of a very large academic department, and the director of an ever-burgeoning research institute. We needed help. Besides, I knew that a good manager plans for a succession of leadership. There should be someone directly behind the leader to take over in the leader's absence so that no hiatus in authority and leadership occurs.

Because of the size of our operation, it made sense to initiate a national search for a new associate dean. Several outstanding candidates emerged, including George Keller, then at the NOAA laboratory in Miami. Because George was a good, longtime friend, I decided to let the faculty decide who the associate dean should be. There was little question in their collective minds: they wanted George Keller. George accepted my offer and joined the School of Oceanography in November 1975. A few months later, another opportunity arose for me at Oregon State.

CHAPTER 10

Joining the University's Administration (1976–1981)

Excelsior

IN LATE 1975, ROY YOUNG, the university's vice president for research and graduate studies, announced he would be leaving Oregon State the following July to become the chancellor at the University of Nebraska. George Keller had requested more duties as associate dean of the School of Oceanography. It occurred to me we might take advantage of Roy's departure to give George the oceanography administrative experience he was seeking.

With George's concurrence, I approached President MacVicar and suggested that he appoint me on an interim basis to the position Roy was vacating and appoint George as acting dean of oceanography while a national search was under way for Roy Young's successor. Conceivably, once we had a permanent administrator for research, we would both return to oceanography, and George would be more prepared for added responsibility within the school. MacVicar bought the idea, and the changes in our assignments were made effective July 1, 1976. For the 1976–1977 year, I served as acting dean of research while a national search was under way. As it turned out, I was selected to do the research job full-time.

When I moved into the university's Research Office, I felt I was leaving the field of oceanography for good. That was not the case. I continued to be active on several National Science Foundation committees and also added to my national committee list with appointments to a number of ocean-related committees and boards for the National Research Council, the National Oceanic and Atmospheric Administration (NOAA), the American Geological Institute, the University Corporation for Atmospheric Research, the Marine Technology Society, and the American Geophysical Union. Membership on these committees and boards were steps toward seniority in the ocean science community. Although I was no longer the director of an oceanographic laboratory, I was still considered part of the oceanographic community.

As dean of research, I became familiar with the full spectrum of research at Oregon State: forestry, agriculture, biochemistry, and microbiology, to mention only a few. The Research Office oversaw all research and education grants and contracts that came to Oregon State from external sources.[1] In addition, the dean of research was responsible for oversight of OSU centers, institutes, and the all-university programs. The centers and institutes provided an integrating mechanism across academic disciplines. As originally established, centers had facilities; institutes did not. Centers included the Marine Science Center, the Radiation Center, and the Environmental Health Sciences Center. Institutes included the Climatic Research Institute, the Transportation Research Institute, and the Water Resources Research Institute. Administrative organizations that impacted the departments on a larger scale included the Agricultural Experiment Station, the Forest Research Laboratory, and the Sea Grant College Program.

A number of these administrative units—Sea Grant is a good example—were established to manage the major federal grants designed to distribute funds to investigators throughout the university. Each of these units had its own director and its own budget. Several directors reported to both the deans of their appropriate academic schools and to the dean of research.

The Research Office budget came from the indirect costs on grants that came to the university and from a major grant from the National Institutes of Health (NIH). Funds from the Research Office were used to stimulate start-up research efforts, provide matching funds for major pieces of equipment, help faculty and departments make up funding shortfalls, and otherwise support research opportunities. The Research Office also helped faculty obtain patents and copyrights that benefited both the faculty member and the university. The dean of research had the opportunity to be helpful to faculty who were active, productive, and imaginative.

The Research Office was in the administration building, next to the Sea Grant and Graduate School offices. I had two assistants, Ruth Jenks and

Mary Perkins (later Mary Nunn). Ruth was a mature woman who could be charming or intimidating. She sat at a desk near the office entrance and was the first person encountered upon entering. Her greeting could be pleasant or stern. Ruth kept track of the Research Office finances. Mary, younger than Ruth, sat farther back in the room and took care of most of the secretarial duties. She was pleasant and businesslike. Both Ruth and Mary were competent and gave a professional aura to the office.

I suppose it was natural that I would be viewed with some skepticism, both by the office staff and by some successful research-minded faculty. Roy Young had created the Research Office, and he had developed most of the office policies and procedures. Roy was a man who went out of his way to avoid contentious situations and, in some cases, tried to avoid making painful personnel decisions. The office had run smoothly under his direction, and I suspect anyone succeeding him would be viewed with a wait-and-see attitude. Two faculty members made blunt comments soon after I took over. I didn't know either of them but soon learned that both were outstanding scientists with minds of their own. Don Reed, a biochemist of some repute, informed me directly that the faculty would be watching me carefully to see how I handled the job. I don't know what he would have done if I hadn't measured up to his expectations. In any case, I intended to do the job as I saw fit. My experience at the NSF and in oceanography was substantial. I had handled difficult people at the Humble Company, in OSU oceanography, and in the oceanographic community at large.

In spite of Reed's initial warning, I had no problems with him. He could be difficult, but he was an outstanding scientist. I respected him, and I think it was mutual.

The other faculty member I had problems with initially was George Pearson, but for very different reasons. George was also a respected scientist and a member of the university's research council. He let me know that the scheduling of my first meeting of the research council was inconvenient for him. He planned to be out of town and insisted the meeting be rescheduled at a time convenient for him. He told me he took his assignment on the research council seriously. His insistence that I change the time and date of the meeting gave new meaning to the word *insist*.

With some difficulty, I adjusted the schedule so George could be there. He proved an effective member of the council. Once over the hurdles with these two faculty members, it was clear sailing. I saw the Research Office as a place to help faculty enhance their creativity, and I think I gained their respect.

Stimulating new research was a challenge because of limited financial resources, but the funds we did have seemed to be effective. Some of the funds generated by the indirect costs on grants, together with a major university-wide public health service grant, were used as start-up funds for new research. Deciding how to allocate these start-up funds was a major task of the faculty research council. The research council was appointed by the faculty senate and met every four or six weeks. The council considered matters of importance to OSU research, including research policies. When I arrived, the dean of research chaired the meetings. In order to be an independent body, I changed the council chairmanship to an elected member of the council.

As time passed, Ruth Jenks and Mary Perkins accepted me. I had expanded the clerical staff and brought in a faculty intern, a practice Roy Young had initiated. The small room off the main office that was used as a library was turned into a private office for Ruth, ostensibly so she could work on financial matters. Mary was moved to the reception desk. The Research Office became a welcoming place for faculty and others.

When I joined the Research Office in 1976, Oregon State had several hundred active grants with a total annual value of about $23 million. About $16.7 million was for research, and the rest was for traineeships, equipment, and educational programs. Virtually all of these funds were generated by individual faculty efforts. The numbers of grants and their value increased every year. When I left after five years, the research volume had increased to more than $35 million, with the total for all grants doubling to more than $46 million. Due to the high productivity of our faculty, OSU was by far the major research university in the state system.

During my tenure, we initiated several programs that probably would not have been possible without the help of faculty interns who volunteered to help with research administration. Larry Kenneke, an intern from the School of Education, was helpful in developing a series of faculty grantsmanship workshops. I presented the initial workshop on the Research Office and funding sources and a later one on complying with federal regulations. Larry was also instrumental in preparing a handbook for faculty on how to obtain and manage grants. In addition to these aids to the faculty, we instituted a series of reviews of OSU's centers and institutes. Occasionally I prepared summary reports of OSU research activities for the higher education chancellor, designed to remind him and his staff of the importance of our research efforts and to brag about Oregon State's research prowess.

Occasional ad hoc assignments added zest to my research position, such as serving as the chair of the higher education system's Marine Science Commission. This commission consisted of selected personnel from OSU and the University of Oregon and representatives of Oregon business. Periodically the commission was asked to review the programs at the various marine centers operated by Oregon's public universities, including OSU's Marine Science Center and Seafood Laboratory and the U of O's Marine Biological Institute in Charleston, Oregon. The commission was asked to look for duplication of effort. After visiting these the facilities, we found little if any duplication and in fact noted that the activities of the two universities complemented each other. Our report was supportive of the marine efforts by both universities.

THE H. J. ANDREWS EXPERIMENTAL FOREST

ONE OF THE FIRST learning experiences that confronted me after becoming dean of research came from the School of Forestry. The dean of forestry or one of his lieutenants had submitted a proposal to the National Science Foundation to establish the H. J. Andrews Experimental Forest—a complete drainage basin on the west flank of the Oregon Cascades—to be designated as a "national center for forest ecological research." Identification as a national center would add considerable prestige to OSU's forestry research efforts. In order to seal the deal with NSF, Carl Stoltenberg, the forestry dean, wanted a financial commitment from OSU in the form of continuing salary, or part of the salary, of the forest manager.

I didn't have a clue as to how much I should commit to the manager's salary, but I did want to help. I also suspected that action on this matter would be the first signal from the Research Office as to how cooperative I would be.

To get a feeling for the project and to see what the terrain looked like, my son, Steve, and I loaded our dirt bikes into the back of our pickup truck and headed up the McKenzie Highway to Blue River. We spent a Saturday afternoon riding our motorcycles around the Andrews Forest drainage basin. We were particularly impressed by the close-up view of the Three Sisters volcanic peaks from the upper edge of the basin. The area was beautiful and appeared to be pristine.

On Monday morning, I called Dean Stoltenberg and told him what Steve and I had done. I told him the Research Office would provide the full salary of the manager. I think Carl was hoping for only half of the salary. A few days later, an NSF officer visited OSU to evaluate the proposal, look at the basin, and determine how committed we were to the project. I had the sense at the time that my pledge to provide the manager's full salary helped carry the day.

Oregon State would operate the Andrews Experimental Forest as an NSF-designated National Center. It was also designated a Biosphere Reserve as part of the United Nations Man and the Biosphere Program and subsequently was recognized as a charter member of NSF's Long-Term Ecological Research Program. The H. J. Andrews Experimental Forest is a successful research site today. Sometimes a person gets lucky, even if he doesn't fully understand what he's doing.

AGRICULTURAL RESEARCH

ANOTHER EARLY CHALLENGE involved the Agricultural Experiment Station (AES). The AES consisted of nine agricultural research stations located throughout Oregon. The stations focused on agricultural research and economic development of Oregon's diverse agricultural crops: wheat in northeast Oregon; fruit, notably pears, in the area around Medford; ornamentals in the area near Portland; and many others across the state. Farmers throughout Oregon depended on the results of Oregon State's agricultural research to improve their harvests. They had a long tradition of turning to the School of Agriculture and its Agricultural Research Stations for assistance.[2]

The Ag Experiment Station director reported to the dean of the School of Agriculture. I thought the dean of research, as the highest-ranking university official responsible for university research, should be aware of all the research carried out by OSU personnel, including research done in the School of Agriculture. So, strictly for information purposes, I proposed to change the reporting pathway: the Experiment Station director would report to the dean of research—me—as well as to the dean of agriculture. There was no personal agenda here. I got along fine with the director of the Ag Experiment Station.

However, when some farmers learned about my proposed change in the reporting structure, they were upset. I think they were concerned that someone outside of agriculture would control research that was of particular importance to farmers. I hadn't intended to change how the research was directed—I just wanted regular reports on the nature and results of the research.

A number of farmers phoned President MacVicar, no doubt calling for my hide. To Mac's credit, he let me handle the situation. He trusted me to take care of it. I called a meeting of everyone involved at OSU and asked that they invite representatives of the agricultural industry.

The meeting room was packed, and few of the people there seemed to be smiling. I explained exactly what I had in mind: reporting, not control. I pointed out that my plate as dean of research was sufficiently full that I didn't have the time, desire, or knowledge to tamper with agricultural research. I simply wanted to know what was going on and to be helpful if I could.

Apparently the meeting cleared the air. It was a slight change for agricultural research, and the farmers present at the meeting accepted the change. It was not the first time I had faced a hostile audience, nor would it be the last.

I think I won over the farmers and the personnel of the research stations by the regular visits I made to the stations to learn what was going on, and then later with an intensive briefing about our wheat-breeding program from the breeder, Warren Kronstad. These actions did a lot to convince the aggies that I was not a threat, but in fact could be helpful to them as they expressed their needs. After I'd spent most of a day with Warren learning about his wheat breeding, he told me that it was the first time any university administrator had spent time learning about his program. His support of me was influential in changing the attitudes of wheat farmers about the new guy in the Research Office.

THE OSU PRESS

OREGON STATE maintained the only academic press in the state of Oregon. I was proud of that. The OSU Press had successfully published some of the classics of Oregon science by researchers at Oregon State and the University of Oregon. Its books, always well presented, included titles on diverse topics of interest and value to Oregonians: the Native American tribes of Oregon, the nineteenth-century journey of Wallis Nash from England to Oregon and back, the scientific revolution of plate tectonics, and many others. It had been a tradition of the press to publish the annual Thomas Condon Lectures and the proceedings of the yearly

Biological Colloquium. The *Atlas of the Pacific Northwest* was updated regularly and was a popular seller.

If the OSU Press had problems, they were usually financial. On several occasions, I was able to help out with funds from the Research Office. The books resulting from the Condon Lectures and the Biology Colloquiums were almost always slim volumes, paid for in part from the endowments that supported those events. Occasionally, though, the leader of the colloquium would be carried away with enthusiasm and would produce a massive, costly volume. After Art Boucot of the geology department had led the thirty-seventh annual colloquium, he teamed up with Jane Gray, director of the U of O's Museum of Natural History, to produce an interesting tome titled *Historical Biogeography, Plate Tectonics and the Changing Environment: Proceedings of the Thirty-Seventh Annual Biology Colloquium and Selected Papers.* I think it was the "selected papers" part of the volume that expanded the book's girth and also its cost. I was able to use Research Office funds to help the press cover the additional expense.

A second case occurred when Joel Hedgpeth, resident director of the Yaquina Biological Laboratory at OSU's Marine Science Center, produced an expensive volume at a time the press was under severe financial constraints. The press told Joel it could not afford to provide him with a complimentary copy of the book he had been so instrumental in producing. You can imagine his reaction to that. I made sure he received complimentary copies.

PATENTS, COPYRIGHTS, AND LICENSES: TECHNOLOGY TRANSFER

BEFORE 1976, Oregon State didn't have much in the nature of patents, copyrights, or commercial licenses, nor did it have the needed policies governing such things. Because the volume of activity was relatively small, OSU sent all its patent and copyright work to a Portland law firm.

That all changed in the late 1970s when OSU scientists Jim Ayres and Bill Sandine were working to develop a cheese starter—a cocktail of microbes that cause milk to ferment and form curds. They discovered a new microbial combination that increased the yield of cheese considerably. A Borden Company subsidiary requested permission to license the process. Suddenly OSU had to obtain patents and copyrights in order to protect the concept and put the university, and the inventors of the process, in a position to receive royalties. Ralph Shay, who had recently stepped down as chairman of the botany and plant pathology department, was assigned to the Research Office and put in charge of the Ayres-Sandine project. Thus began OSU's technology transfer program.

The cheese-starter project, which yielded significant financial returns, forced us to work out a policy for sharing revenues among the originating faculty, their departments, and the university. Shay and I developed a policy aimed at providing as much financial return as possible to the faculty member and his or her department in order to give faculty an incentive to develop ideas that might be suitable for a profitable technology transfer. Bill Hostetler, who became director of technology transfer in 1987, informed me that the cheese-starter license brought about $6 million over several years to the benefit of the university and professors Ayres and Sandine.

DEAN OF THE GRADUATE SCHOOL

IN 1978, the dean of the Graduate School left OSU for what was to be a one-year leave of absence. President MacVicar opted for a short-term and inexpensive solution: he appointed me to cover for the dean of the Graduate School until he returned. Mac was confident I could handle the dean's tasks along with my own. The Research Office appeared to be running well, and because it was right next door to the Graduate School, I should be able to hop back and forth easily between the two offices. Further, Wendell Slabaugh from the chemistry department was serving as part-time assistant dean of graduate programs and spent his mornings in the Graduate School office. I suppose Mac reasoned that the two of us should be able to handle graduate programs with little problem. I started spending my mornings in the Graduate School and my afternoons in the Research Office.

After about a year, the Graduate School dean decided to stay in Washington, DC, and resigned from Oregon State. Shortly thereafter, my title was changed to vice president for research and graduate studies. I was now the full-time dean of the Graduate School and the chief administrative officer for research.

One of my duties as graduate dean was to rule on the many requests for waivers of deadlines and other requirements for the completion of students' degrees. At first I wanted to be lenient when I heard the many heart-tugging stories put forward to justify a waiver of rules, but one of the clerks in the Graduate School office set me straight. She pointed out that every time I permitted a deviation from the long-standing rules of graduate protocol, I was cheating those students who met the established protocol of existing rules. She was correct, of course. It didn't take long for me learn to turn down requests to short-circuit Graduate School requirements. I soon came to regard the Graduate School as my "no" office and the Research Office as my "yes" office. No, you can't deviate from the rules. Yes, I might be able to help with your research project that will move knowledge along.

The graduate dean was required to sign all doctoral dissertations. Usually this was no problem, but I soon discovered that dissertations from a certain OSU school didn't always measure up to OSU's standards of quality or the generally accepted rules of grammar. This presented a problem, because the school's dean had already approved and signed the dissertations. How could I graciously inform the dean that there was no way I, as the final monitor for Oregon State University, could or would accept such poor-quality dissertations?

I fretted for a while over how to respond. Finally, I settled on a short note expressing my regret at not signing the dissertation and pointing out that somehow this particular dissertation had slipped through, probably during a very busy time, and that on the first page or so I had noted several mistakes in grammar or spelling, which were clearly marked in red ink. With the note appended, the dissertation was sent back to the dean. The deans were always gracious in their replies to me.

At commencement in June, it was my responsibility to hand out the master's degrees and to read the names of those graduates who were receiving doctoral degrees. The process was that I would read the name of the new graduate. He or she would receive the doctoral hood and then be escorted by the major professor and greeted by the university president. Many of the recipients were international students with names I found difficult to pronounce. I made it a practice to meet all the doctoral graduates in the queue in the Memorial Union quad before the parade to the graduation site. At that time, I read all of their names aloud and made sure that I had the pronunciation correct. It seemed to work; it put me at ease, and I think it put the degree recipients at ease, too.

UPPER ADMINISTRATION

WHEN I MOVED into the Research Office in 1976, the other members of the administration in addition to the president were the dean of administration, the dean of the faculty, and the dean of undergraduate studies, all members of the president's council. Each week started with a meeting of the president's council, including those deans and an additional half-dozen or so lower-level administrators, together with legal counsel, the summer-term director, the affirmative-action officer, and others. These meetings were primarily for information sharing. For some of the folks around the table, it was their time on stage, and they took full advantage of it, telling us more than any of us really wanted to know. Other regularly scheduled meetings that seemed interminable were those of the dean of faculty, which almost always focused on rules, regulations, and schedules—possibly important to faculty and deans, but not to me. Enough said.

Once a year, a team of the upper-level administrators involved with academic matters met to review faculty dossiers concerning promotion and the granting of tenure (P&T). This was a labor-intensive effort. The dossiers included statements of faculty workloads, lists of publications and often the publications themselves, mentions of other achievements, letters of support from department chairs and academic deans, and letters of evaluation from outside reviewers.

We were all expected to review and be familiar with the materials in all of the dossiers for each of the faculty members being brought forward for review. The academic deans presented the case for each of their faculty members and then left the room. Each faculty member was discussed by the entire group, and then President MacVicar made the final decision. Mac was decisive, but occasionally he reversed his original negative decision if the case was effectively appealed by an academic dean. When he did reverse an earlier decision, he sometimes exclaimed, referring to himself, "Often in error, seldom in doubt." I doubt that Mac was often wrong.

Two other things I experienced with President MacVicar: (1) he insisted on reading and personally signing all faculty out-of-state travel authorizations, and (2) occasionally his temper erupted when someone offered a comment that conflicted with his opinion. With regard to the travel authorizations, he pointed out that he liked to know what his faculty were doing, and if he encountered a person on campus who had traveled, he might be able to ask that person how the trip to Kansas City to the XYZ meeting went. On one occasion, while I was dean of oceanography, he called me personally to ask why an oceanography faculty member was renting a car in New York City to go to a laboratory of Columbia University—inasmuch as Columbia was in New York City. I pointed out to him that the faculty member was going to the Lamont Geological Observatory of Columbia, and that Lamont was thirty or forty miles north of New York City on the west side of the Hudson River. That seemed to satisfy him.

As for Mac's temper, with all the pressure a president experiences, it is amazing he didn't erupt more often than he did. When one of his opinions, unknown to the speaker, was violated, the warning signs began to appear: reddening of the neck came first, then the table was slapped, and then, leaning forward, Mac expressed his opinion in no uncertain terms. At one of the president's council meetings, the dean of undergraduate studies made a comment that Mac strongly disagreed with, and his temper exploded. The dean responded with an explanation of what he meant to say, which made the situation even worse. The dean saved the day—and his own bacon—and interjected humor into the situation when he exclaimed, "I'd like to withdraw my two previous statements."

Within a year of becoming dean of research, I felt comfortable in my position in the upper administration. I continued to be active in the national politics of oceanography, participating on committees and boards that had some influence on the conduct of oceanography. I had chaired major studies of marine activities at the University of Hawaii and at Texas A&M. I'd been considered for leadership positions at the University of California at Santa Cruz, the Woods Hole Oceanographic Institution, the University of Hawaii, and NOAA. Woods Hole and NOAA had recruited me for positions, but I elected to stay at Oregon State. Mac had a hand in keeping me from taking the graduate dean position at Woods Hole by appealing to my ego, pointing out that "Oregon State needs you more than Woods Hole does." I'd had little interest in the position at NOAA, but the recruiting trip introduced me to important people there and increased my awareness of NOAA's importance.

Nineteen-eighty was an interesting year. Mount Saint Helens blew up, but I had nothing to do with that. I was deeply involved in a study of all the marine programs at Texas A&M; I made a trip to Indonesia for the NSF; Ronald Reagan and the Republican Party took control of the White House and became the majority political party of the United

States Senate. The two Oregon senators, Mark Hatfield and Robert Packwood, became chairs of their respective committees: Hatfield of the very powerful appropriations committee and Packwood of the commerce committee, responsible for overseeing the Department of Commerce, which included NOAA.

The ocean interests in Congress clamored for an ocean person to be appointed as the third administrator of NOAA. The Republicans prepared lists of oceanographers who might fill the bill. My name was on those lists, reasonably near the top. It didn't hurt to be an Oregonian while Hatfield and Packwood were influential in the Senate. I described the situation to my good friend, Hollis Dole, who had been an assistant secretary of Interior during the first Nixon administration and, needless to say, was politically astute.

Hollis said, "Let's talk." So we did.

CHAPTER 11

The NOAA Years (1981–1984)

On Dutch Reagan's team

PRESIDENT NIXON HAD CREATED the National Oceanic and Atmospheric Administration by executive order in 1970.[1] That action combined into a single agency the Environmental Sciences Service Administration, which included the weather service, the Bureau of Commercial Fisheries, and the US Coast and Geodetic Survey. The administrator of NOAA was a political appointment requiring the advice and consent of the Senate. The first two administrators had been an atmospheric scientist and an environmental lawyer. The ocean interests on Capitol Hill wanted the next administrator to be an ocean person regardless of political affiliation.

Hollis Dole convinced me I should apply for the NOAA administrator position. He said he would help politically, and he did. This time, President MacVicar convinced me to take the job if it were offered. I responded positively to an inquiry from the White House personnel office: I was indeed interested in the position.

Once the White House personnel folks were satisfied that I was qualified, I was investigated by the FBI. I assume the FBI found nothing about me to stop the process. Interviews followed. I met first with White House personnel, then with the Secretary of Commerce, Malcolm Baldrige, who would be my boss if I got the job.

Mac Baldrige had managed a large commercial firm in Connecticut before becoming Secretary of Commerce. He asked me, "Can you manage an organization as large as NOAA—twelve thousand employees?" I responded, "I don't know. I've never managed an organization that large."

He burst out laughing, possibly not expecting such a forthright answer. The interview must have satisfied him because a few days later, the White House personnel officer called to tell me President Reagan was recommending me for the position of NOAA administrator.

The next step was confirmation by the Senate. The confirmation hearing was scheduled for several weeks later, which gave me a few weeks to prepare. Preparation involved briefings by the leaders of the major parts of NOAA, poring over huge notebooks containing details about NOAA, and the opportunity to ask anyone in NOAA anything about the agency. I stayed in Washington for a week or so while stuffing my brain with all matters of NOAA policy, facts about the agency, how it interacted with the public, and how it provided service to its many constituents. Admiral Stanley of the Sea Use Council had an apartment in DC, and he offered it to me for as long as I might need it during my preparation for the hearings. By taking the apartment, I strengthened my relationship with the admiral, and I saw him often once I became the administrator.

With the NOAA notebooks in hand, I returned to Corvallis for a week or two and studied intensively. Then I returned to Washington to appear before the Senate Commerce Committee, chaired by Oregon Senator Bob Packwood. I prepared for the hearing as I had prepared for my PhD orals many years earlier. I don't remember being nervous, but I suppose I was. I had never met Senator Packwood before that meeting. I remember little about the hearing, but at some point I must have responded to a question in a relaxed, possibly witty fashion, because Packwood turned to his assistant and said, "He has a sense of humor, doesn't he?"

Senator Barry Goldwater of Arizona came into the hearing ten or fifteen minutes after it had started. I was somewhat in awe. Packwood immediately deferred to "the distinguished senator from Arizona" and gave him the opportunity to ask questions. I remember his comments: "Doctor, I note from your resume that you did your doctoral dissertation on the geology of the Gulf of California. That's an area I have special interest in. Please describe for me some of the findings from your research." We talked about the Gulf of California for a few minutes, not NOAA, and then he said, "Well, Doctor, it seems to me you're qualified for the job. You have my vote. Welcome to the Land of Oz!"

LEAVING CORVALLIS

WITHOUT MY REALIZING IT at the time, President MacVicar had put me on leave without pay status, which meant I would be kept on the personnel rolls of Oregon State University while I was in Washington. I'd thought I was leaving OSU forever. I knew the only reason I would return would be to take the position Mac occupied: president of the university.

We had lived in Corvallis for twenty-one years. Our kids had grown to college age there. Corvallis was our home. We owned two pieces of property, our home on Twelfth Street and a condominium my mother rented from us in a neighboring development. We sold both properties a few weeks after they were put on the market. Being appointed administrator of NOAA made me something of a local celebrity, and I was asked to give the commencement address to our son Steve's Corvallis High School graduating class in June.[2] I worked hard on that speech and was thanked with a standing ovation by the graduating class.

It was difficult to realize we were leaving Corvallis, possibly forever. If you ask our kids, they'll tell you that Corvallis is their hometown, even though now they live elsewhere. Our years there were, on balance, good ones—not without problems, but we survived them. An associate professor's salary in the 1960s and 1970s might have been adequate for a single person or a couple, but providing for a family of five, and then six, required a bit of financial management. We learned where the cheapest bread and the least-expensive meat could be purchased. When the weather permitted, I rode a bicycle to campus. Our vacations were almost always camping trips. We never did buy a second home for vacations, as some of my colleagues did; we could never make up our minds whether we liked the mountains better than the coast, we enjoyed them both so much.

Uncharacteristically, I suppose, I took flying lessons during 1965 and 1966 and obtained my private pilot's license. I did this, I think, because I felt a need to do something separate from the family, something to satisfy my male ego. It was something I had always wanted to do. Shirley also got her pilot's license at about the same time. It was easy to drive the fifteen minutes to the Corvallis airport, rent a plane, and be in the air thirty or forty minutes from the time the spirit moved us to fly. It was more difficult to find the time for flying in Washington, DC, when we moved there in 1966, so we gave up flying.

Once the kids were old enough, the family went skiing almost every weekend during the winter. Hoodoo Ski Bowl, near the crest of the Cascades, is about a two-hour drive from Corvallis. Deciding to ski was a good decision; all of our offspring still ski, and Donna, our oldest, has been a ski instructor in a number of places, including the Black Forest of Germany. It was one thing we did frequently as a family. We were the center of a sphere that attracted to its edges the friends of our kids who had the mutual desire to share the exhilaration of skiing and experience the beauty of Oregon's mountains in winter.

For twenty-one years, we were definitely a Corvallis family. When the college years arrived, Donna ended up at Oregon State, the twins found their ways to the University of Oregon, and Steven ultimately received degrees from Central Oregon Community College and Northern Arizona University. When Steve was a senior in high school, Shirley decided it was time to complete her own education. She traveled to Eugene almost daily to earn her master's degree in piano performance and music education from the University of Oregon. At any one time, we had two, three, or four members of our family in college. I have no idea how we found our financial way through all of that, but we did.

I had always felt that my prime responsibility was to my family and then to my job, so I didn't volunteer for many activities in town. I had served on a couple of committees to support Corvallis High School, but not much beyond that. Most of my extra time and efforts were devoted to OSU, principally to the Department/School of Oceanography, helping it grow in stature and quality and visibility within the scientific community and the state of Oregon. I really identified with Oregon State University.

Now, we were leaving Oregon State and Corvallis behind us. Beyond the next few years, we had no idea where life would lead us.

In 1981, NOAA had approximately twelve thousand employees and operated on a budget of slightly less than a billion dollars. It was the largest agency in the Department of Commerce and was viewed by many in the department as one of its best-managed units. Because I didn't arrive until July, NOAA was vulnerable to personnel raids from other parts of the Department of Commerce. Several of the best and brightest people in NOAA's general counsel and congressional affairs offices had been cherry-picked for reassignment to their respective groups in the department. Bud Walsh, deputy administrator under previous administrator Dick Frank, had served as the acting administrator of NOAA for six months until I arrived. Bud served as my deputy while we searched for new leaders for the major parts of NOAA.

As administrator, I was the equivalent of an undersecretary of commerce. In the administrator's office, I had three assistants: Ruth Barritt, my personal assistant, and two secretaries, who handled clerical matters. Ruth had been Bob White's personal assistant when he was NOAA's first administrator. Knowledgeable about NOAA and the ways of Washington, Ruth was particularly helpful as a mentor. Before my tenure was over, Ruth left for another position in NOAA and was succeeded by Colby Hostetler, a political appointee.

Three other staff members were particularly helpful. Jack LaCovey was responsible for public relations, Bob McManus was NOAA's general counsel, and Dick Keating handled congressional affairs and was NOAA's prime contact with representatives and senators. Ruth Barritt had instructions to let LaCovey, McManus, and Keating see me whenever they requested it. These four people were street savvy and knew their way around the federal government. Their primary responsibilities were to keep NOAA, and me, out of trouble. Sometimes that was not possible. On my first day in office as the administrator of NOAA, I was sued by the State of California. I don't recall now what the issue was, nor how the case was settled.

Two things I learned very rapidly: (1) I did not answer mail that was directed to me as administrator, and (2) I did not write my own speeches. When mail came to NOAA, it went directly to the mail room, where someone in charge of the mail operation evaluated it and decided which branch of NOAA was most knowledgeable to draft a response for the administrator's signature. A file for the incoming letter was created, and the file was then sent to the proper office within NOAA, forwarded within that office to the expert responsible for the subject of the letter, who then drafted a response, which was then checked off by the assistant administrator of that part of NOAA, then sent back to the mail room, from which it was then forwarded to the administrator for signing, then sent back to the mail room for mailing. If the letter had been originally sent to the Secretary of Commerce, it was forwarded from the secretary's office to the NOAA mail room. Secretary Baldrige had been an English major at Yale. If he didn't like the draft prepared for his signature, the letter was sent back to NOAA and the process repeated. The result of this process was that a letter from NOAA was substantively correct but the

At my swearing-in as administrator of NOAA, Department of Commerce Secretary Malcolm Baldrige is at the lectern, and Arlene Triplett, assistant secretary for administration, is first in line. I'm eighth in line, standing in front of the farthest window, and Joe Wright, deputy secretary of Commerce, is next to last in line. (Byrne collection)

process of its preparation was maddeningly slow. It took considerable time, sometimes several weeks. In the meantime, the originator of the letter may have assumed, "The government doesn't care, they won't or haven't answered my letter, so to hell with them."

Speeches were another matter. Once an appointment was made for me to deliver a speech, LaCovey's office prepared an appropriate speech or list of talking points. The speechwriter visited with me to determine what I wanted to say, the nature of my speech, the length, and so on. After several tries with different speechwriters, I found someone who came close to thinking the way I did. Roland Paine and I developed a compatible working style, and he prepared my speeches most of the time I was at NOAA. I often used a highlighter to identify the points I wanted to make and used the highlighted text as talking points. This way I avoided reading the speech, making it possible for me to deliver it in an extemporaneous style, as I had done at Hamilton College more than thirty years earlier.

Visits to representatives or senators on the Hill were frequent. These congressional visits were orchestrated by Dick Keating, NOAA's congressional affairs officer. Whether at the request of a representative, senator, or NOAA's assistant administrator, I was told the topic of the meeting and was presented with briefing materials on the major points to be covered. Often, I didn't see these briefing materials until I was in the car on my way to the meeting. I learned to concentrate on the material while

With Shirley standing beside me, Secretary Baldrige presents me with my certificate of appointment. (US Department of Commerce Archives)

John Harley, my driver, took Keating and me, and sometimes others, to the right entrance of the right building on the Hill. John Harley had been the driver for both Bob White and Dick Frank before me. He waited in the car near the entrance to the building until we returned.

Once inside, Keating led us to the appropriate room, and then I took the lead. I had learned the protocol that, when meeting another official or group for the first time, the senior official enters first. By following this protocol—used universally at international meetings—the leaders of each group know who the most important person in the group is. This practice amused me at first, but I soon learned it was a simple way of determining who the principals were at a new meeting. When the principals were acquainted, it was no longer necessary.

During the first few weeks, there were numerous meetings within NOAA and on the Hill simply to meet people and to become familiar with administrative and congressional leadership in the Reagan administration. Even though I had started as administrator on or about the first of July, I wasn't official until I was sworn in on July 24. All the presidential appointees in the Commerce Department were sworn in by Secretary Baldrige in one mass ceremony.

I'm greeted by President Reagan at the president's intimate
breakfast for about five hundred presidential appointees in 1982.
We didn't have much time for casual conversation. (White House)

PARTY POLITICS 101

I SUPPOSE there were other presidential appointees who were as politically naive as I was, but possibly not. My knowledge of party politics
must have classified me as a "babe in the woods," and a young one at that.

In Oregon, I had considered myself to be a true independent voter. I
often changed my party affiliation depending on the issues to be addressed
in primary elections. My most recent party affiliation was Democrat. So
here I was, a Democrat, joining a Republican administration. In official
parlance, I was an apolitical appointee, appointed because of my expertise in oceanography. I rapidly changed my Oregon party affiliation to
Republican. For some Republicans in DC, that was not enough; I was
tainted because I had not worked diligently to help elect Ronald Reagan
to the presidency. One staunch Reagan Republican was the woman who

guarded the entrance to Secretary Baldrige's office. She was extremely reticent to allow me to have appointments with the secretary and was wary of any arguments I made that my appointment was in the secretary's best interest.

I knew that Reagan policies called for reducing the size of government, diminishing the federal budget, handing off programs to the private sector wherever possible, and to charge the user the full cost of the services and products provided by government agencies—and to do all of that in "the American Way," whatever that is. Some of the changes required the approval of Congress. I was part of the Reagan administration and was expected to implement Reagan policies wherever and whenever I could. I had always considered myself to be a good team player, and I intended to be an effective member of "Dutch" Reagan's team, even though implementing parts of the policy could be a headache.

Arlene Triplett, in my judgment a reasonable Republican, had been appointed assistant secretary of commerce for administration. She had been rewarded for being a diligent worker in the national Republican office. She was a nice person; I liked Arlene and felt I could talk frankly with her. About six weeks after I had assumed the administrator's job, I said to her, "Arlene, I have the feeling I'm in trouble most of the time with both the Democrats and the Republicans." She replied, "John, you were in trouble the day you arrived." Then she explained some of the political facts of life to me: Democrats didn't trust me because I was part of a Republican administration, and the Republicans didn't trust me because I hadn't done anything to help elect Ronald Reagan to the presidency. I was in a political no-man's land, at least as far as party politics were concerned.

The conversation with Arlene occurred about the time I was subjected to two other political lessons. The first happened soon after I became administrator. I was asked to testify before the Senate Commerce Committee. This was an oversight hearing in which I described NOAA, articulated my thoughts about NOAA's mission, and explained how I hoped to lead the agency toward fulfilling its mission in accordance with President Reagan's policies. Because this was my first oversight hearing, the room was full. The hearing went well; I had been properly briefed, made my statements, and then it was time for questions.

When it was his turn, Senator Lautenberg of New Jersey asked me, "Doctor, does NOAA have enough money to conduct its research?" I smiled. Before I could answer, Senator Packwood, who chaired the committee, jumped in, "I see by your smile what your answer is." His assumption being that my smile meant, "No, we don't have enough money," which of course would be true but would also be contrary to the president's policy. I immediately responded to Senator Packwood, recognizing that Lautenberg could hear my answer, "No, Senator, I think you misunderstand. Good research usually produces more valid questions than it does answers, so there is never enough money to do all the research that's needed." We then went on to other questions.

No more than thirty minutes later, I was about to enter my office on the fourth floor of the Commerce Building. Ruth Barritt was waiting for me. She said, "Secretary Baldrige wants to see you immediately." I went back down the hall to Baldrige's office. On this occasion, his secretary let me in immediately. Baldrige said he had received a call from the White House and that a report had come in there and been relayed to him that during my testimony I had not adhered to the president's policy about reducing NOAA's budget. I explained to him what had happened, as reported above. He laughed and said, "That was a pretty good answer, John. Thanks."

In the time that elapsed between when I responded to Senator Lautenberg's question and when I returned to my office—roughly thirty minutes—someone behind me in the hearing room had called the White House to report that I was not following the president's policy. That White House person had called and talked to Secretary Baldrige to tell him Byrne was not adhering to the president's policy designed to reduce the budget. Political lesson learned: know who is behind your back, and if you don't know, assume someone will stab you at the first opportunity. I was learning.

The second lesson, which occurred a short time later, was more direct. It involved the selection of my deputy. As I mentioned earlier, Bud Walsh, the deputy administrator of NOAA during the previous (Democratic) administration, had been acting administrator until I arrived. He knew the job, apparently got along well with Secretary Baldrige, had the proper talents for the job, and, to me, seemed a reasonable choice to continue as deputy administrator. I was naïve enough to believe that I, as administrator, would be free to select my own deputy. Worse than that, I made a public statement that Bud Walsh would be my deputy, and my statement was chronicled in *Ocean Science News*, a weekly newsletter that covered matters important to the ocean community nationwide.

A call came to my office from Paul van der Myde, the congressional affairs officer for the Department of Commerce. Senator Trent Lott of

Mississippi would like to meet me. An appointment with Senator Lott was arranged. I should have known something was up when both the Commerce Department's congressional affairs officer and Joe Wright, the deputy secretary of Commerce, were part of the delegation to see Senator Lott.

When we arrived at Lott's office, we were informed that the senator would be a few minutes late due to some Senate activity. This delay gave me the opportunity to note the memorabilia arranged around the senator's office. There were photos of him with his family, with elderly people, with groups of Boy Scouts, and other artifacts that suggested he was a nice person.

After we'd waited about fifteen minutes, Senator Lott arrived. We went directly into his office. He didn't bother to greet me or introduce himself. He simply got red in the face and in a loud voice, in no uncertain terms, he said, "Bud Walsh is NOT going to be the deputy administrator of NOAA. I busted my butt to get Ronald Reagan elected president and no [expletive] Democrat is going to get that job as deputy administrator of NOAA."

His assistant handed him the copy of *Ocean Science News* that quoted me about Bud Walsh. He had already seen the paper. He thrust it at me and, again almost shouting, said he wanted Jim Winchester in that job. Winchester was a Mississippi Republican who had worked on the Reagan campaign and, very clearly in Lott's opinion, deserved an appointment in the Reagan administration.

When we left the senator's office I felt thoroughly chastised. It had been made very clear to me how one element of politics worked at the national level. It was a valuable lesson. I didn't want Jim Winchester as my deputy. But it was obvious Bud Walsh would not be the deputy administrator of NOAA.

I was beginning to understand the nature of the appointment process for positions that came under the purview of the White House personnel office, and I had no choice but to accept it. This wasn't anything new. Bob White had run into the same problem when NOAA was created. He was not permitted to select his own deputy, so he created an associate administrator position, picked a competent person to fill that position, and used the associate administrator as his deputy.

Bud Walsh wasn't surprised that he would not be the deputy administrator of NOAA. He had been in the federal bureaucracy long enough to know the political facts of life. I still needed a deputy administrator. It was suggested to me that Tony Calio, the associate administrator for Space and Terrestrial Applications at NASA, might be interested. Tony had been with NASA since 1964 and knew how to get things done in the federal system; moreover, he had friends in the White House. During a lengthy interview, Tony told me he could have himself assigned to NOAA from NASA on a temporary basis until an appointment at NOAA became a reality. On December 11, 1981, the announcement was made that the president intended to nominate Tony for the NOAA deputy administrator position. Tony was a charming person, had done a fine job at NASA, certainly knew the ropes and the political people to know around Washington. I liked him.

So Bud Walsh would not be my deputy, and neither would Jim Winchester. There was a slot for an associate administrator, however, and with Trent Lott as his champion, Jim Winchester was announced for that position in February 1982. Jim, an engineer with his own consulting firm, had previously been the director of NOAA's data buoy office in Bay St. Louis, Mississippi. He was a Reagan Republican, brought his own staff from Mississippi, and pretty much operated on his own once he arrived at NOAA.

I tried to involve both Tony and Jim in the management of NOAA and to keep them both informed of activities involving NOAA and the Department of Commerce. I worked closest with Tony and solicited his assistance in working with Jim. For the first year or so we managed all right, but eventually the relationship of the three of us became disharmonious. If nothing else, communications between us failed. On his own, Jim Winchester devised a plan to completely restructure the Weather Service, contracting out to the private sector most of the services the Weather Service provided. I couldn't support his plan and I didn't. The Weather Service remained as it had been structured.

Tony and I worked well together at first. Dick Frank, my predecessor, had structured NOAA in a way that neither Tony nor I could understand. I gave Tony the assignment of coming up with a simpler structure for the agency. What he came up with was fine except for one major element. Tony wanted to do away with the office of Ocean and Atmosphere Research (OAR) and assign research to each of the operating divisions of NOAA. I believed that if this were done, research would suffer whenever there was a budget shortfall.

Unfortunately, we didn't have time to discuss the matter because, at the behest of Secretary Baldrige, Tony left for the Pribilof Islands to address another Commerce Department problem. He released his restructuring plan just before he left town, and I felt it necessary to rescind a portion of the plan in order to keep research where it was and to do that imme-diately while Tony was away. It was at this time that communication between us foundered. After he returned, it went from bad to worse. I thought he didn't handle the situation well, but then neither did I.

As time went on, I had the feeling that Tony went behind me to ingra-tiate himself with Secretary Baldrige. It became obvious Tony's personal goal was to be the next administrator of NOAA. He did become the administrator in 1985 after I had returned to Oregon State.

REORGANIZING NOAA

TONY'S PROPOSED reorganization included the National Ocean Ser-vice (NOS), National Weather Service (NWS), National Marine Fisheries Service (NMFS), National Environmental Satellite, Data, and Informa-tion Service (NESDIS). I added the office of Ocean and Atmosphere Research (OAR).

These major elements of NOAA were managed by assistant admin-istrators, and each had its own identity. Although they were all part of NOAA, they often acted as if they were independent agencies. A later administrator of NOAA, Admiral Conrad C. Lautenbacher, attempted to integrate NOAA by instilling the concept that it was the "NOAA Weather Service," the "NOAA Marine Fisheries Service," and so on. Only partially, and perhaps temporarily, did this work. During my watch, the standard saying was: "NOAA really exists only in the mind of the admin-istrator," meaning that the integration of the various elements of NOAA was a myth.

Our attempts at integration were mainly in the form of communica-tions. Tony, Jim, and I met with the assistant administrators for lunch once a month to discuss what was going on in each line office. In addi-tion, all of us and our staffs met monthly as part of our efforts at Man-aging by Objectives, a system of management mandated by Secretary Baldrige. We came to know each other fairly well: Dick Hallgren (NWS), Paul Wolff (NOS), Bill Gordon (NMFS), Dave Johnson, succeeded by John McElroy (NESDIS), Ned Ostenso, followed by Joe Fletcher (OAR).

Dick Hallgren had been with the NWS for years and had assumed the leadership role before I became administrator. One of his goals was to auto-mate the Weather Service so that computers, then in their infancy, would replace acetate and grease pencils as tools in making weather predictions.

Paul Wolff, a retired navy captain, understood oceanography and brought a new level of discipline to the NOS. Bill Gordon had been with NMFS for years and was very popular. He recognized the importance of international connections for fisheries. He seemed to be traveling most of the time.

Dave Johnson ran the satellite operation critical to the Weather Service. He was recognized as an outstanding manager, but he lacked a deputy who was second in command. When Dave retired, John McElroy joined NOAA from NASA. A jovial person, John was an excellent manager, well-liked, and outstanding at explaining complicated matters in simple terms.

Ned Ostenso, a geophysicist I had known for some time from my ocean days at Oregon State, was the acting assistant administrator for OAR. He had been the director of the Sea Grant College Program and went back to that position when Joe Fletcher took over for OAR. Joe was an Arctic oceanographer for whom Fletcher's Ice Island is named.

Joe Fletcher was our first choice for the OAR leadership position, but the White House personnel folks had someone else in mind for that position, probably as some type of political reward. I needed help from the Hill to get Joe Fletcher appointed. I went to Senator Ted Stevens, a senior Republican from Alaska. One of Stevens's assistants, Bill Phillips, told me, "We'll take care of it, John," and he did. Phillips called the person in charge of the White House personnel office and told him, "Senator Stevens wants Joe Fletcher appointed to the assistant administrator for OAR position at NOAA."

A couple of days later, Phillips or one of his colleagues in Stevens's office called again and reiterated the senator's request. A day or so later, there was another call from Senator Stevens's office to the White House, then another. Somehow the White House first choice was lost in the dust. It wasn't long before I received a call from a harried White House personnel officer: "Why haven't you appointed Joe Fletcher to the OAR position? What's taking you so long?" Lesson: if someone is using a hammer on you, use a bigger hammer. Senator Stevens was certainly a bigger hammer.

It wasn't always easy to implement the president's policy of reducing the size of government. I tried, always; after all, Ronald Reagan was the president of the United States, arguably the most important leader in the world, and I was on his team. I didn't always agree with what the president said. His policies in their general form may have made sense, but, as the saying goes, "the devil is in the details." Before I arrived in DC, the president had made a statement to the effect that the trouble with the

United States government was the federal employee, or something like that. Possibly true in some agencies, but not in NOAA. The president's statement was devastating to morale and, in my judgment, unjustified. I was impressed by the quality of NOAA scientists and their staffs and by their dedication to what they were doing. There were innumerable stories of Weather Service employees staying on the job during bad weather for thirty-six hours or more, sleeping in the office when necessary. When I talked to NOAA employees, I always tried to laud the job they were doing. Improving morale was one of my goals. People who feel respected for what they are doing are likely to try harder and do the best they can.

BUDGET

A MAJOR TASK during my first year was the preparation of the NOAA portion of the president's budget. The NOAA business folks, John Carey primarily, did a fine job of formulating a budget with a modest increase. My job was to convince the secretary of commerce our budget should go forward to the Office of Management and Budget (OMB)[3] as part of the Commerce Department's budget.

The task of putting the department's budget together fell to the deputy secretary, Joe Wright. I sat down with Joe in his office and went through the NOAA budget with him in some detail. We came to a line item titled Sea Grant College Program.[4]

Joe asked, "What's Sea Grant?" I explained the program to him in a positive manner.

"Is it a successful program?"

"Yes, it certainly is."

"You said the states put money into it?"

"Yes."

"Let's cut it back to fifty percent. No, let's let the states support it if they think it's so good. Eliminate it from the budget."

I swallowed hard and said, "OK, Joe."

So, in preparation for the 1982 budget, Sea Grant was eliminated. I thought at the time, You're not doing such a great job for your marine constituency, Byrne, but you're certainly learning the ways of Washington.

Several days later, I was making my tour of some of the ocean-supporting senators on the Hill, among whom was Lowell Weicker of Connecticut. Weicker was a liberal Republican and a giant of a man in several ways. At six feet four or more and well over two hundred pounds, he towered over most of the people he met. His ego matched his physical size, but he was a vigorous advocate for virtually any program involving the oceans. He had recently learned to scuba dive and would often point out that "the oceans are in better shape and make better sense than the Senate of the United States."

During our conversation, which was the first of many, Senator Weicker asked me about the budget for ocean programs. When I mentioned what had happened to Sea Grant, he snorted and said, "There's no way we're going to let them eliminate Sea Grant, John." When all was said and done, Sea Grant survived, although its budget did not increase. Lowell Weicker became a steadfast friend to NOAA and particularly to the Sea Grant College Program. I met with him often, usually before any hearing concerning the NOAA budget. As a result, I went into the hearings with Senator Weicker fully informed of the administration's position and feeling confident he would not allow any of NOAA's ocean programs to be seriously jeopardized. No doubt there were several lessons in that Sea Grant episode, but what I was really struck by was the power play between the Congress and the White House.

"FULL-COSTING" GOVERNMENT SERVICES

A year or so later, I experienced another example of democracy and national politics at play, this time involving the Weather Service. One of the administration's high priorities was to privatize government services in order to save tax dollars and enhance the private sector. Unfortunately, sometimes the private sector isn't prepared to take over what the government is willing to give up. The Fruit Frost Warning Program of the Weather Service was popular with growers in the citrus-producing states, California, Texas, and Florida. The program was effective in warning citrus farmers if temperatures were predicted to drop below freezing. The warning gives growers time to put out smudge pots or take other measures to protect the fruit. In the weather stations in those states, it was someone's part-time job to forecast air temperature and issue public warnings whenever frost threatened.

There were two problems with the transfer of this process to the private sector. One, no one person within the Weather Service devoted his or her full time to the forecast and the warning system, and consequently the position could not be easily eliminated. And, two, the private sector was not adequate in number, skill, or desire to take over the system. Apparently the folks at OMB, who were calling the shots, were not aware of these problems. Nevertheless, NOAA was on public record as being in the process of eliminating the Fruit Frost Warning Program so the private sector could take it over—with possibly an added cost to the farmers.

A request came to NOAA's public affairs office that representatives of the Florida Citrus Growers Association were coming to town and wanted to meet with someone from NOAA to express their concerns about this change in the Fruit Frost Warning Program. Staff from NWS and the public affairs office met in my office to talk about who should meet with the citrus growers. Dick Hallgren, NWS assistant administrator, suggested several people in NWS who could do it. We discussed the situation and the qualifications of Hallgren's nominations.

Finally I said, "No. I've never done this sort of thing. Let me talk to them." I don't recall whether those around the table tried to talk me out of doing this. No matter; meeting with the Florida Citrus Growers became one of the more memorable experiences of my time in Washington.

I don't recall where we met, but I do remember there were forty or fifty people in the room, none of whom seemed to be smiling. After I was introduced, I made the usual comments of greeting, telling them how pleased I was at the opportunity to meet with them. Then I reiterated President Reagan's position on reducing the size of government and launched into NOAA's efforts to adhere to the president's policies by eliminating programs, including the Fruit Frost Warning Program. I don't recall whether they hissed or booed first. They did both, but not in good nature. They were angry. I suspect that if they had brought any of their fruit with them, they would have thrown it at me.

As they were exercising their opinions in what I considered a rude manner, I thought, Wait a minute, I don't have to take this from these people; they didn't elect me. I threw my hands in the air and in a very firm voice, almost shouting, said, "Wait a minute! If you don't like what this administration, or any administration, is doing, you have one powerful entry to this government. It's called the Congress of the United States, and it's made up of people you elected to represent you. They are here in Washington to protect your interests and to see that this government acts in a manner that supports you. So if you want to be effective in getting what you want, go right across town and let your representative and your senator know what is important to you."

They, of course, knew all this. That's why they were visiting Washington. When I was finished with my short lecture on the nature of the democratic process, they stood up and applauded me. We never did eliminate the Fruit Frost Warning Program. It was not the last time the folks at OMB would try to force an untenable idea on NOAA.

In December 1982, a committee of the president's cabinet, the Cabinet Council on Commerce and Trade, chaired by Secretary Baldrige, recommended that the Commerce Department "oversee the transfer of the civil operational weather, land and future ocean satellites to the US domestic private sector as soon as possible."

Operation of the weather satellites was a big, big deal. Announced in March 1983, this recommendation created a firestorm of resistance from users of weather information, significant members of Congress, journalists, and editorial writers. Political cartoonists had a field day. The recommendation quickly ballooned into the thought that this was merely the first step by the Reagan administration to sell the entire Weather Service to a for-profit business, which undoubtedly would have increased costs to taxpayers wanting weather information. Pundits questioned how much would be charged for the forecast of a snowstorm, a thunderstorm, or a hurricane. It seemed that only potential bidders were in favor of the idea, organizations such as Comsat, which would have gained from the sale. The transfer of this service to the private sector required congressional approval, and that was not about to happen.

As the messenger of this White House decision, I was regarded sympathetically by the media. They realized my position required that I be an advocate for the decision. It was clear from the beginning that Congress would not buy the idea. The operation of the satellites remained within NOAA. In defending the administration's position on the transfer of satellite operations to the private sector, I gained national attention and was credited by *USA Today* with the "quote of the week": "The private sector is what made this nation great."

Another money-saving idea promulgated by the OMB was to full-cost the products we produced. For NOAA, the first products that came to mind for full-costing were the nautical charts of the waters around the United States and its territories. In the early 1980s, a nautical chart sold on average for about six dollars. The initial reaction within NOAA was that if we charged the full cost of printing and packaging, that chart might cost as much as twenty dollars.

But that is not what the folks at OMB had in mind when they referred to full-costing. They wanted us to include the full cost of the hydrographic survey, the cost of operating the survey vessel, crew salaries, depreciation of the cost of the vessel, and so on. Add to these the cost of drafting the charts as well as printing and distribution. If we sold the same number of charts as we did at the six-dollar price, the cost for each chart could easily exceed $1,000. We surmised that at $1,000 per chart, we would sell far fewer charts, so the cost per chart would skyrocket, possibly going as high as $40,000. Further, we assumed that at $1,000 or more, users would not purchase new charts; they would continue to use older, outdated charts, possibly resulting in serious navigation problems with damage to vessels and danger to lives. Full-costing nautical charts did not make sense to those of us at NOAA. But OMB didn't give up easily and recommended further study of the concept. Full-costing of nautical charts did not happen on my watch at NOAA.

REGULATING FISHERIES

TO ME, fisheries problems presented the most interesting issues. When those problems reached my desk, it was obvious they had no easy solution—if the solutions had been easy, the National Marine Fisheries Service would have solved them, and I would not be hearing about them. By the 1980s, most of the major fisheries of the world were in serious trouble; they had already been depleted or were being harvested at an unsustainable level. Where the fish stocks were still capable of being exploited, there were often conflicts between fishermen seeking different types of catches, e.g., crabs versus fin fish. Occasionally the conflicts resulted in physical violence. Also at the time, environmentalists had become concerned about the by-catch of dolphins in the purse seines used by the tuna industry and the capture of turtles in the nets of shrimp trawlers. The scientists and technicians at NOAA devised devices and processes to minimize the taking of dolphins and turtles.

Sometimes there were solutions to such problems, but often there were not, or they were lose-lose solutions. In most instances, the president's administration left us alone to resolve these situations. Sometimes the OMB interfered. The most egregious interference by OMB during my watch involved the halibut fishery in the waters off Alaska.

The Alaska halibut fishery, like most fisheries, was an open fishery; anyone with a boat and financial backing could fish for halibut. It was becoming clear to fisheries biologists in the NMFS that halibut were being overfished. There were obvious ways of cutting back on the number of halibut being caught: create a "limited-entry" fishery and limit the number of fishermen licensed to catch halibut, shorten the fishing season, or do both.

NMFS opted first to shorten the season to three days. After several years, it became obvious to NMFS that, even with the three-day season, halibut were still being overfished. They concluded that the best way to regulate the catch was through a limited-entry fishery, which would be one of the first federal limited-entry fisheries in American waters.

Limited-entry fishing was a controversial concept that was not new to Alaskan fishermen. The Alaska legislature had limited entry for some other fisheries in Alaskan waters. A federally imposed limited-entry system would mean that some fishermen who had been fishing for years might be excluded. Questions abounded. Who would be included, who excluded? Once included, how long would a fisherman be included? Would quotas be established, and how would they be determined? Would vessel size be a factor in determining individual quotas? Would prior longevity in the fishery be a factor? Was the amount of fish an individual caught in the one, two, or three seasons before the initiation of limited entry to be a factor in determining his or her quota?

NMFS administrators communicated with Alaska fishermen, explained the plight of the halibut fishery, and asked the fishermen for their advice. With as much information and advice as they were able to obtain, NMFS made its decision, formulated a plan, and brought it to me for approval. The NMFS folks explained the precedent the first federal limited-entry fishery would create and the associated public-relations problems.

Were the plan and its execution viable? Yes. Was there any alternative if we were to maintain sustainability of the Alaska halibut fishery? Not that we could think of. Will the Regional Fishery Council for Alaska go along? Yes, they have been fully informed.

OK, I said, let's do it.

As part of its plan, NMFS had decided that a person's prior catch would be a factor in determining who would be licensed and how quotas would be determined. Believing their last season's catch would determine their eligibility for inclusion in the limited-entry fishery, the fishermen worked hard to catch as much halibut as possible. That was understandable.

Not so understandable was the position taken by the OMB. Literally a day or so before limited entry was to go into effect, OMB refused to allow it. "OMB does not approve the application of limited entry to the Alaska halibut fishery," read their ruling. "It is not the 'American Way.'"

No explanation, no reasoning, no logic, just: "Americans have never done business that excludes a sector of its population. It's simply not the American way." We at NOAA were shocked.

We relied on our friends in Congress to provide support. Even so, sometimes the executive branch of our government succeeds in blocking Congress. A limited entry to the halibut fishery did not happen, at least not at that time.

I tried to support the policies determined by the Reagan administration of which I was part. Because some of those policies were counter to the wishes of representatives and senators trying to support their own constituencies, I occasionally found myself a target for criticism, sometimes vitriolic.

Senator Stevens, whom I considered a friend, was particularly hard on me in a hearing concerning the elimination of the vessel buyback program. I was there to explain why the Reagan administration was eliminating this program from the federal budget. The buyback program had been created to help fishermen who, in order to buy new boats, had overextended themselves financially. Some were not able to make their bank payments and were being forced into bankruptcy. The vessel buyback program provided federal funds to buy the vessels back from the fisherman, thereby relieving them of their loan commitments. It was a program created by an earlier administration, and it was strongly supported by Senator Stevens.

The senator had no qualms about publicly attacking the messenger: me. He was so vehement in his attack that several of his staff apologized to me after the hearing. It was obvious he really cared about that program and its benefits to his constituency. Truly, his attack did not bother me. I realized the situation, and I was there on behalf of the administration, which was really his target. To me, it was all part of our democracy, another example of the frequent tension between the executive and the legislative branches of government.

The personal involvement of representatives and senators in support of their constituencies was impressive. I saw this again when we attempted to streamline the Weather Service to reduce the need for meteorologists in small, one-person weather stations serving underpopulated areas.

The streamlining involved the use of computers and remote sensing and called for reassigning personnel. Valentine, Nebraska, one of the small stations, was serviced only a few times a week by a meteorologist from the North Platte Weather Station. The Valentine station seemed to be a logical choice for the elimination of personnel, particularly if weather data for Valentine could be obtained remotely via the magic of electronics.

The Valentine, Nebraska, station was in the congressional district of Representative Virginia Smith. Representative Smith was not about to see the Valentine station closed or its services reduced. Somehow her resistance came to the attention of Secretary Baldrige. Mac Baldrige was from Connecticut, a graduate of Yale University with a major in English, but as an undergraduate, he had spent his summers in Nebraska working as a cowboy. He had an affinity for cowboys and liked the range on which they roamed, the plains and hills of Nebraska. He still participated in weekend rodeos as the heel-roper of a roping team. In his office, he had a saddle that he had won in a rodeo. He loved Nebraska, and he was convinced he could win over Representative Virginia Smith.

He was wrong. Even though he admitted he knew Valentine, Nebraska, and in fact had spent a night in the Valentine jail while he was a cowpuncher, Representative Smith would not budge. She, too, loved Nebraska and Nebraskans, and the one-person weather station at Valentine. We never did close that station. Such was the power of one legislator.

When Rick Spinrad, a recent OSU PhD graduate in oceanography, left Oregon to take a position in Washington, DC, in the late 1980s, he asked me if I had any advice for him. My response: "Yes. Be careful. Watch your back. There are folks in Washington with agendas different from yours, and they won't hesitate to be rough in order to achieve their agenda."

I then went on to say, "You can survive. I survived, and I have the scar tissue to prove it—mostly on my back, with some on my stomach from turning around quickly."

An example: early during my tenure, I was asked to serve on a multiagency task force to provide information for the president on the United Nations Law of the Sea Treaty to help him decide whether the United States should sign it. We were charged with identifying all the options open to the president. Those in our group who prepared the draft report omitted an obvious option that, if taken by the president, would be detrimental to their agency. To me, the omission was so obvious that I concluded the writers were attempting to skew the president's decision in their favor. I knew I would have to identify the omission and reject the draft paper. This was a paper designed to be read by the president's advisors in the White House and possibly by President Reagan himself.

I was nervous about making the challenge. I needn't have been. James L. Buckley, State Department undersecretary chaired the committee. As soon as the committee convened to discuss the draft, Jim Buckley said some nice words about the draft and then added, "But, it's incomplete. You haven't included all of the options. Please go back and complete the draft and then we'll meet to discuss it. This meeting is adjourned."

If there were contentious issues, they seemed to arise on Friday afternoons. Naively, I assumed that if I could get through Friday afternoon, the weekend would be smooth sailing for me and the family. This was not always the case. One Friday afternoon about six, as I entered the front door of our home on Quesada Street, Shirley greeted me with, "Senator Packwood wants you to call him as soon as possible."

Of course I called him immediately. The senator had learned that NMFS scientists were working on a project with Japanese scientists and intended to kill a number of Dall's porpoises in the North Pacific. He didn't know why they would do this, but insisted that I stop them.[5]

I didn't have a clue what he was talking about but told him I would find out and report back to him on Monday morning. He said, "Call me in my office at ten o'clock Monday morning." I responded, "Yes, sir."

It being after closing time on Friday, I had no success in finding anyone in NMFS to help me. I had better luck on Saturday and again early Monday morning. I learned that the project was designed to learn about the little-understood life cycle of the porpoise in order to protect it. The scientists believed that to fully understand the Dall's porpoise life cycle, they needed to "sample" (or, less euphemistically, kill) porpoises at different life stages. Killing mature porpoises was bad enough, but killing the juveniles, the porpoise "babies," was unthinkable.

I called Senator Packwood at the appointed time on Monday morning and tried to explain to him the scientific reasons for killing the porpoises. Our scientists were in Japan and were ready to go to sea on Monday morning. Leadership at NMFS had called them and told them to delay their excursion until we cleared them to go.

Senator Packwood said, "John, we don't agree on this, and if you let them sail with the intention of killing the porpoises, I'll have you for breakfast, lunch, tea, and dinner on the front page of the *Washington Post* and the *New York Times* before you can turn around," or words to that effect. "See me in my office at five o'clock."

I was in his office slightly before five o'clock, ready, I thought, to convince him of the necessity of "sampling" the porpoises. No way. He seemed serious about plastering me all over the front pages of the newspapers. When he had made his points very clear to me he said, "Now, let's go next door and see the television people." He had alerted the local TV news people so that he could be televised telling them how he had stopped the unnecessary slaughter of countless numbers of Dall's porpoises in the North Pacific Ocean, and he did it, probably in time for their six o'clock news broadcast.

We brought the NMFS scientists home from Japan. The Japanese scientists collected the porpoise "samples" and shared them as appropriate with our NMFS scientists. No American scientist was involved in killing porpoises. Senator Packwood seemed pleased that he had stopped the "taking" of a number of marine mammals.

Yet another lesson concerning the nature of politics in Foggy Bottom occurred in 1984, when Shirley and I were invited to dinner at the Moroccan embassy. Also invited were Senator Charles H. Percy and his wife. I was invited because, in 1983, NMFS director Bill Gordon had asked me to lead a group of American fishermen on a trip to Morocco to work out relationships between our two countries concerning fishing and marketing.

While in Morocco on that trip, I was expected to make opening remarks at a plenary session of the meeting between American and Moroccan fisheries folks. NMFS would prepare my remarks, and they suggested that the opening sentence or two be in French. I said, "No, let's make the remarks brief, and let's do the entire talk in French." French had been the language I studied in high school and practiced speaking whenever opportunities presented themselves. Fortunately, the wife of one of the Fisheries Service administrators taught French in a local school. She translated the talk prepared by NMFS and recorded it on cassette for me to listen to. I practiced delivering the talk.

Our first stop in Morocco was a visit with the US Ambassador, Joseph V. Reed. At the opening session of the fisheries meeting, Ambassador Reed made a few opening comments. He then turned the meeting over to Moroccan Fisheries Minister Smili, who tossed the ball to me. I began, "*Mesdames et Messieurs*," and continued to explain in French why we had come to Morocco and what we hoped to achieve during the next few days.

My brief talk was well received—a great beginning to a successful conference. I was told afterward that Ambassador Reed was slack-jawed at

I'm at the very successful joint US–Morocco fisheries conference with the US ambassador, Joseph V. Reed Jr., and the Moroccan minister of fisheries, Smili. (NOAA)

the fact that I had delivered the entire talk in French. To my surprise, just before the final meeting of the conference, I was asked to give a summary of the conference—and it was expected to be in French. Somehow, I managed to do that. Again my talk was received with pleasure by all, particularly the Moroccans. During the conference, I spent time with Minister Smili. We warmed to each other, and that also contributed to a successful conference.

Back to Senator Percy. At the reception before the dinner at the Moroccan embassy, it was interesting to see how Senator Percy and his wife separated when they entered the room and each moved around the reception hall, meeting individually with each of the guests.

Dinner was arranged at a number of low round tables, each seating six people. Shirley and I were seated at different tables, as were Senator and Mrs. Percy. Minister Smili was at the table with Shirley. I was at the table with Senator Percy. An attractive young woman was seated between Senator Percy and me; she captured virtually all of Senator Percy's attention during the meal.

After dinner, the Moroccan ambassador welcomed the guests and then asked Minister Smili to say a few words. Smili spoke about the successful fisheries conference, giving me credit for much of the success of the conference and lauding me profusely. Senator Percy leaned forward to look beyond the young lady between us, noticing me for perhaps the first time that evening. Following the conclusion of the dinner, Shirley came over and I introduced her to the senator. He told her in glowing terms how proud they all were of me and the splendid job I had done, as if he had known it all the time. I was amused by his performance.

CHAPTER 12

The International Whaling Commission (1981–1985)

No more "Thar she blows"?

MY JOB AS NOAA ADMINISTRATOR included appointment as the US commissioner to the International Whaling Commission (IWC). Although my knowledge about the oceans seemed reasonable for someone about to be the administrator of NOAA, my knowledge of whales and whaling in general put me at the low end of a learning curve.

The IWC was created by whaling nations shortly after the end of World War II to "provide for the proper conservation of whale stocks and thus make possible the orderly development and sustainability of the whaling industry." The United States became a member of the IWC in December 1946 by signing the International Convention for the Regulation of Whaling (ICRW). At that time, we were a whaling nation with a long tradition of killing whales, well documented in Herman Melville's *Moby Dick*.

One of the major activities at IWC meetings was determining quotas of whales permitted to be killed by each whaling nation during the coming year. A scientific committee collected data for each whale stock and then advised the IWC of the maximum number of whales that could be harvested without affecting the stock's sustainability. The ICRW also included provisions for scientific research and aboriginal subsistence whaling.

By the late 1960s, a conservation movement was under way to protect whales. Organizations such as the American Cetacean Society mounted efforts to stop whaling globally and permanently. The sustainability of most whale stocks was never in question. Scientists on the IWC committee who evaluated them pointed out that the whale stocks were robust and there was no scientific reason to stop the harvesting of a reasonable number of whales, but those conclusions were often ignored by the non-whaling nations in their efforts to protect whales.

The movement to "save the whales" was strong, and in 1972, delegates to the United Nations Conference on the Human Environment held in Stockholm proposed an intermediate step: a ten-year moratorium on commercial whaling in order to let over-harvested whale stocks recover. Because the moratorium applied only to commercial whaling, both research and aboriginal whaling would be permitted to continue. This proposal was brought to the attention of the IWC, where the power to implement the proposal supposedly rested.

Though the IWC determined the number of whales each nation could harvest during the coming year, if a nation disagreed with its assigned quota, it could file an objection within ninety days and continue to harvest whales as it did before the quota was applied. The IWC itself had no power to enforce either the quotas or the moratorium.

However, pressure could be exerted by individual member nations on other member nations. For example, through amendments to two US fisheries laws, the Pelly Amendment to the Fisherman's Protective Act of 1967 and the Packwood-Magnuson Amendment to the Magnuson Fishery Conservation and Management Act, the United States had the ability to compel nations with fishing rights inside US waters to comply with the moratorium. Under both amendments, the Secretary of Commerce was responsible for recognizing a nation whose actions inhibited the effectiveness of an international fisheries agreement, including IWC quotas, and to "certify" that nation. Certification carried implied sanctions under the Pelly Amendment and specific sanctions under the Packwood-Magnuson Amendment, which mandates a reduction by 50 percent or more of the offending nation's fisheries allocation inside the US exclusive fishery zone. To whaling countries with fishing rights inside US waters— such as Japan—the Packwood-Magnuson Amendment had teeth.

The IWC met annually, usually in England (Brighton or Bournemouth), and once during my tenure in Buenos Aires, in deference to the chairman of the commission, an Argentinian. Before each IWC meeting, the US delegation met two or three times in Washington, DC. These meetings provided an opportunity to share information, develop our agenda, and discuss strategies for achieving our goals at the IWC meeting.

Because I would not arrive in Washington until July 1 and the 1981 meeting of the IWC would be held in late June, the deputy commissioner,

Tom Garrett, handled the chores of US commissioner at that year's meeting.[1] I assumed responsibility as the US whaling commissioner shortly after I arrived in Washington in July.

My first IWC meeting was a special convening in February 1982 to address the Japanese taking of western Pacific sperm whales. I met the other commissioners and learned about the protocols of IWC meetings. What I learned at that first meeting prepared me for the most important meeting of my tenure as IWC commissioner: the July 1982 meeting at which the moratorium on commercial whaling was passed.

The US delegation to the IWC was a mixed group of federal agency people, representatives of environmental nongovernmental organizations (NGOs), Alaska Eskimos, and others with interests in whales. Because of this diversity, there were often a number of agendas at play within the delegation. Some members of the delegation were at odds with other members and wouldn't speak to each other. Some of the staunchest whale lovers would not share information with the Eskimos or with federal agency people interested in maintaining harmonious relations with the Japanese. I was the chairman of this delegation.

Although we were once a whaling nation, the primary goals of the United States were now threefold: stop commercial whaling by passing the moratorium, obtain as large a quota as possible of bowhead whales for Alaska Eskimo subsistence whaling, and limit the quotas of whales to be killed by each commercial whaling nation. The United States was both a nonwhaling nation and, in the matter of aboriginal whaling, a whaling nation. The delegations of other nations were more focused: they were either a whaling nation or not. In addition to the United States, only the Soviet Union attempted to obtain a quota for their aboriginal people.

Our IWC gatherings began with a meeting of the full US delegation, followed by a meeting of the like-minded commissioners from nonwhaling nations to develop a common strategy. I explained US intentions to my nonwhaling-country colleagues and indicated that, on the aboriginal whaling agenda item, I would not meet with them. I came to like and respect my commissioner colleagues from both whaling and nonwhaling nations: Kunio Yonezawa and Saito from Japan, Per Tresselt of Norway, Ian Stewart of New Zealand, Eduardo Iglesias from Argentina, and others whose names are buried in memory.

Japan, Norway, Iceland, and the Soviet Union were our major opposition at the IWC meetings. The delegation spent most of its time discussing how to handle Japan. Norway came next. Although Norway didn't take

Kunio Yonezawa of Japan, a fellow IWC commissioner, and I became friends, although we were constantly on opposite sides of whaling issues. Here we are at the 1983 annual meeting of the IWC. (Byrne collection)

many whales, we estimated that they sold about 85 percent of the whales they caught to Japan. Iceland was perhaps the most independent-minded of the four nations; if they didn't get their way, they simply dropped out of the IWC.

The Soviet Union had an aging whaling fleet and dropped whaling for economic reasons; however, they continued to act as a whaling nation. Prior to each IWC meeting, I was briefed by navy intelligence on what they had learned about Soviet intentions for the meeting. Nikonorov, the Soviet IWC commissioner, was instructed to oppose all US positions. I took some delight at IWC meetings in agreeing with Soviet statements and positions whenever possible, often stimulating a glare from my esteemed Soviet colleague.

As the IWC existed in 1972, there were not enough nonwhaling votes to pass a moratorium. During the ensuing ten years, nonwhaling interest groups recruited and paid the dues of nonwhaling nations to join the IWC, thereby increasing the number of nonwhaling votes on the moratorium. The commission had grown from the original fifteen whaling nations in 1946 to thirty-seven nations in 1982: it was clear there were enough nonwhaling votes to pass the moratorium.

At the meeting in July 1982, it was obvious that enough nonwhaling nations would be present to pass the proposed moratorium. Although the whaling nations—Japan, Norway, Iceland, and the Soviet Union—argued forcefully and logically against the moratorium, they didn't stand a chance of defeating the moratorium proposal. In spite of a report from the IWC scientific committee that scientific evidence did not support a widespread moratorium, the votes were there to pass it.

The meeting room was crowded with conservationists looking forward to passage of the moratorium. A cheer went up when the final vote was announced: twenty-five for the moratorium, seven against, and five abstentions.[2] The moratorium supporters rushed from the chamber, presumably to pop open champagne bottles. The commissioners sat quietly and addressed the next agenda item. The moratorium was scheduled to begin in 1986 and last five years, until 1990, at which time the scientific committee would assess the recovery of whale stocks and recommend further actions to IWC membership. So there was still much to be done to bring commercial whaling to a close.

A subsequent item on the agenda was the quota of bowhead whales for the Eskimos of Alaska. For this agenda item, the United States was a whaling nation. My role as an advocate for killing whales was difficult. I think I may have been too rigid in holding the line for the Eskimos, and consequently the negotiations on aboriginal whaling issues took extended periods of time.[3]

Since the time petroleum was discovered and produced from the north slope of Alaska and the wealth of the Eskimos thereby increased, the subsistence argument has not carried the same weight as it had earlier. Before the July 1982 IWC meeting, the US delegation determined what quotas we would attempt to obtain for the Eskimos. The numbers were always greater than the nonwhaling nations agreed to. Negotiations with the nonwhaling commissioners were intense. The fact that the bowhead was considered by the National Marine Fisheries Service to be an endangered mammal made the negotiations more difficult. I argued that the Eskimos needed the whale meat for subsistence and that whaling had been part of their culture for thousands of years.

Neither the subsistence nor the cultural arguments carried much weight with the commissioners of nonwhaling nations. Ian Stewart, the commissioner for New Zealand, said to me, "John, cultures can change. In my country, our native population used to eat each other as part of their culture." He, of course, was referring to the Maoris, who at one time were cannibalistic.

At the 1982 IWC meeting, the determination of the bowhead whale quota was argued from about ten at night until three or four o'clock the following morning. The quota issue was resolved when Chairman Eduardo Iglesias proposed a compromise that called for quotas for two years, with a carryover provision for quotas that were not reached during the first year. During subsequent years of negotiations, the debate on bowhead quotas remained intense.

Back to the moratorium. Within the ninety days following its passage, Japan, Norway, Iceland, and the Soviet Union all filed objections with IWC headquarters. Although the moratorium had passed, IWC rules allowed those nations to hunt whales as long as their objections existed. Between 1982 and 1986, whaling quotas were still needed, and the United States had a new long-term goal: persuade the Japanese to withdraw their objection to the moratorium.

The leverage the United States had on Japan was the allocation of fish in the US national fishing zone around Alaska. The value of the fish the Japanese were permitted to take in Alaskan waters easily exceeded the value of the whales they harvested. Under the Pelly and Packwood-Magnuson Amendments, the United States would be forced to reduce the Japanese fishing rights by at least 50 percent if they were certified by Commerce Secretary Baldrige. The situation was complicated by the fact that, independent of the whaling situation, Senator Stevens of Alaska wanted to eliminate Japanese fishing in Alaska's waters. If the amendments were to have any value as leverages, they needed to be used quickly while Japan still had fishing rights around Alaska.

As the date for implementation of the moratorium approached, we continued to put pressure on Japanese whaling quotas. I assigned Bob McManus, NOAA's general counsel, the task of working out the legal aspects of certification and pressure on the Japanese. It seemed we were entering the endgame concerning Japanese whaling—or at least that is what I thought at the time.

In preparation for the IWC meeting of 1984, we held our delegation meeting in Washington, DC. When I entered the room, Craig Van Note, a staunch whale conservationist, led the delegates present in a standing ovation for me because he and they thought we had achieved our goal to end whaling. I quickly tamed the crowd and told them what I thought would happen. We weren't where we wanted to be yet. I knew the Japanese prime minister was coming to Washington to talk to President Reagan on a number of matters important to maintaining cordial relations between our two friendly nations. Whaling would be on his agenda. What I told our delegates was that, because of the importance of the US relationship with Japan, as we came closer to implementing the moratorium, the US State Department would probably take over the whaling negotiations.

I was right; the State Department named an undersecretary to take over the negotiations. He met with me individually, then with me and the delegation. He quickly realized that whaling issues were extremely complex and arcane and that there wasn't enough time for him to learn all of the nuances and complexities of the negotiations. He asked me to continue in the leadership role.

Under US pressure—including the possible loss of fishing rights— the Japanese withdrew their objection to the moratorium before it went into effect, though they did continue to harvest minke whales from the waters around Antarctica under the research provisions of the ICRW. The efforts to persuade the Japanese to withdraw their objection were among my final endeavors as I left NOAA in November 1984 for a new opportunity: the presidency of Oregon State University.

CHAPTER 13

Selecting a President for Oregon State University (1984)

In quest of the brass ring

SHORTLY AFTER ROBERT MACVICAR, president of Oregon State University, announced his retirement in 1983, I received a letter from Milosh "Poppy" Popovich, former OSU vice president for administration, who was chairing the presidential search committee. He said a search for Mac's successor was beginning and asked if I would be interested.

Of course I was interested. I had already devoted twenty-one years to Oregon State. Since my days as a graduate student at the University of Southern California, I had aspired to be a college or university president. When I took on the NOAA position, I realized it was quite possible that my career was taking a change in direction and I might be leaving higher education, or at least Oregon State University. I accepted that possibility. I also felt that if I didn't return to OSU, I might search for a presidency at another university or college when my NOAA days were over.

Succeeding Mac as president was something I had thought about before leaving for Washington, but once at NOAA, I didn't have much time to dwell on it—until the Popovich letter arrived.

I knew little of the specific search procedures, but I assumed someone within OSU submitted my name. I was sure there would be many candidates; I learned later there were about one hundred applicants. In view of my longevity at Oregon State and my knowledge of the institution and its culture, I considered myself to be both an inside and an outside candidate: I certainly knew OSU from the inside, but I was definitely outside the university at the time.

I responded to Poppy's letter with an application stressing my strengths: I knew the university well, and I'd gained leadership and administrative experience at NOAA. I knew I might not be selected, so I continued to do my politicking to stay on as the administrator of NOAA during President Reagan's second term, assuming he would be reelected.

I called Joe Wright, former deputy secretary of Commerce who was at that time the deputy director of the Office of Management and Budget, and asked him to discover if there was any reason I would not be acceptable as the NOAA administrator during the second term. We had lunch together in the White House dining room. He said he had asked around and there was no reason I would not be acceptable. I had proven myself, and he thought I could continue in the position.

I was chosen as a semifinalist for the OSU position and was asked to come back for an interview, which involved a public presentation devoted to my vision for the university. Naturally I was pleased, but whether I got the job or not, I was determined to make my interview a noteworthy event. There was much I thought OSU faculty, staff, and students needed to hear, and to change, if OSU were ever to come close to achieving its potential. I was convinced changes were in order, and I had learned while in DC that, with a will, big changes were possible.

Before the search process reached the finalist stage, two of the candidates withdrew. Both would have taken substantial reductions in pay if they were to accept the Oregon State position. I wasn't concerned about the pay; I wanted the job.

As a semifinalist, I met with the search committee consisting of faculty, administrators, and a student or two, and then with groups of student leaders, community leaders, members of the board of the private foundation that supports the university, and a group of alumni. I gave a public speech titled, "A Plan for Excellence." Then, as a finalist, I met again with the search committee, a group of alumni, and finally with the full Board of Higher Education, which is responsible for selecting the new president. My wife, Shirley, was invited to participate in some of the interviews when I reached the finalist level.

The sessions with each group were question-and-answer affairs: they asked, I answered. My answers often evolved into minilectures on academic affairs, racism and diversity, intercollegiate athletics and their place in an academic institution, public relations, the mission of a land-grant university, and so on. Each group's questions followed the group's bias: students were concerned about grading, dull professors, intercollegiate athletics, parking on campus. Faculty questions focused on pay, promotion and tenure, diversity, competition with the University of Oregon, OSU's academic stature, the inadequacy of the library. Alumni were concerned about the relative excellence of OSU in athletics (particularly football) and academic matters. Academic deans wanted to know why they weren't permitted to solicit private donors for money for their college.

If time permitted, I was asked how I would manage the university, increase the state budget for OSU, improve the library, and generally what changes I would make throughout the university. I tried not to hedge on any of my answers, although when asked about individuals, particularly in intercollegiate athletics, my answers avoided specificity. The participants of the groups told me exactly how they felt about certain matters, usually telling me exactly what I should do if I were selected as president.

Two sessions stand out: the first with alumni and major donors and the second with students. Shirley and I had dinner in the basement room of the Gables, one of the finest restaurants in Corvallis, with a group of a dozen or so alumni and donors and their spouses. It appeared to be a social occasion, but it was in reality an interview. The discussion rapidly focused on the public image of Oregon State University. We talked about the land-grant role of OSU throughout the state and the importance of agricultural research at the various experiment stations. We talked about the role of the Extension Service in every county and its importance in influencing legislators to support OSU when the budget was decided in the legislature.

It didn't take long before the discussion turned to a comparison of OSU with the University of Oregon. There was agreement that the U of O's image was better than its substance, whereas at OSU, it was just the opposite: the substance of the institution was far better than its image—but not in football. In football, OSU had a real problem with both substance and image. Joe Avezzano, the football coach, and Dee Andros, athletic director, were specifically mentioned as contributing to the substance/image problem. Strong opinions and several anecdotes were shared with Shirley and me. As we listened, I realized more than I had previously that, for the next president, intercollegiate athletics was on the "major problem" agenda.

As I remember, the one-hour session with the students was a positive one. Forty or fifty students were present. I was introduced by a student member of the search committee, and then I made a short opening statement about the mission of Oregon State University as a land-grant

Finger in air, I make a specific point to students during my interview for the OSU presidency in 1984. I may have been telling them that if I become president, we will increase the rigor of your education (namely tougher grades). (OSU Special Collections and Archives Research Center)

university and the importance of the teaching part of that mission. I told them a bit about myself, my job at Humble Oil and my leaving that job because I wanted to teach, coming to Oregon State College, receiving the Carter Award for inspirational teaching, and so on.

I was attempting to establish my credibility with them as someone who truly cared about the educational mission of Oregon State. I told them if I were chosen as the next president, they could expect a reevaluation of the core curriculum. I told them that, although I was a scientist, I was convinced liberal arts were important to every graduate of Oregon State, and that a strong dose of liberal arts should be part of every student's core academic program. I supported increased rigor in the evaluation of students, having witnessed a case of severe grade inflation by one of OSU's colleges when I was dean of the Graduate School. We discussed briefly the role of students on faculty committees and the importance of students in affecting the curriculum and, by their performance, the academic reputation of the university.

I thought my interview with the students went well. I was relaxed, they were well-mannered and attentive, and we had a few laughs together. Apparently some students thought I would make grading too tough and they might have to work much harder to get good grades. Who knows? I guess I did all right, though, because following my interview, the student newspaper, the *Barometer*, publicly endorsed me as the leading candidate for the presidency of Oregon State.

I was one of three finalists. The others were Cliff Smith, who held a position in the chancellor's office and had been dean of administration at Oregon State when I was dean of research, and Hans Mark, deputy administrator of NASA. Before the final interviews were held, Hans Mark withdrew, leaving only Cliff Smith and me as finalists. I thought the Board of Higher Education should extend the search in order to increase the finalist pool—I thought there ought to be more than two options when selecting the president of a major university. But the board did not extend the search, and on April 10 Chancellor Davis called me in Washington to inform me that I would succeed Robert MacVicar as the president of Oregon State University. My annual salary would be $72,528, and I would be provided with a house and an automobile for university business. I thought the salary was modest for the president of a significant land-grant university, but that wasn't important to me. I was pleased to be selected. I had enjoyed the years I had spent at Oregon State, I knew the institution could be improved, and I was confident I could make a positive difference. Cliff Smith was very gracious about my selection, and within hours of the announcement, he called to congratulate me and offer his best wishes.

President MacVicar had announced that he would retire at the end of December, or earlier if his successor were ready to take over. I told Chancellor Davis there were a number of things I wanted to complete as administrator of NOAA and as the US whaling commissioner, and that I would prefer to start the job in mid-November, after the US presidential election. The chancellor assented, and Shirley and I made plans to leave Washington shortly after election day in November 1984.

As it turned out, continuing as administrator until that date wasn't as easy as I'd anticipated. When I informed Secretary Baldrige of my intention to take on the presidency of Oregon State in mid-November, he balked. He didn't like lame-duck positions, particularly ones that would last six months, May to November. He urged me to step down as administrator of NOAA and serve as an advisor to Tony Calio, who he assumed would be the acting administrator, until I departed.

That was the last thing I wanted. Tony Calio and I did not get along well, and I could certainly not see myself reporting to him. Further, I argued that negotiations with the Japanese on whaling issues were at a critical stage, and it would be disadvantageous to those negotiations if I stepped down as whaling commissioner. In fact, I told Secretary Baldrige I thought I should continue as whaling commissioner for another year after I left Washington. I called on my friends in Congress for support, notably Oregon Senators Packwood and Hatfield, as well as Lowell Weicker and Ted Stevens, of Connecticut and Alaska, respectively. Result: I continued as administrator until I left Washington, and I continued as whaling commissioner during my first year as president of OSU.

Shortly after my appointment as OSU president was made public, I was called on to make several decisions. What changes would I like made to the president's house? What kind of automobile did I want? Were there any administrative changes I wanted made before I arrived?

I knew some new presidents had gotten into trouble by demanding too much concerning the president's house, their car, and other perquisites, and also by making changes too rapidly. I suppose the changes I requested were conservative, but changes needed to be made if we were to improve the efficiency of operation and to improve the image of OSU. Some of the quality of life in Washington had rubbed off on me. I wanted OSU to be a classier institution than it had been. By becoming more efficient in our operations, we would be changing the image of Oregon State from that of a folksy nineteenth-century land-grant university into an efficient, businesslike modern university. That was what I hoped for, and that was my plan.

The president's house required upgrading. It was a two-level house built on a hill, and the lower level had never been completed. I decided the lower level should be turned into a complete apartment and that my mother would live there. No one seemed to complain about that. Working with university physical plant employees, Shirley oversaw the remodeling and the decoration of the public part of the house. Unfortunately, the house, built in the 1950s, was not insulated or air-conditioned, and it was impossible to correct that deficiency. Result: it was cold in the winter and very hot in the summer. We managed to live with those conditions for the eleven years I served as OSU's president.

The choice of a car was a different sort of problem. Having lived in Oregon through the gasoline shortage of the 1970s, I was well aware of how sensitive and critical the Oregon public was of what they considered an unnecessary perk for the president of the university. I decided I wanted a state vehicle that looked like other vehicles in the OSU motor pool—plain and serviceable. The motor pool ordered a Chevrolet Caprice full-size sedan for me. Perfect.

Perhaps the most image-changing decision I made was to request a reserved parking space close to my office. No university administrator before me had ever had a reserved parking place. President MacVicar was often forced to search for a parking place whenever he returned to campus from an off-campus trip. The search took time and often resulted in his parking some distance from his office. I thought the decision to have a reserved parking space would increase the efficiency of the president's operation. That simple decision was noticed and was favorably regarded by a number of faculty.

One other decision that changed the efficiency of operation and also OSU's image involved the president's spouse. Shirley realized what her role as the "first lady" of Oregon State would be, but she also knew she wanted a career of her own; she intended to teach piano privately. She knew she would need help in managing the university-related social events held in the president's house. She needed an assistant who would attend to those details and would have an office in the president's house. In the mid-1980s, not many university presidents' spouses had such an assistant, but the trend was developing. Shirley got her assistant.

As November approached, Shirley and I did the normal things to prepare to leave Washington and move back to Corvallis and OSU. I sent my official letter of resignation to President Reagan, pointing out the reasons that I thought were important for me to continue for one more year as commissioner to the IWC. I said my official goodbyes to the people I had come to like and respect in the Congress: Senators Hatfield, Packwood, Stevens, and Weicker, and Representatives George Brown and

Ron Wyden. Goodbye receptions were the order of the day, and NOAA employees presented me with gifts of appreciation.

Meanwhile, we put our house on Quesada Street on the market. It sold the first day it was officially for sale. We shipped our Toyota Corolla to Oregon and packed my mother's Cadillac for the drive across country.

Living in Washington, DC, had been expensive. We were now essentially broke, but there was no way I would have traded the NOAA and International Whaling Commission experiences for anything. I had learned so very much about our nation and how it works, what it is like to manage a large agency, and how many decent, hardworking individuals make up our government. President Reagan's assessment that the problem with the national government was its size and the "bureaucrats" who make it up was simply wrong. I'd started as NOAA's administrator as a naive and unknowledgeable individual. I was returning to Corvallis more seasoned and more savvy.

On Election Day, November 6, Shirley and I were ready to head west. We drove out of DC the next day. President Ronald Reagan had defeated Walter Mondale by a landslide and was ready for a second term—a term without the Byrnes. As we headed across the country, I thought about my unfinished task of ending Japanese whaling. I kept in touch with Bob McManus, NOAA general counsel, who was working with me as I continued my role as whaling commissioner.

The long drive also gave me time to reflect on the three-plus years I'd just completed as a presidential appointee. I remembered the difficulties I'd encountered during the early days of my tenure as administrator. I was appointed to the NOAA position because I was an oceanographer, not because I was a Reagan Republican. I remembered the resistance I encountered from both Reagan Republicans and Democrats, but I was part of the Reagan team, and I did what I could to implement the president's policies.

I was proud of the NOAA employees and how dedicated they were to their jobs. They, as government employees, were not "the problem," as the president had proclaimed. I thought about my efforts to improve their morale. I appreciated the dedication of members of Congress. I reflected on the no-holds-barred efforts of some political appointees to achieve their own personal agendas. I also reflected on the number of good friends Shirley and I had made in Washington, DC.[1] Those years had been good ones for both of us. And as we neared the end of the journey, my thoughts turned to the new challenges I was about to face.

CHAPTER 14

Oregon State University President (1984–1995)

New beginnings

WE ARRIVED IN CORVALLIS midweek, a few days before the Civil War football game between OSU and the University of Oregon. That year, the game was to be played at OSU. My first official day on campus was Saturday, November 16. It was a full day, including a meeting with representatives of the local Republican party in the morning, the football game in the afternoon, and a retirement dinner for the MacVicars that evening. The reception by the Republicans was overwhelming. To those gathered, I was a hero, I guess, and with the incredible acclamation I received, I understood how some people can be caught up in party politics. The football game didn't turn out well for Oregon State—the Ducks prevailed. Shirley and I were misinformed about the starting time for the MacVicar dinner and arrived late.

My job as president really started two days later, on Monday, November 18, 1984. At that time, OSU had approximately sixteen thousand students, undergraduate and graduate, from all fifty states and seventy-five countries. The university was divided into two colleges—the College of Liberal Arts and the College of Science—and ten professional schools.[1] In addition to the four-hundred-acre campus in Corvallis, the university operated the Hatfield Marine Science Center in Newport, the Seafood Laboratory in Astoria, nine agricultural experiment stations located throughout the state, and Extension offices in each of Oregon's thirty-six counties.

LAND-GRANT COLLEGE

Oregon State University's ancestor was Corvallis College, established in 1858. Ten years later, it was designated by the state legislature on a temporary basis to be the agricultural college of Oregon—its de facto land-grant college. Land-grant colleges had been established in 1862 by the federal Morrill Act and given the mission of teaching the applied arts of agriculture, science, engineering, and military matters.

Two years later, Corvallis College's land-grant designation was made permanent. Following a series of name changes over the years, Oregon State College was named Oregon State University in 1961 and given authorization to offer degrees in sciences, liberal arts, and the ten professional areas. Since that time, OSU has been designated by federal agencies as a Sea Grant, Space Grant,[2] and Sun Grant University,[3] with the mission of conducting applied aquatic, space-related, and energy-related research, and sharing the results of that research with the public through Extension programs and teaching.

I inherited three of President MacVicar's assistants: Irene Sears, Keith Mobley, and Stefan Bloomfield. Irene was to be my personal assistant and secretary. She had been Mac's secretary for most of the fourteen years he served as president. Irene clearly knew the ropes, and she provided considerable assistance to me, particularly during the first years of my presidency.

Keith Mobley was new to me. He had served as the president's assistant for legislative matters and knew his way around the politics of state government and the relationship of OSU to the legislature. Keith was particularly useful when it came to traveling around the state to meet legislators in their home districts. He had grown up in Oregon and was savvy about the ways of rural Oregonians.

Stef Bloomfield was a faculty member in the School of Business who had obtained an American Council on Education (ACE) fellowship to serve as a presidential intern at Oregon State. An ACE fellowship was a way for rising academics to prepare for management careers in higher education. Stef accompanied me to meetings of the Oregon State System of Higher Education and the legislature, and he served as my general assistant for a number of matters.

The university had done well under President MacVicar, but I knew it could do better to meet the challenges of our changing times. We were a good early-twentieth-century land-grant university, but this was the late twentieth century. We had an outstanding faculty that was significantly underpaid—our faculty salaries were well below the average for comparable universities. Raising faculty salaries was a high priority.

Our management style seemed outdated. I thought Mac tried to do too much himself, delegating very little. By delegating responsibility, we could speed up decision-making because decisions would be made by those closest to the action. We needed a strategic long-range plan for the future. The curriculum needed to be modernized and academic rigor increased. Funding for the library and for computing was shamefully inadequate and needed to be boosted.

In spite of more than a decade of affirmative action, we had made little progress in enhancing the diversity of the faculty and staff. We needed a new approach for achieving greater diversity. Campus buildings were badly in need of repair or replacement. Intercollegiate athletics appeared to be a mess, particularly the football program.

It was a challenging and exciting agenda, and I was eager to get started. I felt we should be one of the nation's leading land-grant universities as we approached the twenty-first century, and I was absolutely confident that was possible. I suspected there would be surprises, and I was right—there were many.

In March 1985, I was inaugurated as the twelfth president of Oregon State (fourteenth if interim or acting presidents are counted) and, as it turned out, the first OSU president ever to be formally inaugurated. Because my inauguration would be an opportunity to showcase Oregon State, an entire week in March was set aside for the festivities. We put on a series of public lectures, panels, and symposia, all of which emphasized the excellence of Oregon State University. The *Gazette-Times,* Corvallis's local newspaper, recognized what we were attempting to do in an editorial: "Inauguration Celebrates Oregon State University Instead of Crowning a President." The week culminated in a ceremony that included students, faculty, and alumni. Dignitaries included Governor Vic Atiyeh, Chancellor Bud Davis of the State System of Higher Education, and my predecessor, Robert MacVicar.

I delivered an inaugural address, "Preparing for the Future"—a theme I intended to carry out throughout my presidency. I stressed the special responsibility OSU had to the people of our state and our unique position of privilege as Oregon's land-grant university. I emphasized the importance of innovation—we needed to free our thinking from traditional ways; we needed to create new ideas and act on those ideas. As I told students on many occasions, "Life doesn't come in three-credit-hour units; it comes in challenges and opportunities for those who are willing to think creatively."

I emphasized that Oregon State was an international university, and we had a responsibility to share our expertise with the people of the world. We also had a responsibility to help US students experience the world and realize that they were citizens of the world, not just Oregon and the United States. I stressed the importance of a liberal education and the place of liberal studies in the curriculum of every student.

Finally, I addressed diversity at Oregon State. "All our achievements are tarnished," I said, "if, as an institution, we lack integrity or respect for the dignity of the individual, or if we fail to do our best." I challenged all who were present to join me in doing everything possible to make Oregon State University the university it was capable of being.

Complicating my first weeks as president, I was still serving as the US whaling commissioner to the International Whaling Commission. When I'd left Washington, negotiations with the Japanese had been well under way. I'd left them in the capable hands of Bob McManus, the NOAA director of legal affairs. Once I was in Corvallis, many of the other whaling issues were handled by phone with Dean Swanson, an invaluable assistant to me at NOAA on all IWC matters. It was necessary to travel to Washington a couple of times to meet with the US delegation to the IWC, and I had one special meeting with Saito, the Japanese whaling commissioner, at IWC headquarters in Cambridge, England.

Whale quotas for the whaling nations continued to be contentious until the moratorium would go into effect. The biggest issue for me as US commissioner was the quota of bowhead whales for the Eskimos of northern Alaska. The discussions with the US delegation about the bowhead quota had been leaked to David McTaggart, chairman of Greenpeace International.

Shortly after my inauguration, David called me at OSU. It was a month or two before the IWC meeting, to be held in July 1985 in Bournemouth, England. He warned me that if I pursued the quota we were thinking about for the Eskimos, Greenpeace would hold an anti-Byrne demonstration on the Oregon State campus right outside the administration building. He was sure I wouldn't want that. I told him, "David, do what you feel you should do, and I'll do what I need to do." I had met David several years earlier and enjoyed seeing him at the annual IWC meetings.

President Bill Clinton wanted to talk about forestry issues in Oregon when he met me during a meeting of the Board of Directors of the American Council on Education in 1993. I was a member of that board. (ACE)

I considered him a friend. Shirley and I had dinner with him in July at the meeting in Bournemouth. During that dinner, he received a phone call informing him that the Greenpeace vessel, *Rainbow Warrior*, had been bombed in the harbor at Auckland, New Zealand. He left the dinner and the IWC meeting. It was the last time I saw David McTaggart.

OPERATING AS PRESIDENT

PRESIDENT MACVICAR operated not only as president, but also as his own academic vice president and provost. He took on the day-to-day details of managing the university from within, while at the same time being responsible for presidential duties outside the university. By my count, he had twenty-nine people who reported directly to him. For Mac, that management style seemed to work; the people who reported to him did their jobs well but were rarely held accountable for their actions. He had no designated second-in-command to handle most academic matters but was assisted by a dean of undergraduate studies, a dean of the Graduate School, and a dean of faculty. Most academic matters were handled by the academic deans of the schools and colleges. He personally received most, if not all, of the requests from academic deans. Rarely did he pass such requests to a subordinate for a decision. As an example, he personally signed all out-of-state travel requests, reading them in detail before signing.

I think he enjoyed doing this, but attending to that level of detail required an inordinate amount of his time. That was not how I planned to use my time as president. I had learned while I worked for Humble Oil that people closest to the working level usually made better decisions than people higher in the management structure. I intended to delegate as much responsibility as possible and to personally pursue those things that only the president can do. I would focus on improving the substance and the image of Oregon State University, attending to the legislature, developing partnerships with the private sector, and raising money for the improvement of the university.

I soon learned that the job of the president required keeping a number of balls in the air simultaneously and being available at all times. Being president wasn't a job; it was a way of life. I forced my agenda into the time available and set things rolling in a number of areas: introducing my management style to the university, reorganizing the upper administration, developing long-range plans, improving faculty salaries, and addressing the situation in intercollegiate athletics.

I had my own agenda, but other people had theirs, too. Managing my time and energy was important, and deciding whose agenda had priority was essential. During my first week, one academic dean urged me to fire a high-level administrator with whom the dean had personal differences. It was his agenda, not mine. I took no action on his request.

There was no doubt in my mind about the importance of maintaining harmonious relations with the general public. This was a larger task for the land-grant university than for other public universities due to the presence of Oregon State faculty and students in every county within the state. It took special attention from the president to avoid problems in interactions with the public and resolving any issues when they occurred, and to keep the public informed of university matters that might be of interest. The relationship of OSU to the Corvallis community was particularly important. OSU was a relatively large entity in a relatively small community—analogous to the elephant in the living room. Day-to-day issues such as ample parking for students and staff on or adjacent to campus, noisy parties involving students, off-campus housing for students, and a host of other interactions needed to be addressed, and promptly.

Responsible involvement by faculty and staff with local citizens was always important, as was keeping the public informed of changes on campus.

It was always best to head off problems before they arose, but we were not always successful in doing this. I hadn't been president very long when an upset local business owner insisted on seeing me. He operated a local retail store that sold computers and other office equipment. He alleged that the OSU Bookstore on campus was taking unfair advantage by being part of a state-supported university. The bookstore's pricing of computers resulted in sales he couldn't possibly match. He claimed the OSU Bookstore could undersell him because its overhead costs were lower than his, and that the manager of the bookstore knew this and was purposely trying to undersell him. He pointed to bookstore ads in the local newspaper as an attempt to solicit purchases from townspeople who were not faculty, staff, or students. He insisted that I put a stop to this unfair practice.

To maintain harmonious relations with the people of Corvallis, I gave his agenda a high priority. I took action on it right away. I met with him, listened to him, and pointed out that the OSU Bookstore was not an official part of Oregon State University. It was independent and had its own board and manager. It was located on campus as a convenience to OSU students, and we certainly didn't want it to be in competition with local businesses. I told him I would look into the matter and report back to him. I suspect he thought I was whitewashing the issue, but nothing was further from my mind.

I asked Keith Mobley to look into the allegation and report back to me soon. Keith reported quickly. Yes, the bookstore's computer prices were lower than those in town, but whether the manager was intentionally trying to drum up local citizen purchases was open to question. The issue was sufficiently important that OSU should act quickly to resolve it. I directed Keith to suggest the membership of a committee of local citizens and OSU faculty and staff to look into the charge and to address other matters concerning the relationship of OSU to the Corvallis business community—a Town and Gown Committee. I appointed faculty to the committee with Keith as chairman and invited several townspeople to serve on it.

The committee included the merchant who, since his moment of ire, had calmed down. The committee resolved the immediate situation to the satisfaction of all. The OSU Bookstore stopped advertising in the

Gazette-Times, and its manager examined the inventory of items that might be considered to compete with products sold by local merchants and adjusted their prices. Looking into bookstore practices in greater detail, the committee discovered that the manager was indeed an aggressive marketer. He was informed that his practices were not appropriate for a university bookstore and asked to revise his practices. A short time later, the manager left the university to pursue other opportunities.

Citizens and faculty had no reticence in writing to me to express their opinions and concerns. Occasionally their notes praised something about the university or the actions of faculty or staff, but mostly they complained about something: the lack of a Russian language program, alcohol at football games, handicap access on campus, inappropriate advertising by the athletic department (e.g., football players carrying submachine guns), comments by me reported by the *Gazette-Times*, fees for copying material in the library, faculty working as consultants, student drinking during commencement, snow-covered sidewalks, high tuition, and more. I took all of the notes seriously. Although some of their comments may have been disturbing, I realized the authors cared about the university and the image of OSU. They wanted us to be perfect, and so did I.

I was anxious to make as many changes as quickly as possible, but I had seen examples in other universities where a new president had immediately made changes, not all of which were welcomed by the faculty, students, or alumni. Often the changes were made before the new president had established his own credentials and become familiar with the personnel on hand. Chaos often resulted, and the new president's tenure at the institution was short-lived; he was fired before getting much accomplished.

If I had an advantage, it was that I was already known to the OSU community. For twenty-one years, I had worked with many faculty one way or another; I had been one of them. I was reasonably familiar with the nature and traditions of Oregon State. Even so, I learned quickly that some problems didn't wait for a solution or for their turn in the queue of things to be done.

Intercollegiate athletics was one of those issues. It cut into line before I had a chance to address the management philosophy or administrative structure of the university or faculty salaries or diversity or long-range planning. The question of what to do with the football coach, Joe Avezzano, was the catalyst for bringing intercollegiate athletics to the head of the queue. In fairness to Joe, who knew his tenure at Oregon State was in jeopardy, the football program, and consequently some aspects of inter-collegiate athletics, had to be considered before anything else. I tell that story more fully in chapter 17.

At the time I focused on athletics, I made it known that our management style had changed. I delegated management responsibility to the appropriate officers of the university. That meant we needed to address our administrative structure.

Athletics, management style, administrative structure: three balls in the air simultaneously—an introduction to being president.

Was this my honeymoon?

RESTRUCTURING THE ADMINISTRATION

I DID NOT INTEND to monitor the activities of the more than two dozen people who previously had reported to the president. In a university, the process by which changes are made is important, as is the style used in making those changes. Academe had traditional ways of making changes, and I intended to adhere to them. I brought three well-respected higher education consultants to Oregon State to review our administrative structure. With their ideas, a group of faculty and administrators could then plan a more effective structure and put that structure in place. The team I brought in consisted of Bob Clodius, president of the National Association of State Universities and Land-Grant Colleges (NASULGC), Harold Enarson, former president of the Ohio State University, and Charles Sturtz, vice president for administration at the University of Maryland.

The team came in March and spent three days visiting with academic deans, administrative deans, department chairs, faculty, and student leaders. Within two weeks each member of the team submitted an individual letter report. Each letter reflected the expertise of the individual and each recommended an administrative structure of five vice presidents, with the vice president for academic affairs serving as provost, at least when the president was away from campus. The team also made recommendations concerning the president's cabinet and which staff, in addition to the vice presidents, should report directly to the president.

With these recommendations in hand, my assistants and I drafted a new administrative structure, one that, although it appeared to be revolutionary for Oregon State University, was the standard for most major universities in the United States. There would be five vice presidents: one for finance and administration; one for student affairs; one for research, graduate studies, and international programs; one for university relations; and one for academic affairs. The VP for academic affairs would serve as provost. Because of the sensitivity of some areas of responsibility, the university's legal advisor, director of affirmative action, and athletic director would also report to the president.

The new structure meant only eight people would report directly to me, in addition to my three assistants. For this to be effective, I delegated responsibility and authority. Each vice president was given the right to make his or her own mistakes. I had a few of my own rules that accompanied their right to make mistakes: (A) when recognized, a wrong decision was to be corrected by a second decision as soon as possible; (B) no mistake was to serve as a precedent for future decisions; and (C) never give away the authority to make a decision, no matter how difficult the decision; don't buck the tough decisions up the line.

In other words, if a decision is a mistake, correct it. If help is needed, ask for it. Delegation of authority was not to be abused from above; micromanagement was not to be tolerated.

When this structure and these rules were presented to the academic deans in April, acceptance was not universal. Several deans were concerned about the delegation of authority to vice presidents. Would the vice presidents serve as a barrier between the deans and the president? How would the deans get to the president for a decision on their request? Answer: the new president would not be making decisions on the deans' requests. The appropriate vice presidents would make those decisions.

It took a month or two of my refusing to consider such requests and referring the deans to the appropriate vice president before the new management style sank in. It was not business as it had been. It was a new era of responsibility. This system also required that I, as president, stay out of each vice president's area of responsibility. I had to remain merely an observer when I thought a vice president was making a mistake, unless I considered that mistake to be detrimental to the entire university. That never happened.

Staying out of VP issues was difficult at times. Example: the Survey Research Center, which operated under the vice president for research, was important to a number of faculty researchers. Shortly after I introduced the new delegation style of management, George Keller, the vice president for research, closed the center for budget reasons. Having been in George's position in the research office at one time, I thought closing the center was a mistake. The reaction by faculty and deans to the vice president's decision bordered on revolution. I stayed out of it. If anything, I may have asked George if he really wanted to close the Survey Research Center. The new management system was being tested.

George subsequently reversed his decision and found another way to adjust his budget. Our new system was working.

In June, the Board of Higher Education approved our administrative reorganization and the creation of new vice president positions. It was time to fill those positions.

Jo Anne Trow and George Keller were already in charge of student affairs and research and graduate studies. It was a simple matter to change their titles from "dean of" to "vice president for." Tom Parsons was already handling finance and administration at a vice presidential level, so I designated him as vice president for those functions. Dave Nicodemus had been MacVicar's academic personnel officer. I made him my VP for academic affairs. Both Parsons and Nicodemus were about to retire, but I wanted to put them into these vice presidents' slots for the time being, so the reorganization could be done without major upheaval while we initiated national searches for their successors and for a new vice president for university relations.

The university had never had a single person in charge of university relations, so that position needed to be created anew. The person in this position would be responsible for the image and marketing of the university, for overseeing the alumni association and the OSU Foundation and the coordination of those two organizations, and for major university events.

Tom Parsons continued as VP for finance and administration while the search for his successor was under way, but we needed interim appointments from within the university for the vice presidents for academic affairs and university relations. I appointed Bill Wilkins, dean of liberal arts, as the interim vice president for academic affairs and Rob Phillips as the interim vice president for university relations. Phillips, a faculty member in journalism, had managed the summer term and overseen Seatauqua, the program of lectures, events, and short courses at the Oregon coast. He also had experience managing the *East Oregonian*, a newspaper in Pendleton, Oregon.

When we completed the national search for the VP for academic affairs, we intended that the position would include the title and duties of provost—a position OSU had never had before. I thought that someone coming in from outside would not be aware of the values, principles, and traditions of Oregon State, so important to those of us who had been here for some time. Until that person was comfortable with those values and traditions, I would personally serve as provost.[4]

We started the full-scale national searches for the three positions early in the 1985–1986 academic year. In summer 1986, we hired Graham Spanier,[5] the vice provost for undergraduate studies at the State University of New York at Stonybrook, as vice president for academic affairs and provost. About a month later, we attracted L. Edward Coate to the vice president for finance and administration position, and in September we brought in Bill Slater as vice president for university relations. Ed Coate had been a deputy regional administrator for the Environmental Protection Agency and an adjunct professor at the University of Washington. Slater had been dean of liberal arts at Eastern Washington University. By conducting three major searches simultaneously, we were able to fill the upper administrative positions in as short a time as possible.

Graham's title, VP for academic affairs and provost, was changed after a couple of years to provost and VP for academic affairs. This may seem a subtle change, but it reflected my confidence in him and sent a strong signal that he was second in command. He brought several new ideas to OSU, including the creation of distinguished professorships for OSU's outstanding faculty, the reintroduction of the honorary doctorate at commencement, an annual *Oregon State University Fact Book*, and a spousal hiring program.

Spousal hiring programs did not exist nationally in academe. Ours was a direct outcome of the hiring situation for Graham and his wife, Sandra, a recognized scholar in literature. In a small town such as Corvallis, the employment opportunities for a two-professional family are limited. To make our situation attractive to the Spaniers, I created a position specifically for Sandra. Subsequent to our hiring both Spaniers, Graham initiated a program in which professional opportunities were identified within commuting distances of Corvallis, and the information shared with other organizations faced with similar hiring problems, both academic and commercial.

When the position was created for Sandra Spanier, a number of faculty objected to the spousal hiring program, insisting that national searches must be conducted before the position created specifically for her could be filled. They didn't seem to understand that the reason we were creating a position within the university specifically for Sandra Spanier was to attract Graham to the vice president position. The pragmatic creation of the position in order to attract the Spaniers seemed to make little difference to those faculty members.

Our administrative team seemed compatible and worked well together. The balance of two vice presidents, Trow and Keller, who were comfortable with the existing values and traditions of Oregon State, and the three who were new to campus—Spanier, Coate, and Slater—provided both stability and innovation. All of the vice presidents contributed to the agenda I had set; all were important in implementing my agenda. Of no less importance were the vice presidents who succeeded the original vice presidents during my watch. Roy Arnold, the dean of the College of Agricultural Sciences, succeeded Spanier when he left in 1991. Lynn Spruill moved from the deanship of the College of Business to become the vice president for university relations when Bill Slater left, and Lee Schroeder left engineering to succeed Ed Coate as vice president for finance and administration.

CHAPTER 15

Looking Ahead: Long-Range Planning at OSU

"Planning is everything."
—Dwight D. Eisenhower

SINCE MY DAYS IN OCEANOGRAPHY, I believed if you were going to improve an organization for the future, you needed a written plan, a template to be used for budgeting and for governing day-to-day operations. I also thought that at a university it was important to have the faculty heavily involved in creating that plan. I called on the faculty to help develop possibly the first long-range plan in Oregon State's history. I intended to use the plan to shape the biennial budget, and use the budget to help implement the elements of the plan. We would plan on a biennial basis and develop our budget on an alternate two-year cycle.

Before we could even begin to plan, we needed to know the condition of the university today. I appointed three faculty committees: one to look at OSU's mission, another to judge OSU's strengths and weaknesses, and a third to assess the external environment in which we operated.

I gave the committees six weeks to report back—ample time, I was convinced, in spite of the glacial pace at which academe often operates. During the first week, I heard numerous complaints that six weeks wasn't enough time to do an adequate job. To the faculty's credit, I received all three reports before the deadline. I was told weekend meetings were required, even Sundays, but that the faculty felt good about working hard and beating the deadline.

With those basic background papers in hand, I asked the Faculty Senate to appoint a five-person long-range planning commission. The commission met with me on November 1, 1985. I told them I wanted the plan to represent all of Oregon State. It was to be the faculty, staff, and

Presidents of land-grant universities are often required to demonstrate
agricultural skills. Here I'm attempting, unsuccessfully, to milk an OSU
cow (ca. 1994). Alumni Director Don Wirth looks on from outside the
fence before he takes over and fills the pail with milk.
(OSU Special Collections and Archives Research Center)

administration's plan, and if it was to be effective, everyone had to have a sense of ownership. It was important to involve campus leaders and to invite participation by all who wanted to be involved. It was to be a bottom-up, democratic process.

The planning commission invited everyone at Oregon State to contribute ideas. Committees and task forces were organized to develop goals and objectives for alumni relations, conference services, continuing education, curriculum, graduate programs, interdisciplinary programs, extension and outreach, research enhancement, marketing, minority issues, space allocation, student advising, the summer term—just about everything OSU did. Specific responsibilities were assigned to 152 people, including deans, department chairs, faculty, students, staff, and alumni.

The commission, cochaired by Kinsey Green and Bud Weiser, included Warren Hovland, Pete Fullerton, Steve Lawton, and my assistant, Stef Bloomfield, who served as liaison with the administration. Once all task-force reports were in, the commission assembled the plan, which was then distributed to OSU faculty, staff, students, and external stakeholders for comment.

The final plan, published in September 1987, listed twenty-one goals grouped in four categories: fostering human development, creating knowledge and beauty, assisting the economic and social development of Oregon, and establishing an environment for success. These goals were supported by ninety-eight specific objectives. I thought it was an outstanding plan. By 1990, more than seventy of its ninety-eight objectives had been achieved or were close to achievement. The plan had provided guidance but also made provision for unexpected events that might benefit the university. As important as the plan was, of greater importance was the method employed in preparing it. A great number of faculty and administrators had been involved in the plan's preparation, and anyone who was so inclined was able to offer input, all of which was taken seriously. Dwight Eisenhower, preparing for the invasion of Europe during World War II, was correct: plans were nothing; planning was everything.

Watching the planning commission in action, it became obvious to me that OSU faculty and staff often performed exceptionally well and achieved outstanding results in areas not directly part of their normal assignments. I thought they needed to be recognized, so I created the Oregon State University President's Award for Outstanding Effort and Achievement of Excellence, also termed "The Beaver Champion Award."

Each recipient of the award received a bronze casting of a beaver at work in its own environment, a sculpture created by Oregon artist Kenneth M. Scott. At University Day in September 1987, I announced the award for the first time and presented one to each member of the long-range planning commission. I began the tradition of making the award as a surprise at the University Day event. The recipient was not announced until the presentation of the award.

Our first plan, "Preparing for the Future," had been a bottom-up effort that served as an effective foundation for the second planning process, which resulted in a revised and refocused strategic plan, "Creating the Future." This process evolved as a hybrid, both bottom up and top down. Lessons had been learned in creating the first plan. So, before beginning to draft the second plan, the commission identified a number of planning principles: Everyone should be involved in the plan's development. Much of what a university engages in doesn't change from year to year, so the plan should focus on the margins of what a university does. The plan should be realistic, flexible, and should emphasize things that can be done immediately. Finally, as we had learned with the first plan, the process of planning is more important than the final product, the plan itself.

As the plan was developed, four themes emerged that tied it together: (1) Good teaching, fundamental to an excellent university, should be promoted and rewarded. (2) Inadequate facilities can be impediments to teaching and research. (3) Cultural diversity is essential to enhancing an international focus and a diversified curriculum. (4) Good relations with constituents are the foundation of marketing Oregon State University.

Goal statements are usually fairly broad and, for universities, sufficiently general that they can apply to virtually any institution. Oregon State's were no exception, but they did serve as reminders and vehicles for the more specific action objectives. Our goals were: Serve people through instruction, research, and extension. Maintain a high-quality and nurturing educational environment that aids students in achieving their fullest potential. Sustain and expand research excellence and artistic creativity. Attract, develop, and retain faculty and staff who are committed to excellence (a particular objective was to bring faculty salaries to competitive levels). Expand educational and professional opportunities for members of minority, female, disadvantaged, and disabled populations. Increase the enrollment of outstanding students. Sustain, coordinate, and sharpen an international focus. Improve facilities and equipment. Expand and improve library and computing services. Improve relations with the university's constituents.

PLANNING AND UNIVERSITY ACCREDITATION

ACCREDITATION of institutions of higher education is a form of quality control that has been in effect in the United States since the end of the nineteenth and beginning of the twentieth centuries. Colleges and universities, including Oregon State, are accredited every ten years, with a mid-decade progress review. Our accrediting agency, the Northwest Commission on Colleges and Universities, agreed that our strategic/long-range planning could be a major element in our 1990 accreditation review. Focusing on planning was unusual in an accreditation review, but the reviewers apparently thought that planning for the future was worthy of inclusion in the process. Inasmuch as we were involved in the planning process at the time, Oregon State's accreditation could be a good test case for applying such an evaluation to other colleges and universities. Consequently, our accreditation visiting team included an expert on long-range plans and planning.

The accreditation process began in late February 1990, with a four-day visit of a fifteen-member team that included university presidents, deans, vice presidents, professors, and special assistants to presidents. The review went well: The team was impressed by our planning efforts and the adjustments we had made to meet our budget. They noted that we were following our two planning documents with the clearly stated goals and priorities in the plans.

The team concluded: "The final result has been a 'closet cleaning' that has left OSU a much better, more efficient and more clearly directed institution." I think they were impressed by our efforts to manage OSU more efficiently. They did note, however, that our buildings were in need of repair and that the OSU library and campus-wide computing needed attention— items we were all well aware of and were already working to rectify. It is quite possible that the team's particular attention to those deficiencies, over which we at OSU had little control, were included as a message to the State Board of Higher Education and the chancellor's office. We were very pleased with the visiting team's report and the positive attention they gave to our planning efforts.

TOTAL QUALITY MANAGEMENT

In 1989, Oregon State awarded an honorary doctor of science degree to W. Edwards Deming, the quality guru who is largely credited for developing the quality improvement program known as Total Quality Management (TQM) used by the Japanese to improve their automobile industry to a position of world leadership. Deming noted the importance of management in improving systems of production and service by which employees operate. He knew that employees could be doing an exemplary job, but the systems by which they operated could be improved.

A few days after the commencement at which Deming was honored, I mentioned to Ed Coate, our VP for finance and administration, that I would like to "Demingize" Oregon State University. Coate was aware that the Hewlett-Packard operation in Corvallis employed a number of Deming's methods in its quality-improvement program. He arranged for several of us to have lunch with a group of HP people to learn how they were doing it. As a result of that luncheon, the HP quality-improvement folks agreed to create an evening course for educators on the systems and techniques of quality improvement as they might be applied to educational programs. The course met one evening a week. Participants, who were from OSU and Linn-Benton Community College, were tasked with creating a quality-improvement program using Deming's techniques.

Coate and I decided to test TQM in the nonacademic part of OSU, specifically the physical plant department. We started by asking the academic deans to identify their biggest problems with the physical plant. At the top of the deans' list was the length of time it took the physical plant folks to complete a project from the time a request was submitted to them.

Using Deming's statistical methods, Coate and his team learned that the average time to complete a project was 270 days. The next step was to diagram the system of work that included every step in the process, no matter how small the step. This required talking to the workers involved in the process. At one point, Coate and his team learned that a clerk in the physical plant office was stamping the date an incoming work order appeared on her desk, filing it, pulling it from the file ten days later, and then passing it on to the next step in the process.

When they asked her why she did this, she replied that when she first started in her job, she was told to delay every work order for ten days.

She had done this on every work order for the past ten years that she had been in her position. The clerk had been doing her job; it was the system that was at fault.

By eliminating that delay, ten days were shaved from the total project time. By further streamlining the system, it was possible to reduce the total project time by twenty-five days—almost ten percent of the total time from the initial work request to job completion.

Based on our experience in streamlining operations in the physical plant, we were convinced the Deming TQM model would work for the rest of the nonacademic side of the university. Under Ed Coate's leadership, quality improvement was instituted as a major management concept, using the TQM guidelines provided by Deming.

It was more difficult to persuade faculty to adopt TQM practices to their teaching. We heard arguments that teaching was not like manufacturing things; working with students was not the same as turning out widgets; and furthermore, no one is going to tell me how to manage my courses. But some faculty did pick up Deming's techniques and worked with their students to improve their courses. In those courses, we observed that both faculty and students benefited, and the relationship of student to teacher improved. Eldon Olsen, a professor in the School of Forestry, joked that before he introduced TQM to his courses, students crossed the street to avoid meeting him. After they worked with him on quality improvement, those students still crossed the street, but because they wanted to encounter him. The students had learned something about quality management, and they had learned that all manner of things can be improved by working cooperatively.

Others had learned that sharing results among quality-improvement teams and celebrating those results was important. We did, too. We held a TQM celebration every year to share different quality-improvement projects through presentations, poster sessions, and awarding of prizes. People felt good knowing they had helped to improve Oregon State University. At the TQM fair in 1992, we honored Eldon Olsen, Edward McDowell, associate professor in industrial and manufacturing engineering, and Dave Gobeli, professor of business administration, for their leadership in implementing TQM principles on the academic side of the university.

Ed Coate developed a national reputation for his TQM work at OSU, and so did our university. The *Chronicle of Higher Education* named OSU as one of the leaders in the application of TQM principles to higher education. Thank you, Ed Coate.

ASSESSING MANAGEMENT AT OSU: THE PEAT MARWICK REPORT

ALSO AT THIS TIME, we were coping with fallout from the passage of a far-reaching property tax limitation measure, Ballot Measure 5. Passed in 1990, Measure 5 was an initiative that amended the Oregon constitution to limit local property taxes. The limitation, amounting to 1.5 percent per $1,000 of assessed value of real estate, effectively transferred support of K-12 schools from local communities to the state without increasing the size of the state's budget. As it was phased in over three biennia, Measure 5 resulted in financial chaos for higher education, triggering significant cuts to academic programs at Oregon State and at other public colleges and universities.

The passage of Measure 5 had caused the legislature to become increasingly sensitive to budgetary and management matters, particularly in higher education. At the end of the 1991 legislative session, the legislature passed a budget that included a note calling for a review of the administrative and support services of the entire State System of Higher Education.

It is a rule of survival in state government that budget notes are not ignored if you anticipated being around for the next legislative session. To comply with the budget note, the higher education board immediately created a Board Administrative Review Committee (BARC) to conduct a comprehensive review of management of the entire system and to direct each institution to develop scenarios for cutting administrative costs by 10, 20, and 30 percent, with an assessment of the impacts of each reduction level.

At my direction, Oregon State University played a lead role in working with BARC to begin the review. The review was intended to be intensive and to include all aspects of administration, from the department level to president's office. I requested that Oregon State be the first institution to be reviewed. This was in keeping with my belief that OSU should be the best-managed university in the system. BARC identified KPMG Peat Marwick, a management consulting firm, to provide advice as the administrative review was initiated.

Being first among the universities of the state system turned out not to be as advantageous as I had anticipated. In fact, it seemed to put Oregon State in some jeopardy, because the legislature might consider the Peat Marwick recommendations to be a mandate, even those recommendations that were unworkable for a university. And that is exactly what the legislature attempted to do.

The Peat Marwick consultants assigned to Oregon State knew very little, if anything, about how a university functioned. They were at the bottom of a steep learning curve, and I suppose we were, too, in terms of working with private-sector consultants. It was critically important that university folks work directly with the consultants, so we created our own administrative review committee (ARC), consisting of fifteen OSU faculty, staff, and administrators. Beginning in early 1992, the consultants and the ARC looked at all aspects of administrative and support services. They examined our organizational structure and processes, explored opportunities for contracting out or eliminating services, and looked for ways to eliminate duplication of administrative efforts.

It soon became obvious that the consultants could not do their job without the assistance of the ARC. Early in its deliberations, the ARC developed guidelines to help identify potential cost savings: define administrative support; use the same criteria to evaluate all units; look for university-wide and cross-function solutions; benchmark against the private sector and comparable universities; begin with a clean slate; and avoid protecting sacred cows and turf.

The consultants and the ARC worked hard for a full five months and in July delivered their voluminous report, "An Administrative Cost/Structure Assessment of Oregon State University." The group commended OSU for steps we had already taken, such as restructuring the administration, adopting Total Quality Management, merging colleges, strategic planning, and so forth. It was obvious to the Peat Marwick group that OSU was moving in the right direction toward improved management efficiency.

Their report included major recommendations and numerous supporting recommendations. One key recommendation was to limit the major management positions reporting to the president to two: the provost and the vice president for finance and administrations. The other VPs would report to the provost as associate provosts. The report recommended similar adjustments concerning the assistant and associate provosts. Additional recommendations included:

- consolidating academic departments, colleges, and programs, thereby reducing the number of colleges to eight or nine, eliminating unnecessary duplication of services;
- consolidating business activities such as purchasing and accounting into a central office;
- outsourcing as many services as possible (such as the bookstore and food services);

- eliminating nonessential units, including the Horner Museum, OSU Press, the Portland Center, and the aquarium at the Hatfield Marine Science Center;
- upgrading computing services throughout the university; and
- linking the Extension Service to research under the associate provost for research.

The Peat Marwick/ARC group recognized that some of their recommendations could not be implemented if the university was to sustain its mission of service to the public. They made those recommendations anyway. The report included estimated financial savings of 10, 20, and 30 percent for each of the recommendations, totaling $14 to $19.7 million. A possible implementation plan was included.

My initial reaction: some of the recommendations made sense; others were out of the ballpark and there was no way we would even consider them. Much of what the team had proposed was unworkable for a university; their recommendations seemed more appropriate to the needs of a corporate organization. It was obvious the team didn't realize the magnitude of the duties assigned to each of the vice presidents, or that transferring those duties to a subordinate of the provost would diminish the authority of the vice president to whom the responsibility had been delegated. Our administrative structure was an innovation developed by a team of well-respected academic leaders. We would not change our administrative structure.

We were already combining various departments. Further consolidations of academic support units under an associate provost would require study. Their suggestion of linking Extension with OSU's research function told me that the consulting group did not understand academic research and certainly had little understanding of the nature of Extension or of its importance to a land-grant university. The role of Extension and its position in the university hierarchy required more attention.

The other recommendations made sense in general, but details needed to be evaluated. The recommendation to outsource some activities seemed a good idea, but the examples cited in the report were additional evidence that the Peat Marwick folks didn't understand the university. The bookstore was already a nonuniversity operation, and the Hatfield Marine Science Center aquarium was a low-cost part of the center's operation. The future of the Horner collection and of the OSU Press would be considered.

We were already doing everything our budget allowed to upgrade computing services campus-wide.

While I had my own thoughts about the report, I knew that in a university it is important to follow due process and involve faculty and staff in major decisions. Consequently, when I received the report in the summer of 1992, the provost and I immediately formed a leadership implementation team (LIT) to review it and determine which recommendations could work for Oregon State University.

With the provost's guidance, the LIT worked hard for a full two years at a detailed assessment of the report. In the meantime, in response to the urgency of adjusting the OSU budget, we merged several academic units, restructured some administrative functions, and eliminated programs. The College of Education was folded into the College of Home Economics, faculty in the Department of Religious Studies were transferred to the Department of Philosophy, and the Departments of Geology and Geography were merged to form the Department of Earth Sciences.

THE EXTENSION SERVICE AND EXTENDED EDUCATION

WHEN I FIRST came to Oregon State in 1960, I had little knowledge of what the Extension Service was, how it functioned, or how important it was to Oregon State and to every land-grant university in the United States. But I did believe fundamentally in the philosophy of Extension: people helping people by sharing knowledge. Over the years, I came to regard Extension as one of the great attributes of the land-grant university system. I became impressed at the ways in which Extension forged direct, practical, and highly useful relationships between the university and the citizens it served. Extension added a dimension to land-grant universities that other types of universities did not have.[1]

Traditionally, Extension had been associated with colleges of agriculture, home economics, and engineering and was administratively under the dean of agriculture. Over time, I came to believe that the Extension mission should not be limited to these domains. Extension agents, I thought, should have access to, and should be given the capacity to disseminate, the knowledge that existed throughout the university, if that knowledge could be helpful to Oregon's citizens.

The Cooperative Extension Service at Oregon State University was administered from the College of Agricultural Science, and the Extension director reported to the dean of agriculture. Extension agents were located in every county in Oregon and served the people of those counties in resolving local problems and issues. These county Extension agents held academic rank within the Extension Service, but not in academic departments. They were reviewed for promotion and tenure within the Extension Service. Extension specialists, located within academic departments on campus, served to link the county agents with the expertise that existed within academic departments on campus. Most of the Extension specialists were faculty members in academic departments within the Colleges of Agriculture and Home Economics.

O. E. "Ernie" Smith, director of the Extension Service during my tenure as president, helped to educate me about Extension and its wide reach. He accompanied me on trips throughout the state to visit county agents. He pointed out to me that the challenges these agents faced had changed over time. During the early twentieth century, Extension's focus had been on agricultural production and how to increase crop yields. During the 1930s, the emphasis had shifted to the marketing of agricultural crops. Later, as the rural economic environment changed, the issue became one of financial and social survival for farms and farm families.

The county Extension agent was expected to address all these issues, be they agricultural, economic, or social. To be most effective, the county agent needed access to expertise in areas that were not part of Extension's traditional academic territory. This had been made clear to me by the time I initiated the Extension program in the Department of Oceanography. I was one of the first oceanography leaders nationwide to make Extension part of the department's mission.

I remembered Ed Condon, the second Extension agent I added to the oceanography department. Ed was a former naval officer who had been in charge of the naval shipyard in Portland, Maine. He was used to working with the maritime industry, and he directed his Extension efforts to helping that industry in the Portland, Oregon, area. Ed's nontraditional background meant he was not steeped in the traditions and culture of Extension. He had no reticence in reaching beyond agriculture, engineering, and home economics for help. If the dimensions of a problem included forestry, science, or business, Ed sought out the experts in those areas to assist in solving the problem.

Ever since I'd become president of Oregon State, I'd had the goal of elevating Extension to a higher position in the university's administrative hierarchy. This would help bring Extension agents into contact with expertise throughout the university, and it would also send a strong signal of the importance of Extension at this university. But where? Should

Extension become part of the Research Office, where it would have access to new knowledge as that knowledge was being created? Or, would it be more effective in another part of Oregon State's organization—possibly reporting directly to the provost?

Moving Extension's administration from the College of Agriculture to somewhere else would involve a number of complexities that required careful thought and critical analysis. I knew someone I could trust to provide such thought and analysis, if he would agree to take on the task. I had known Emery Castle since the late 1960s, when we were both department chairmen and were active in establishing the Oregon Sea Grant Program at OSU. I knew him to be thoughtful and thorough, familiar with problems of administration, knowledgeable about the needs of Oregonians, and well aware of the nuances of both the Extension Service and of the academic environment at Oregon State University.

Emery had come to Oregon State College in 1954 as a faculty member in the Department of Agricultural Economics. During his tenure, he had served as dean of the faculty, chairman of the department, and dean of the Graduate School. In 1976 he left Oregon State to join the highly regarded think tank, Resources for the Future (RFF), in Washington, DC, serving first as vice president and later as president. RFF was, and still is, a tax-exempt public policy institute specializing in environmental and natural resources. Emery retired from RFF in 1986 and returned to OSU with a half-time appointment as director of the Economics Core Program, a program designed to coordinate the several economics programs at OSU.[2]

Still digesting the Peat Marwick report, I invited Emery to my office. We talked about Extension and how important it was to the people of Oregon and to Oregon State University. I told him that I wanted to move Extension's locus of operation out of the College of Agriculture and to position it at a higher level. I reviewed the Peat Marwick recommendation for him and told him I was not sold on the idea of having it report to the vice president for research. Yet I hadn't decided in my own mind where I thought Extension should fit.

After I explained all this, I said, "Em, I need your help. If you will look at Extension with its administrative location in mind, I will sincerely appreciate it." I knew Emery to be a careful man and was not surprised when he said he would like to reflect on the assignment before deciding. I was confident he would give the task careful consideration, and if he thought it was important to the university and to the people served, he would take it on, no matter how difficult.

Emery came back to see me several days later to discuss my request and the assignment. He pointed out that there were a great many dimensions to the problem, not just the administrative placement of the Extension Service or to whom the director should report. What we ultimately decided could have an impact not only on Extension personnel, but also on academic faculty. How such a change would be received by the citizens within the counties was another important dimension. Emery saw it as essentially a top-to-bottom issue involving all levels within the university, from the upper administration to the individual faculty member.

In spite of the complexities that we talked about, he was willing to study the situation and to provide his advice. I was delighted he'd accepted the challenge, and I told him I would help in any way I could.

Emery sought information at every level, from the US Department of Agriculture to Oregon's county Extension agents. Over several months, he visited with academic deans, faculty, and nonuniversity stakeholders. He talked to ninety people in all, individually and in groups. His report, "On the University's Third Mission: Extended Education," took my breath away. It was visionary—far more than I had anticipated when I had presented the challenge to him. If his recommendations were implemented, they would change not only the Extension Service but the entire university.

As I studied it, I realized Emery's analysis was right on target.[3] His report focused on the Extension Service, but it went well beyond Extension in acknowledging the other outreach units of Oregon State, such as continuing higher education, the Hatfield Marine Science Center, and the efforts of the College of Engineering in the Portland area. His perceptive analysis placed all these outreach units within a larger framework of extended education and challenged everyone at the university to recognize that extended education—education outside the confines of the campus—was an essential part of Oregon State's mission.

In his characteristically thorough fashion, Emery also addressed in detail such practical questions as the administrative location of the Extension Service, title of the officer in charge (dean and/or director), relationship of Extension to the academic units, assignment of county agents to academic units, recognition of Extension personnel for promotion and tenure, and even other "recommendations requiring decisions by the president." While these matters were important and were in fact exactly what I had in mind when I asked for Emery's help, his analysis went beyond the role and nature of Extension. In its forward-thinking recognition of the changing needs for access to higher education, the report provided the foundation for Oregon State's subsequent embrace of a larger vision of extended education and engagement with society.

"Oregon State University must continuously assess how it can best serve the changing educational needs of the people of the State," he wrote in his introduction. "Consistent with its Land Grant responsibilities, the University should consider these needs regardless of geography, occupation, economic class, race, or gender."

Before issuing the final report, I shared preliminary versions with some academic and Extension personnel and with other stakeholders. There was considerable discussion and some concern about the concept of including county Extension personnel in academic units. (Extension *specialists* had been members of academic departments for some time.) After discussion and some amendment to the original version of the report, the final report was released. It included a "President's statement of decisions on the placement of the OSU Extension Service within the University."

In my statement, I affirmed the recommendations of the Castle report and created an Office of Extended Education, which included the administration of the Extension Service. The office would be administered by a dean/director who reported to the provost. I outlined the academic dimensions of the new extended education function, including the assignment of all Extension faculty to academic units. I set forth reward systems (salary and promotion and tenure) and specified that they would be reviewed and possibly revised. I directed the provost to implement my decisions and begin a nationwide search for the first leader of the new Office of Extended Education.

The report and my decisions received a mixed reception. Many county Extension agents were concerned they would not receive equal treatment with academic faculty for promotion and tenure consideration. Some academic faculty were concerned their disciplines would be diluted, or that they would be required to take on extra duties related to offering courses in the extended-education mode.

The provost and I, and others, recognized that the Extension agents in academic colleges needed to be protected from unfair treatment, intentional or unintentional. Promotion and the granting of indefinite tenure were of primary concern; promotion and tenure policies and procedures were reviewed and changed. The dean/director of Extended Education was made a member of the provost's promotion and tenure review committee to ensure equitable treatment of Extension faculty.

Fortunately, there were people in both Extension and academic departments who saw the value of the new mode of outreach and extension and who were willing to support and advocate for the changes. Our innovation was noted throughout the national Extension community, viewed with interest, then eventually applauded and imitated at other universities. It was a significant step toward revising the role of the land-grant university for the twenty-first century—a role that now seeks ongoing and practical engagement with citizens. It was a major change in the face of the American public university, and Oregon State helped lead the way.

Our work got the attention of the W. K. Kellogg Foundation.[4] Several foundation officers paid us a visit. The Kellogg Foundation had already invited ten universities to be part of a program addressing the educational requirements for careers in food systems in the twenty-first century. When the Kellogg Foundation leaders discovered what we had already done to make Oregon State more effective as a modern university, they were especially impressed with our new Extended Education office, also with our long-range planning efforts and the implementation of TQM. As a result of their awareness of OSU, they increased the number of institutions in their food-systems program from ten to twelve in order to include us. As it turned out, OSU became one of the leaders in this program.

The Kellogg Foundation's food-systems program led to the creation of the Kellogg Commission on the Future of State and Land-Grant Universities.[5] The Kellogg Commission comprised the presidents of twenty-five public universities dedicated to promoting the reform of public higher education in order to meet the demands of and challenges to global society in the twenty-first century. Oregon State University was one of them.

LONG-RANGE PLANNING: MEASURE 5 AND A VISION FOR THE FUTURE

ONCE THE ACCREDITATION effort was behind us, we took actions according to our second strategic plan. We'd been doing reasonably well until November 6, 1990, when Ballot Measure 5 was passed. The third planning committee, called on to develop our final strategic or long-term plan, the successor plan to "Creating the Future," balked, insisting it was impossible to plan under such future financial uncertainty. I sympathized, but I felt that, now more than ever, it was crucial that we have a clear sense of direction for Oregon State University. If a plan was impractical, a clear vision statement was not.

In January 1992, we turned our efforts to producing a vision statement for the university. It was not as easy as I had anticipated. I appointed a committee that included two deans, a department chairman, and a couple of staff members, chaired by the president of the Faculty Senate. I assumed that it would be a quick, relatively easy undertaking—after all, I thought, OSU is a land-grant, public research university, and seemingly well understood by everyone on the committee.

The group agreed that the statement should be brief, general enough to encompass the breadth of the institution, but specific enough to differentiate OSU from other Oregon universities. That's about where broad agreement ended. As the process unfolded, the committee met two challenges. First, apparently all members of the committee desired to see themselves and their program in the statement. The drafts of the statement became biased toward affirmation of the value of each of the colleges and units represented by committee members. Second, progress in the statement's development bogged down as the committee members became wordsmiths. Their continual fussing over the verbiage began to muddy the original message.

However, in spite of continuing differences of opinion, eventually the vision committee produced a draft they all agreed on. I released a draft of the vision statement text through the staff newsletter, OSU this Week, on February 20, and invited comments. We held two open-house forums and welcomed written comments. We received hundreds of comments, and it seemed that almost all of them expressed some disagreement with the vision statement. Most of the respondents did not seem to have a problem with the vision per se—they were more concerned about sections of the report that alluded to reducing and eliminating programs. They also expressed doubt about the increasing role of administration in making those decisions.

Even so, I felt the draft text was successful in several ways. For one, it demonstrated how diverse OSU is: many faculty and staff read it and few if any approved, but everybody had the opportunity to comment. The democratic process is important, but so is persistence. The committee persisted, and, based on the comments received, produced a new vision statement document.

"Oregon State University: Beginning the 21st Century" was released to the campus community on April 30, 1992. The document presented a "vision of the future, a picture of what Oregon State University should look like as the twenty-first century begins." Our vision was that OSU will be a comprehensive Land Grant, Sea Grant, and Space Grant university whose student body will be strongly undergraduate, racially diverse, and international. OSU will maintain a strong emphasis on scholarship, including research, at the graduate level, maintaining an emphasis on interdisciplinary and multidisciplinary instructional programs, including the liberal arts and science. OSU will be recognized as the leading institution in the state for its outreach and international efforts and will continue to emphasize its strengths in the natural physical environment.

Like many documents of this nature, the mission and vision are general enough that they might apply to any land-grant university at almost any time, even decades later. However, the discussions of context, implications, and strategies were sufficiently specific to pertain only to Oregon State University, Oregon's land-grant university, under the conditions in Oregon at the end of the past century and the beginning of this one.

At the time of the statement's release, I stated publicly that I thought it was an excellent vision statement and, on the basis of the comments received that led to its modification, it included "wisdom and advice" and affirmed that "we really are a university." Further, I stated, "It emphasizes that we are a land-grant university, and to be a strong land-grant university, we must have strong arts, humanities, and sciences. The liberal arts help turn an otherwise good scientific and professional school into a university."

As is often the case, the process by which such a document is produced is more important than the finished document. Many faculty and staff were involved in its creation and no doubt felt more committed to Oregon State University as a result. Those who read the vision statement today will most likely agree that it works for OSU today just as it did in 1992.

UNFORESEEN OPPORTUNITIES: THE PAULING PAPERS

LINUS PAULING, the world-renowned chemist and peace activist, was a 1922 chemical engineering graduate of Oregon Agricultural College (OAC). Although he had not graduated from high school, the admissions people recognized him as an outstanding student and accepted him into the college. Later, when Pauling was faced with dropping out of college due to financial difficulty, a perceptive faculty member of the chemistry faculty arranged for him to teach introductory chemistry to home economics students.

One of those students was Ava Helen Miller, who later became Pauling's wife, and who had a major influence on his subsequent career. Pauling's scientific accomplishments earned him a Nobel Prize for chemistry in 1954, and his untiring work for world peace brought him the Nobel Peace Prize in 1962.

Linus Pauling maintained a positive relationship with his alma mater over the years. I approached him to ask if he would consider archiving his and his wife's papers at Oregon State University. He responded to my letter positively. I wasn't the first to ask him; similar requests for his papers had been made by Presidents James Jensen and Robert MacVicar before me. Perhaps the timing of my request was more appropriate, or possibly it appealed to Pauling that I asked for his wife's papers, too. In any event, in 1986, OSU became the repository of the Ava Helen and Linus Pauling Papers in the special collections of the university's Valley Library.

Soon after we corresponded about the papers, Pauling made several trips to Corvallis. One of them was on or about the time of his ninetieth birthday. The Oregon State students put together a fine birthday celebration, complete with a large birthday cake, in the lounge of the Memorial Union, and they serenaded him with a rousing chorus of "Happy Birthday." This gave Pauling the opportunity to interact with students, an activity he clearly relished.

On another trip, he visited a class being held in the room in Education Hall in which he had met his wife. He was introduced to the class just before the end of the class period. As the students filed out, one young woman student approached him and said, "Dr. Pauling, I think you knew my grandmother when you were a student here." Pauling asked the student the name of her grandmother. The student told him; Pauling hesitated for a moment and then said, "Yes, I remember her. She had red hair and I think she was from Tillamook." The student affirmed that Dr. Pauling was correct.

On another occasion, I was driving him to visit a potential donor of funds to OSU. The donor was located in a rural area southwest of Portland, an area I was unfamiliar with. After becoming lost, twice, and stopping for directions each time, I apologized profusely to Pauling. He said, "Oh, no, don't apologize. I'm enjoying this ride immensely. I haven't seen this part of Oregon for years. Not since I was a lad."

I always enjoyed my time with Linus Pauling. We had the opportunity to talk about scientific matters, particularly if they referred to mineralogy and X-ray diffraction and the analysis of minerals, an area of overlap

It was fun celebrating OSU alumnus Linus Pauling and his daughter, Linda Kamb, center, at a recognition dinner for him in 1992. We were joined by Norman Cousins, optimistic author and longtime editor-in-chief of the *Saturday Review* (far left), and Bud Clark, Portland mayor and Goose Hollow tavern owner, and his wife, Sigrid, to my right. (OSU Special Collections and Archives Research Center)

with my early geology education. Also about this time, two faculty members at the University of Utah had claimed they had discovered a method of inducing atomic fusion in the laboratory and at room temperature. Pauling didn't believe it and had a way of explaining what those researchers had witnessed. He was right.

We hoped that, when the time came, not only their papers but also the family's photographs and memorabilia would be included in the Pauling collection. It was about this time, in the summer of 1994, that Pauling died. His daughter, Linda Kamb, wanted to retain family ownership of the photographs. Linda's brother, Linus Pauling Jr., Pauling's eldest son, felt the photographs should be part of the collection. It was during this period of negotiations that we all came to know each other better. I made several trips to Pasadena to visit with Linda Kamb in order to convince her that the photographs and memorabilia would be more important as a memorial to her father if included in the collection.

Ultimately, the photographs and the memorabilia, including the two Nobel Prize gold medals received by Pauling, became part of the Pauling

Collection. Cliff Mead, the director of the library's special collections, played a significant role in the negotiations and in the physical collection of the Pauling materials.

After Pauling died, the future of the Linus Pauling Institute of Science and Medicine in Palo Alto, California, became uncertain. Steve Lawson, who headed the institute at that time, had indicated that the institute would have to move because of city zoning changes. That, together with funding problems, led the institute's board to consider whether to seek affiliation with a university or other nonprofit organization.

We were interested, but only if the institute's work would mesh with the biochemical, biomedical, and nutritional research under way at Oregon State. We already had the Pauling papers. Having the Pauling Institute would bring us even more recognition, but more importantly, we anticipated that the institute's research would benefit people all over the world—and that was part of our land-grant mission.

Working with OSU dean of research Dick Scanlan, we dispatched a team of faculty researchers to Palo Alto to report back on their assessment of the "fit" of Pauling Institute research with that under way at Oregon State. The team included Scanlan, Don Reed, George Bailey, and JoAnne Leong. I particularly wanted Don Reed on the team because I regarded him as an outstanding scientist and one who would make a critical, hard-nosed assessment.

He didn't let me down. The assessment was generally positive: the Pauling Institute's research would mesh with what we were doing at Oregon State. Apparently there was discussion about the quality of some of the research, but any equivocation was resolved when Don Reed stated firmly as reported to me, "This is a lifetime opportunity for Oregon State; we would be crazy not to seize it."

The report was good news to me. I knew I wanted the Pauling Institute to be part of OSU. But when we called the deans in to discuss the question, they were not all in agreement. Some were strongly opposed to the addition; others favored it equally strongly. I suspect that the opponents saw the institute as competition for funds, space, and possibly prestige.

In my mind, there were no show-stoppers expressed at the meeting. We would proceed with negotiations with the institute leadership. We did not know at the time that the University of Oklahoma was interested, too, and in fact had made a firm offer to the institute that involved significant funding. They had money; we had the Ava Helen and Linus Pauling papers and the attraction of an alma mater.

After preliminary discussions with the folks at the Pauling Institute, Dick Scanlan and I arranged to meet with the institute's board at its Palo Alto headquarters. We walked into the meeting not realizing that there would be another presentation by a representative from another competing organization. A Portland group was eager to attract the Pauling Institute to Portland and set it up in the southeast Portland house that Pauling had lived in during his high-school years. After his father died, his mother had used the family home as a boardinghouse to support the Pauling family, and Linus had set up a chemistry laboratory in the basement.

Dick and I made our presentation in the morning. I talked about OSU, its land-grant history and philosophy, and the importance of research to the OSU mission. Dick Scanlan talked about the centers and institutes that were already at Oregon State and how they were organized and staffed. We talked about the departments that focused on nutrition research: exercise and sports physiology and medicine, pharmacy, biochemistry and biophysics, environmental and molecular toxicology—all strong programs that seemed compatible with the institute's mission. After a few questions from the directors, we recessed for lunch.

The representative for the Portland group had the floor after lunch. He had been there in the morning and listened to our presentation. During lunch, my mind was occupied by how I would counter whatever he presented. The Portland group would have to start from scratch to develop a supporting infrastructure for personnel matters, purchasing, public relations, and fundraising—all things that already existed at Oregon State, not to mention support that would be provided at OSU by the science departments, colleges, centers, and institutes.

I needn't have been concerned. The representative of the Portland group spent much of his time demeaning colleges and universities, emphasizing how university bureaucracies weighed down scientific interests with bureaucratic overkill, how any funds brought with the institute would be dissipated for other university needs. His presentation was extremely negative with respect to what Oregon State had to offer, and was insulting to universities in general. He had little positive to offer on behalf of the Pauling House group.

As I listened to him talk, I realized he was digging a hole deeper and deeper for himself. It soon became apparent the directors were being turned off by his presentation and were asking him challenging questions he was unable to answer. He seemed to be attacking higher education in general, an approach that was not at all well received by a couple of directors who held faculty positions at Stanford and the University of California. The meeting concluded in midafternoon, after which the directors met to discuss the situation and possibly make a decision.

Dick Scanlan and I returned to Corvallis feeling fairly confident that we had done as well as we could. I had barely returned home when Linus Pauling Jr., the board's chair, called to inform me that the directors had decided that Oregon State University was their preferred home for the institute.

There was much to be done to prepare for the transfer. The next step was to bring some of the Pauling Institute's scientists to Corvallis to meet their counterparts at OSU. After a number of meetings, it became clear that we had a good fit. It was time to work out details of the merger: how many people would come from Palo Alto and who they would be; where the institute would be housed; who would direct it; what it would provide and what Oregon State would provide; and much more.

With the merger, Dick had a lot added to his plate in addition to the regular duties as dean of research. He worked directly with Steve Lawson, the institute's manager, to work out the details of which researchers should be given the opportunity to come to Oregon State to work as initial members of the Pauling Institute at OSU. About half a dozen scientists were given the opportunity to join the Oregon State faculty.

Because I was approaching retirement by this time, Dick Scanlan took over the task of bringing the Pauling Institute to OSU. Working with our legal office, he developed a memorandum of understanding (MOU), and began the search for a permanent director for the Linus Pauling Institute. Dick had served as president of the Faculty Senate and knew how to short-circuit faculty bureaucracy for the OSU approval needed in order to appeal to the Board of Higher Education for permission to create this new institute at Oregon State. We were on a fast track.

The MOU was drafted by Dick Scanlan and Caroline Kerl, Oregon State's legal officer, representing OSU, and by Steve Lawson and Linus Pauling Jr., representing the Linus Pauling Institute of Science and Medicine. The purpose of the Linus Pauling Institute (LPI) at OSU was simply stated as "to advance knowledge in areas of interest to Linus Pauling." All assets of the institute, including about $1.5 million and its donor list, would be transferred to the OSU Foundation and were to be used solely for support of the LPI, principally as support for an endowed chair for the scientific director. OSU would supply space, facilities, and faculty positions for LPI researchers in the appropriate academic departments. OSU (or the OSU Foundation) would supply a major-gift development officer, and a campaign would be initiated to raise funds for a permanent facility to house the institute.

This MOU was available for signature the first week in January 1996. I had retired from OSU less than a week before, but everything leading up to the signing had occurred while I was president, so I was asked to sign the MOU together with OSU president Paul Risser, my successor.

I think all of us who were involved with the transfer of the institute to Oregon State realized there was some risk, but we all envisioned a success that tied the successes of Oregon State's most illustrious alumnus more closely to OSU. As this is being written in 2015, the Pauling Institute is a major success. Balz Frei was secured as director. Steve Lawson continues as the administrative officer of the Linus Pauling Institute, which moved into a major new building funded through the OSU Foundation. Institute scientists do outstanding research that benefits people everywhere. Dick Scanlan, Steve Lawson, and Balz Frei each provided the leadership that brought all of this about. They deserve the credit for it.

CHAPTER 16

Academic Matters

"to promote the liberal and practical education . . ."

THE ACADEMIC PROGRAM at Oregon State University was mandated in general terms by the first Morrill Act of 1862, the Land-Grant College Act: "To teach such branches of learning . . . in order to promote the liberal and practical education of the industrial classes in the several pursuits and professions of life."

Research and Extension were added to the missions of the land-grant universities later, but the academic program came first; it has always come first. If OSU were to achieve excellence as an academic institution, we needed to improve the student experience, bolster the liberal arts, improve the library, and internationalize the university. As a public land-grant university, we had a responsibility to all students regardless of their academic talents—a responsibility to the average student as well as to the intellectually gifted. I would like to think the faculty and the academic administrators (deans and department chairs) received and internalized this message.

IMPROVING THE STUDENT EXPERIENCE

BASIC TO the quality of the student educational experience was the curriculum. About the time we started our long-range planning effort, the faculty directed their attention to improving the baccalaureate core. By 1988, the academic core requirements for the bachelor's degree were modified, giving students greater flexibility in choosing courses to meet the basic requirements. Further, through the efforts of the faculty and academic administration of the College of Liberal Arts, graduate degree programs were established in applied anthropology, economics, English, and scientific and technical communication.

Approval by the Board of Higher Education of the granting of graduate degrees in these areas was a significant breakthrough. During earlier times, proposals for new degree programs by one college or university in the state system could be effectively blocked by another. Several requests by Oregon State to offer graduate degrees in traditional economics were all blocked by the University of Oregon. However, board approval did not guarantee the long-term success or survival of such programs. Differences of intellectual opinion and budget constraints served as hidden threats to the survivability of otherwise worthy programs.[1]

BOLSTERING THE LIBERAL ARTS

IT WAS NOT until 1962, after Oregon State College became Oregon State University, that the liberal arts and humanities programs were authorized to offer upper-division undergraduate programs. Several decades would pass before graduate programs in liberal arts and humanities were authorized. Until then, faculty in the College of Liberal Arts were precluded from some of the benefits associated with teaching in a graduate program, such as time for scholarly research, postdoctoral fellowships, and places in which to pursue scholarly creativity. To provide such benefits, the Center for the Humanities was conceived as part of a major fundraising program called Project Foursight. I had a hand in completing the fundraising for Project Foursight and procuring a facility to house the center.

The center's program was funded by an endowment grant from the National Endowment for the Humanities. The endowment's proceeds provided annual funding for about a dozen fellows, chosen competitively from faculty at OSU or other universities. The funding allowed the fellows to spend up to one year conducting scholarly work on time released from their regular teaching duties. For OSU faculty, funds were provided to the fellow's academic department to enable the department to find substitute teachers. Frequently, the fellows selected were on sabbatical leave at the time. Fellows from outside OSU were provided with a small stipend and were asked to conduct a seminar course at Oregon State. Most of the OSU fellows were from the College of Liberal Arts.

The center's program initially operated from Peter Copek's office in the English department. Peter was the center's first director, and soon after the program began, a former sorority house owned by the OSU Foundation became available. Located about halfway between the OSU campus and downtown Corvallis, the building was just right as a home for the Center for the Humanities. The rooms made perfect offices for the fellows, the living room served as a reception area, and the dining room was ideal for seminars. Each fellow was provided with an office and a computer. An area was set aside as a support office, and there was a small pantry with microwave, refrigerator, and coffeepot. The center was a quiet place to do scholarly work. What more could any faculty member desire?

The house was for sale from the OSU Foundation for $200,000. I approached Tommy Autzen, director of the Autzen Foundation, for a grant of $200,000. I had met Tommy and felt we had good rapport. When I made my request, Tommy considered it and then replied, "No, but the Autzen Foundation will give you $50,000 and you can use it any way you want."

Learning from that event, I asked the Autzen Foundation for $50,000 each of the next three years, with success. Over a period of four years, we saved the grants from the Autzen Foundation and then bought the house. At the time, the University of Oregon seemed to make a big thing of their Autzen football stadium, for which the Autzen Foundation had made a significant gift. Somewhat childishly, I suppose, I wanted the Autzen name visible on our campus, too. After all, Tommy Autzen's father was a graduate of Oregon Agriculture College, an early forerunner of OSU. I asked Tommy if we could name the building Autzen House. He agreed, and the Center for the Humanities became officially located in Autzen House.

The Center for the Humanities became a successful adjunct to the humanities and liberal arts at Oregon State University—so much so, that once faculty discovered how much they enjoyed and benefitted from their time at the center, they were often eager to repeat the experience.

EXTENDING THE UNIVERSITY THROUGH THE LIBERAL ARTS

Even before there was a College of Liberal Arts, the arts and humanities at Oregon State demonstrated excellence, with visiting lecturers, musicians, thespians, and artists sponsored by liberal arts departments sharing their expertise with the public. Before the construction of the LaSells Stewart Center, public events were held in the Home Economics auditorium or in Gill Coliseum, the basketball pavilion. More important than the venue was the opportunity to share with the public the high-quality performances of visitors and OSU faculty. Dramatic production continued to improve under the direction of Charlotte Headrick and drew the public to Mitchell Playhouse and subsequently to a new location in Withycombe Hall.

Artists of the art department were among the most prolific in the Pacific Northwest. The department drew to OSU aspiring young artists who were inspired by the art faculty and in their turn added to the creative environment of the Northwest.

The music department, through its public musical offerings, both vocal and instrumental, exhibited the outstanding quality that was developing in music at Oregon State. The symphony orchestra grew to excellence under the direction of Marlan Carlson. By recruiting outstanding high school musicians and enabling them to perform with professional musicians from Corvallis, Eugene, and Portland, Carlson not only improved the performance of the orchestra, but also gave the students musical experiences they could not obtain elsewhere. Many of these students were majoring in the sciences, engineering, or liberal arts rather than in music. I encouraged the development of music at every opportunity. Following one excellent performance of the symphony, I sought out Maestro Carlson in order to tell him, "Marlan, I feel that we are finally a first-class university."

CREATING AN HONORS COLLEGE

OREGON STATE had offered an honors program for students who were qualified and who wanted an extra intellectual dimension to their education. This program had always existed during my time at OSU, at least dating back to 1960 when I first arrived as a faculty member. The program included specialized seminars for small groups of students, high-level lectures, and other intellectually challenging experiences. Participation in the program by faculty was voluntary. Thus the faculty of the honors program included faculty who truly wanted to teach and to engage students who were serious about their education. It was a highly successful program, managed well by Margaret Meehan and, after her retirement, by Gary Tiedeman of the sociology department.

In 1991, the honors program was eliminated, a victim of the Ballot Measure 5 budget reduction. Almost immediately, faculty called for its resurrection. They felt that the honors program was important to OSU's best and brightest students, and many believed that it added to the intellectual prestige of Oregon State University. With the assistance of Bruce Shepard, in the office of the vice president for academic affairs, a number of faculty focused attention on bringing the program back.

Although stressful, crises are often occasions to create new programs from the remnants of what previously existed. Some faculty saw this as a time to create something more than an honors program: namely, a degree-granting honors college. Faculty drafted proposals for an OSU Honors Research College or for a Linus Pauling Honors College (1992). They were optimistic in thinking that somehow OSU could find the funds required to support an honors college, and they were stimulated by the challenge. In September 1993, the provost appointed a working group to draft a proposal: "The Honors College of Oregon State University." At my direction, the proposal was shared the following January with the OSU faculty. Most of the comments received were positive, but there were some objections. Because it was a sensitive time financially, some faculty and academic administrators thought an honors college would drain funds from existing academic departments and colleges.

Several proponents mounted a campaign to convince their colleagues that such a college could work and that it could be formulated in a way that would not threaten existing academic units. In February 1994, a faculty-generated proposal was submitted to the Faculty Senate. The proposed honors college would provide its high-achieving students with experiences designed to be interdisciplinary, integrative, and intercultural. It could be successful only with the cooperative efforts of all the academic deans and their faculties.

The Faculty Senate passed the proposal, I approved the college, and the Board of Higher Education concurred. In fall 1995, the Honors College opened its doors to 185 students.

With my approval, Joe Hendricks, who had been the chair of the sociology department, was appointed by the provost in April 1995 to be the first dean of the Honors College. Joe was given the responsibility to create a new college within the university. Among other things, Joe spent his time selling the concept that the Honors College was a degree-granting college. He developed a system of "buying" voluntary faculty from the academic colleges by providing funds to the deans, which enabled them to release faculty from their normal teaching duties so they could teach in the new Honors College. Joe worked to establish for the students an "honors college community" that included a residence hall, a newsletter, student barbecues, student trips, and even a special study hall in the basement of Strand Agriculture Hall that the students dubbed the SLUG, for Students Learning Under Ground. Joe was also responsible for recruiting intellectually successful high school graduates to the program.

In order to graduate with an honors degree, seniors were required to write a thesis based on their own original research. For some, the thesis represented an insurmountable barrier and they dropped out of the program before graduation. But even those students who did not receive the honors degree experienced innovative teaching by some of the best teachers at Oregon State.

The Honors College became an attraction for bright high school students—a gem in the array of educational programs at OSU. It was a great success. The initiative for the creation of the Honors College had come from the faculty. My role as president resided in taking the financial risk at a financially sensitive time. The success of the Honors College is clearly due to Joe Hendricks and his colleagues, who had my enthusiastic support. I consider the creation of the Honors College to be one of the signal events during my administration

IMPROVING THE LIBRARY

FROM THE BEGINNING, one of my major goals was to enhance the holdings and quality of OSU's library, then called Kerr Library. Still somewhat naive about my relationship with the news media early in my tenure as president, I spoke openly about this during an interview with the Corvallis *Gazette-Times*. When the reporter asked me about the adequacy of the OSU Library, I said, "In some areas of longtime expertise at Oregon State, the library isn't too bad." I was probably referring to agriculture, engineering, and forestry. Oceanographers had their own system of sharing information that didn't involve the library.

Unfortunately, all the *G-T* printed was that I had said, "The OSU library isn't bad." As a result of that article, the letters I received from librarians and faculty in the College of Liberal Arts ranged from, "I kept waiting for your statement retracting what the *G-T* printed" to, "Dr. Byrne, I can't believe you said that. In my field, the library holdings are deplorable, miserable, inadequate, a disaster."

The fact that I had initiated a self-imposed reallocation of the OSU budget in order to put more money into the library, and that one of my goals was to bring the library's base budget up to standard, had apparently not resonated with or possibly not even reached those faculty. I was learning. Although we seemed to suffer from budgetary restrictions during my whole tenure as president, I attempted to raise the base budget for library acquisitions whenever possible. The increases never seemed to be enough. Eventually we did manage to generate the funds needed to completely remodel the library and to rename it the Valley Library in honor of Gladys and Wayne Valley. The Valley Foundation was the primary donor to the library fund-raising campaign—a story I tell more fully in chapter 18. I have always believed that a university's library is at the university's intellectual heart.

INTERNATIONALIZING THE UNIVERSITY

ANY MODERN UNIVERSITY must recognize its responsibility to educate students for a global future. The university must do everything it can to be a world player, encourage its faculty to participate in global and international matters, and prepare students for lives as citizens of the global society. My recognition of the importance of international education was probably generated by my own experiences: my experiences in the Bahamas and French Oceania and my roles as science advisor to the US delegation to the United Nations Law of the Sea Conference and US commissioner to the International Whaling Commission. To a great extent, my role as an oceanographer involved with the world oceans and participating in the international dimensions of the NOAA programs also played a part, as well as witnessing the experiences of our oldest daughter, Donna, as an OSU exchange student to the University of Freiburg in Germany.

For some time, OSU had attracted students from Asia, Europe, and the Middle East to study agriculture, engineering, forestry, and home economics. While I was president, about 10 percent of the OSU student body came from some ninety countries throughout the world. During the 1988–1989 academic year, about fifteen hundred students from other countries were registered at Oregon State, the highest number of international students in OSU's history up until that time.

OSU's home economics and agriculture programs had gained international reputations both in education and research long before I became president, and student-exchange programs began to develop in a formal way after World War II. Our first strategic plan (1987) called for broadening the university's global perspective and focusing our international activities. Fortunately, Oregon State was blessed with two exceptional leaders in the international sphere: Jack Van de Water, responsible for international education, and Ed Price, who led international agricultural and other development efforts. In 1976, Jack Van de Water came to Oregon State to direct the university's recently created Office of International Education. When he arrived, most of the office's activities were focused on our existing study-abroad programs, providing support for international students and scholars, and managing the activities of an English Language Institute. By the time I arrived as president, the Office of International Education was an effective organization, and Jack's leadership was readily apparent. Jack had my unqualified support. In his words, "This was the beginning of a long run of innovative ideas, new program development, curricular change, attracting external funding, and the director of the international office becoming an effective change agent."

Educational exchange programs were of two types: direct student exchanges and nondirect study-abroad programs. In the direct student exchanges, the same number of foreign students and American students were exchanged between Oregon State and the partner institution overseas. The students paid tuition to their home institution and took courses and resided at the exchange institution. This type of exchange required careful management in order to ensure a direct swap in the number of students going each way. A resident director from OSU or one of the other Oregon institutions was assigned to an office in the host country.

When I became president, OSU had two direct exchange programs: one with the Universities of Baden-Wurttemberg in Germany and another with the University of Poitiers in France. During my time, new exchange programs were created in France (Lyon), China (Beijing), Korea (Seoul), Hungary (Szeged), Ecuador (Quito), and Japan (Tokyo-Aoyama Gakuin University). The Office of International Education also supported students in the nondirect study-abroad programs by helping them apply to overseas institutions and by counseling the international students who were attending OSU.

Recognizing that the international students coming to Corvallis were experts in what it was like to grow up in their home countries, Jack created the International Cultural Service Program. In this program, outstanding international students were trained as "ambassadors" of their countries and provided with tuition support, in exchange for which they acted as cultural and educational resources for local K-12 schools, community service organizations, and courses at OSU.

A second program, the International Internship Program, was created when it was noted that some Oregon students elected to spend more time in their host country after their formal stay was completed, working in business, government, and nongovernmental organizations before returning to Oregon. Under Jack's leadership, this activity was formalized, and the international office organized the effort to match students with overseas internship opportunities.

The crowning international education achievement was the creation and implementation in 1992 of OSU's international degree, a second bachelor's degree in international studies. Candidates were required to complete the primary baccalaureate in a particular discipline and then take thirty-two or more credits in international and cultural courses selected from the baccalaureate core. In addition, they were required to be proficient in a foreign language, show increased cultural awareness based on significant experience in the country of their language proficiency, and complete a senior thesis on global issues or on the international dimensions of their primary degree.

A great deal of work went into the development of the proposal passed by the Faculty Senate, and much of the credit must be given not only to Jack Van de Water, but also to Dianne W. Hart. In a November 6, 1990, memorandum signed by Van de Water and Hart, the proposal was shared with the deans and department chairs, asking for their comments.

Later, when I asked Jack if there were any problems in implementing the international degree, he replied that it had faced several problems: "The dean of the College of Business was not interested; the initial budget was wildly optimistic; and there was opposition to the language requirement. The keys to the successful initiation of the degree were that the deans of the Colleges of Science and Liberal Arts were staunch supporters, and it was known the president favored the concept. Dianne Hart was effective in advocating for the international degree and revising it several times."

By October 1992, the program had been approved, students were enrolling, and a search was under way for a coordinator. The first international degree was awarded in 1994, and as of 2013, more than three hundred had been awarded, all as second baccalaureates.

The eleven years I served as president saw the broadening and strengthening of the student-exchange program, the creation of the International Cultural Service Program, initiation of the International Internship Program, and the implementation of an international baccalaureate degree. All of these served to elevate Oregon State University to the high ranks of internationally focused universities in America. All were the direct results of Jack Van de Water's leadership, which had my enthusiastic support.

INTERNATIONAL RESEARCH AND DEVELOPMENT

On November 3, 1961, President John F. Kennedy created by executive order the United States Agency for International Development (USAID) in response to the requirements of the Foreign Assistance Act of 1961. USAID was formed to provide civilian assistance in disaster relief, poverty relief, and other global issues. During the 1970s and 1980s, the agency provided funds for basic human needs and increasingly for economic growth.[2]

It should be no surprise that funds designed to enhance the economies of developing countries focused heavily on agricultural research, education, and infrastructure development. To a great extent, the land-grant universities of the United States were the best-equipped American organizations to provide the technical workforce needed for such assistance. No institution was better equipped or more philosophically prepared to participate in USAID-sponsored programs than Oregon State University. OSU possessed the mindset, the manpower, and the leadership needed to meet USAID needs. Under the leadership of Ed Price of the College of Agricultural Sciences, OSU intended to be a major player in international assistance funded by USAID.

By 1990, OSU had become the nation's top-ranked land-grant university in overseas research work, both in the number of staff abroad and in the amount of USAID contract and grant money administered. In terms of total federal funding for overseas programs, OSU was surpassed only by Harvard and MIT. Oregon State administered major projects in Africa, the Middle East, and Latin America. The projects were almost exclusively agricultural, or at least food-related. In one sense, those projects were simply an international extension of what OSU had been doing for almost a century in Oregon.

These research and development activities were located in Third World nations, nations that were desperately trying to raise the standard of living for their people. I felt a need to learn firsthand about the conditions OSU faculty were exposed to in their international work. I also felt it was important to see the study conditions that we were sending

OSU domestic students overseas to experience. Consequently, I made five international trips for Oregon State University during the 1980s. Shirley accompanied me on all but one. Without exception, these trips were learning experiences for the Byrnes, and they helped boost faculty morale and cement relationships with international alumni. I believe they sent a strong signal that we were serious about strengthening the international aspects of Oregon State. Four of the trips focused on international education; the fifth was in support of the USAID-sponsored, OSU-managed projects in the Middle East and Africa.

THE MIDDLE EAST AND AFRICA

The most physically demanding trip was my 1987 three-week visit to Oman, Egypt, North Yemen, Malawi, and Tunisia. It was an opportunity to visit a part of the world that few Americans ever see and to support the many OSU faculty who had committed themselves to assisting development in the Middle East. The trip was arranged and managed by Ed Price and his associates from the College of Agricultural Sciences.

We were always treated as VIPs. We met with the important people working on the OSU projects, American and otherwise, and with high-ranking officers of the countries visited. We visited universities, attended many official receptions and dinners, and frequently were feted by Oregon State alumni. Gifts were shared at appropriate occasions; we received local crafts, they received Benny Beaver memorabilia.

TRIPS IN SUPPORT OF STUDENT-EXCHANGE PROGRAMS

In 1985, Shirley and I traveled with Jack Van de Water and his wife, Nancy, and daughter, Jill, to Poitiers and Lyon in France and Stuttgart and Tubingen in Germany. We reviewed the student-exchange programs in those cities and met the faculty at those institutions. The trip led to the creation of the student-exchange program between OSU and the University of Lyon and served as an introduction to the international leadership of OSU's educational partners.

Two years later, we returned to Stuttgart and Tubingen to celebrate the twentieth anniversary of the Baden-Württemberg exchange program, initiated in 1968 by OSU's Walter Kraft, of the foreign language department, and Gordon Gilkey, dean of the College of Liberal Arts. As a celebration of this landmark anniversary, a delegation from the Oregon State System of Higher Education visited the German institutions participating in the exchange program.

A delegation from the universities in Baden-Württemberg came to Oregon on the twenty-fifth anniversary of the program. Their visit to the Oregon State campus coincided with a meeting of the trustees of the OSU Foundation, which resulted in a shared luncheon. That occasion served to impress the foundation of the merits of international exchange programs. For the Germans, it was apparently an eye-opener to learn about private fundraising, American style, from alumni and friends of the university. Fundraising was an activity that did not occur in Germany.

In 1986, I led a team of colleagues from the State System of Higher Education to Fujian Province, China, to set up a student exchange between institutions there and those within the Oregon State system. Three years later, Shirley and I were joined by Jack Van de Water and Don Wirth, the OSU alumni director, on a trip to Japan, Korea, Hong Kong, and Thailand. This trip was in support of student-exchange programs in those countries and served to enhance alumni connections in those places.

Establishing the pathways for such exchanges is important. Students who participate in overseas experiences learn firsthand about other cultures and other countries. They learn about themselves. It takes a special courage to leave one's personal comfort zone and enter an unknown social, cultural, economic, and political environment. Persuading students to take the personal risk of studying in another country, particularly a non-English-speaking country, is one of the major challenges facing American educators today.

It is disappointing that more American students do not become proficient in a foreign language, and it is disappointing that more American students do not take advantage of overseas study opportunities. For every ten international students who came to Corvallis to study at Oregon State, only about one American student traveled overseas for an international learning opportunity that was there for the taking. Those opportunities still exist. Not much has changed since my days as OSU president.

The international alumni of OSU are among its greatest recruiters of international students, both graduate and undergraduate. OSU alumni overseas expressed love and appreciation for their alma mater beyond the ordinary. Several international alumni went out of their way to tell me that their years at Oregon State and living in Corvallis were the high points of their lives. I firmly believe the international alumni of American universities and colleges can be a strong tool in the improvement of American prestige throughout the world, particularly among those nations we identify as developing countries. Today, there are many challenges to sending American students overseas for a part of their education. These challenges are worth addressing.

CHAPTER 17

Intercollegiate Athletics

". . . not that you won or lost—but how you played the game."
—Grantland Rice

I SUSPECT THAT NOTHING a university does receives as much public attention as intercollegiate athletics. Competitive sports in America, in fact in the whole world, grab the emotions of the masses. In the United States, regardless of the sport, alumni are attracted back to their alma mater through athletics. They are hungry for their college or university to win. How their teams win may be of secondary importance. Yes, most alumni want their teams to play fairly, to represent their alma mater with class—but above all, they want them to win.

Oregon State did reasonably well in men's basketball, but over the years prior to my return to campus as president, it did miserably in football. Unfortunately, football and men's basketball are the revenue-producing sports on which all other sports depend.

At the time our football team was struggling, we operated under a mandate from the Board of Higher Education that intercollegiate athletics at Oregon State University, the University of Oregon, and Portland State University must be self-supporting, with no state funds used for direct or indirect support. This meant that we could not divert state general funds to athletics, nor could we use other university services supported by state funds to help athletics. It meant that, although we had a physical plant staff that took care of the campus, we were forced to have a separate physical plant organization for intercollegiate athletics.

Survival of the intercollegiate athletics program depended on ticket sales and financial contributions to a private fund for athletics. Football ticket sales were directly correlated with wins on the gridiron, and to a

One of my first jobs as president was to tell the press why Coach Joe
Avezzano's contract was not being renewed. Joe left OSU and went
on to a successful career as a coach in professional football, notably
with the Dallas Cowboys and the Oakland Raiders.
(OSU Special Collections and Archives Research Center)

great extent so were donations to the athletic fund. Once our football
team began to lose, following the period of competitive football under
coaches Tommy Prothro and Dee Andros during the 1960s, most OSU
athletics programs were in financial trouble.

Because of the board's mandate and the lack of nonstate revenue, our
program could not afford to pay a football coach a competitive salary.
Craig Fertig, who succeeded Dee Andros as the Oregon State football
coach, had a three-year contract at $26,000 a year, and Joe Avezzano,
who succeeded Fertig, was on a four-year contract at an annual salary
of $40,000. The coaches OSU was able to hire were understandably out-
matched by the coaches earning at least three or four times as much at
other NCAA Division I schools, where constraints on the athletic budget
were minimal or nonexistent. All we could really hope for was to attract
a coach near the beginning of his career, a coach who could see that Oregon State as a member of the prestigious Pac-10 conference could be a
step upward, provided the team won most of its contests.

Having been at Oregon State for a long time, including five years in the upper administration, I had a reasonably good idea of the situation facing intercollegiate athletics. Although I wasn't aware of some of the details of the athletics operations, I had heard rumors about the football coach and the athletic director. As soon as I became president, I received a number of personal letters advising me what I should do concerning OSU athletics. I suspected that any problems involving intercollegiate athletics would require my early attention. I was right.

PERSONNEL CHANGES

MY FIRST DAY on campus as president was a Saturday in November 1984. It was the day of the annual Civil War football game against the University of Oregon, being played at Oregon State. For Coach Joe Avezzano, it was the final game under his initial contract. We lost 31–6. After the game, I visited with Coach Avezzano and suggested that he come and see me the following week.

Joe and I met for more than an hour on the first or second day I was in my office, talking about the football program and general conditions in intercollegiate athletics. We met the next day for another hour or so, and I promised Joe I would have a decision on his future at Oregon State by the end of the week.

Thursday was Thanksgiving. To keep my promise to Joe, I needed to make a decision and announcement by Friday, November 23. During my deliberations with Joe, I kept our athletic director, Dee Andros, informed, but it was obvious the decision regarding Avezzano's future was being made by the president and not by the athletic director. I think Joe had known for some time he would not receive a new contract from Oregon State. I also think he realized that under our financial constraints there could not be much of a future for him or for any other football coach at OSU.

Joe's record as a football coach at Oregon State was six wins, forty-seven losses, and one tie, the so-called Toilet Bowl tie, 0–0, with the University of Oregon in 1983. I like to think the situation might have been different if I had been president while Joe was the football coach, but I'm not sure it could have been. Mac, my predecessor, had told me that he had never understood football, and consequently he didn't feel as close to football as he did to basketball. He relied heavily on the Board of

Intercollegiate Athletics to advise him on what to do in athletic matters. This board functioned as a buffer between the president and the Department of Intercollegiate Athletics and made many of the decisions about the athletics programs.

The day after Thanksgiving, I called Joe and informed him OSU did not intend to give him a new contract. He was not surprised. Then I called Dee and informed him of my decision, and we arranged for a public announcement and press briefing. At the briefing, I read a statement I had prepared earlier: (1) Joe Avezzano's contract would not be renewed; (2) it was time for a change of football leadership; (3) we hoped to announce the name of the new coach by mid-December; (4) the search would be absolutely confidential; (5) I thought there had been some progress in the football program during Avezzano's term as coach; and (6) I would have no further comments to make about the matter until it was settled.

The news was no surprise. The need for a change in football leadership was obvious, and we were optimistic in the extreme if we thought we could do a reasonable search and have an announcement in three weeks. Joe and I parted on good terms, and he subsequently went on to a successful career as an assistant coach for the Dallas Cowboys and the Oakland Raiders professional football teams.

Before I'd even arrived on campus, Dee Andros, suspecting that the football situation would be an early agenda item, had written to me urging that if we did need to find a new football coach, I should declare an emergency, waive affirmative action procedures, and move as rapidly as possible in order not to lose a player-recruiting period. This was not my style. I intended to find the right person for the coaching job regardless of the time it took. After twenty years of losing football, I was willing to move deliberately to find the right person, regardless of the urgency to recruit next year's players. Furthermore, waiving affirmative action—a mandate with which many of the faculty and administrators had been struggling for a number of years—would send a negative message to the rest of the university. We would conduct the search according to my principles.

I told Dee I would be more involved in the search than my predecessor had been. The selection of the last two football coaches had not worked out well. Both Dee and I realized that win-loss records of 6–47–2 and 10–34–1 were unacceptable. Dee prepared a list of possible candidates. We would not use the athletics board for the search; rather, I appointed an ad-hoc committee to advise on the most suitable candidates from the list Dee was preparing. The committee consisted of seven people from the athletic and the academic communities. I assumed that when it came to a vote, at worst it would be a four–three vote.

The committee recommended three finalists: Dennis Erickson of the University of Idaho, Dennis Raetz of Indiana State University, and Gene Murphy of California State University at Fullerton. All three were head coaches at smaller institutions that were members of less-prestigious conferences. Each had turned a losing program into a winning program, and each had taken his team into a conference championship or bowl game in 1983 or 1984.

We invited each finalist to campus for interviews with the committee and members of the athletic department, the Beaver Club booster organization, and others at OSU. Erickson was Dee's favorite and the favorite of the athletic types on the committee; Raetz was the first choice of the academics. Murphy was a late addition to the list of finalists, and it was not clear to me who might have favored him.

The process was taking longer than I had anticipated, largely because of our desire to interview each candidate on our campus. I was looking forward to a four-to-three vote, but sometimes expectations don't materialize, and that was the case when the committee's votes came in: Raetz, three votes; Erickson, three votes; Murphy, one vote. Dennis Erickson called Dee and told him that he couldn't wait any longer; he had to start his recruiting trips, and unless we made a decision—presumably to pick him—he was pulling out. As I recall, he gave us a deadline. No matter, because two other events took place about that time that caused the process of finding a new football coach to stretch out even longer.

I asked Dee to see if the Beaver Club would add $25,000 to the salary of the next football coach regardless of who it might be. Dee was pressing hard for Dennis Erickson to be the next coach, and the Beaver Club supported him. I received a phone call on Sunday afternoon from someone close to one of the Beaver Club members, informing me that Dee had called a "private" meeting of selected Beaver Club members; they had met in his living room, and he had lobbied for Beaver Club support of Dennis Erickson. The Beaver Club leadership present at the meeting indicated that if anyone other than Erickson was selected, the Beaver Club would not support him with funds for a salary increase, for recruiting or for anything else. Was this intimidation, blackmail? No matter.

A day later, I called Dee into my office and confronted him with what I had learned about the meeting and his role in the final Beaver Club decision. I pointed out that the conversation we were about to have was not between John Byrne and Dee Andros, it was between the president of the university and the athletic director. I was very clear that I didn't think it was proper for the athletic director to lobby behind the president's back; that I had expected better of him and that I felt I must issue him a letter of reprimand which would be placed in his personnel file. I then handed him the letter of reprimand, which he accepted gracefully. I think he recognized that I was right.

We still didn't have a football coach. Dennis Erickson had pulled out, and a short time later so did Dennis Raetz. Before Dee and I could go back to the original pool of candidates, I received another phone call. The call was from Rich Koeper, a former Beaver all-American and professional football player who had been an assistant coach under Dee Andros. Rich indicated that Sam Boghosian might be interested in the coaching position. Boghosian had been an assistant coach at Oregon State under both Tommy Prothro and Dee Andros and was then the offensive line coach for the Oakland Raiders. Boghosian and Koeper were good friends, having both been assistant coaches at Oregon State at the same time.

As soon as I hung up after Koeper's call, I called Dee and we agreed I should see Sam Boghosian. I flew to California and, after talking with Boghosian at some length, offered him the job. Sam was popular with Beaver fans, and I was confident his choice as football coach would be well received.

Sam was interested and told me he would give the offer serious consideration. He did, but it took time. As we approached three weeks from the time the offer was made, I became anxious for a response. Those three weeks were interesting, as I received more and more press coverage in the sports pages of a number of Oregon newspapers. "Why is the president taking so long to make a decision?" "Why is the president doing the job the athletic director should be doing?" "The president is really screwing up the selection process." "If he can't make such a simple decision, maybe he shouldn't be president." And so forth. During that period of time, I stopped reading the sports pages, and my mother started to read them, no doubt wondering what the press was going to say next about her son.

Finally, Sam called. He had seriously considered the offer, had talked with his wife about it, knew it would be a challenge, an enjoyable one, but he had finally decided to stay with the Raiders.

I immediately called Dee and told him to get the applicant file out again. Dee and I sifted through the files together and found that Dave

Kragthorpe, who at the time was the athletic director at Utah State, wanted to get back into coaching. He had been at Utah State for two years as athletic director, a position he took after his Idaho State Bengals won the Big Sky Conference Title and then took the National Collegiate Athletic Association (NCAA) Division I-AA Championship in 1981. Using an offense that depended on the forward pass, the Bengals had outscored all of their opponents 422–172 on their way to the national title. Just possibly Dave Kragthorpe could turn the Oregon State program around. Dee and I agreed: this could be the man. We hired him.

Well, ultimately Dave did not turn the program around, but his team did record one of the greatest upsets in modern college football history. It happened on October 19 at Husky Stadium in Seattle. The smart money had the University of Washington a 38-point winner over Oregon State. The press had a field day, saying that Oregon State was an embarrassment to the Pac-10 and should get out of the conference. It was a surprisingly close game, and OSU was acquitting itself well. With about a minute and a half to go in the game, Washington, leading 20–14, found itself deep in its own territory and was forced to punt. Almost miraculously the punt was blocked and the ball, which had bounced into the end zone, was recovered by Oregon State: touchdown! The extra point was good and the final score of the game was OSU 21, UW 20. It was without question Dave Kragthorpe's biggest win as Oregon State University's football coach, memorable for everyone who was there. As he and I walked off the field together, he said to me, "That was a great win. It's good to have that monkey off our back." Yes, indeed. I hoped he was right.

Back in Corvallis, I was learning more and more about how intercollegiate athletics was managed, or not managed. In the past, the president had relied on the athletic board not only for advice, but also for making de facto decisions. Apparently the board had jurisdiction over athletic-related clothing and mementos sold through the OSU Bookstore. The income from those sales constituted income that was unrelated to the operation of the tax-exempt university. Unrelated income was subject to federal taxation. Bob Gutierrez, the legal counselor to the president, had been in communication with the Internal Revenue Service concerning this unrelated income of the athletic board on which income tax was, and had been, due for some time. It appeared that no one was managing the activities of the athletic board, or even paying attention.

The result of the discussions with the IRS caused me to eliminate the athletic board. I probably would not have used the board in any case, certainly not as a decision-making entity. Further, I discovered that intercollegiate athletics had its own private foundation for raising private funds for athletics. This foundation operated independently of the university's fundraising activities, which were managed out of the president's office.

Those of us in the administration of the university also learned how the athletic department was able to balance its budget annually. By looking into the details of bookkeeping within athletics, the vice president for finance and administration discovered that any financial deficits for the year in question were being covered by the advance ticket sales for athletic contests to be played during the next year—hence each year more of the coming year's income was being used to balance the current year's budget. Finances for athletics were on a downward spiral. By stopping the clock and looking only at the income and expenses for the year under examination, it became obvious that intercollegiate athletics was operating at a deficit. They were in the red and had been for a number of years.

Obviously we had a management problem. A decision concerning the future of the athletic director was appropriate, possibly overdue.

Terry Baker, 1962 Heisman Trophy winner, receives the NCAA's Silver Anniversary Award in 1988. Tommy Prothro, Terry's football coach at OSU, joined us for this event. It was an honor for Terry and for OSU—and for me, too. (NCAA/OSU Special Collections and Archives Research Center)

President MacVicar had worked out a retirement plan with Dee Andros that called for Dee's retirement in several years. In consultation with Dee and his lawyer, we agreed that he would retire as athletic director immediately but continue on the payroll as a development officer—the fundraiser—for intercollegiate athletics, primarily football. The agreement indicated that Dee's tenure as athletic development officer would be the same as specified in his original retirement plan. This agreement allowed for an immediate change in the management of intercollegiate athletics but retained Dee, who was effective in raising funds for intercollegiate athletics from his friends.

While the search for a new athletic director was under way, I appointed Dee's deputy, Sylvia Moore, as interim athletic director. Sylvia had been the gymnastics coach from 1967 to 1975 and then athletic director for women's sports. When men's sports and women's sports were merged in 1982–1983, she became the deputy athletic director. She held the interim athletic director position for nine months while a search was under way, until Lynn Snyder from Marshall University was appointed as the new athletic director.

ELIMINATING TRACK AND FIELD

TITLE IX required that women's and men's athletic programs must be equitable. In order to be a member of the Pac-10 conference, all institutions were required to maintain a specific minimum number of sports, and to remain a Division I school under the NCAA, a similar number of sports were required. But we still needed to balance the budget. We could not count on additional funds from a losing football program or from private donations, so something had to be eliminated. Support services within the athletic department had already been trimmed to the bone. One sport needed to be eliminated, and it must be a sport with a substantial budget. The amount of money needed was about equal to the baseball budget and also to the track and field budget. Either baseball or track and field would have to be eliminated.

Both sports had long and valued traditions at Oregon State. Elimination of the baseball program would solve the financial situation, at least temporarily. Because baseball was a men's program, its elimination would not jeopardize OSU under Title IX requirements. The budget for track and field was about equal to the baseball budget, and its

elimination would also solve the financial problem. But women participated in track and field, so its elimination would affect OSU under Title
IX requirements, and an additional low-cost women's sport would need
to be added in order to comply with Title IX.[1]

So it seemed baseball would have to go. However, the University of
Oregon, facing a similar financial problem, had already eliminated their
baseball program. If OSU eliminated baseball, there would be no Division I intercollegiate baseball in the state of Oregon. This was an important factor in any decision I might make.

Athletic Director Snyder came up with a solution: eliminate track and
field and begin a low-budget program in women's soccer. OSU would
thereby solve the financial problem, satisfy Title IX requirements, and
meet the minimum number of sports requirements of both the Pac-10
and the NCAA for Division I status.

But what about the kids who wanted to major in engineering and at
the same time participate in track and field? OSU was the only public
university in Oregon with an engineering program at the time. The same
question could be asked if baseball were eliminated. Unfortunately, not
every solution is perfect, and this one certainly was not perfect. Sometimes the president of a university is forced to make such undesirable
decisions, and this was one of those times.

I knew the decision to eliminate track and field would be unpopular, at least with its devotees, and it certainly was unpopular. It was not
the last unpopular decision I would be forced to make. That decision
did, however, save the baseball program for future success and glory.[2]

A FINANCIAL PARADIGM SHIFT

IN SPITE OF the temporary reprieve in the athletic department's
finances, the situation in football did not help to resolve the longer-term
financial problem. The mandate of no state support for athletics at the
three universities continued to contribute to our financial malaise.
Morale was flagging, and Athletic Director Snyder was not successful in
changing the attitudes. By 1990, the athletics deficit had climbed to over
$2 million. Ballot Measure 5 had passed and promised to impose sub-
stantial financial pressure on all of public higher education. The financial
straits of athletics at all three universities—Portland State, the University of Oregon, and OSU—were in desperate shape. Our Faculty Senate

was becoming increasingly agitated about athletic finances, and several members were calling for OSU to resign from the Pac-10. It was time for the Board of Higher Education to address the situation.

At the board's September 1991 meeting, the chancellor's staff reported on the financial crisis facing athletics at the three universities. Under the leadership of board president George Richardson, the board created a fifteen-member task force chaired by board member Herbert Aschkenasy, the CEO of Oregon Freeze Dry. The task force included Board of Higher Education members, legislators, a representative of the state's Executive Department Division of Budget and Management, a member of the student lobby, a representative of the Interinstitutional Faculty Senate, a university president (me), a college president, and representatives of each of the university-affiliated private foundations. Sally Plumley represented the OSU Foundation, and Robert Frank, chairman of OSU's English department and our faculty representative to the NCAA, served as staff of the task force.

Richardson's instructions to the task force, on February 13, 1992, included a review of prior efforts to solve the financial problem. In June 1990, the board had required institution presidents to balance their athletic budgets, using institutional funds for one year if necessary. That didn't solve the problem. After another review and public hearings, the board had considered the matter again in November 1991, reaffirmed its commitment to intercollegiate athletics, voted to sustain each campus's conference affiliation, and created the current task force to find an acceptable way of funding athletics at the three universities.

In April 1992, after meeting three times, the task force made a number of recommendations to the board of higher education that were complex in the aggregate. These recommendations called for the foundations affiliated with the universities to make significant financial contributions; the addition of surtaxes to tickets; the reduction of athletic budgets; the waiving of some of the budget shortages; and permission to use institutional funds to cover parts of athletic budgets.

Because the estimated total fell short of the monies needed to cover projected operating deficits for the years 1992–1995, the difference could be covered by using institutional funds for support of women's athletic programs, support for men's and women's nonrevenue sports, coaches' salaries in nonrevenue sports (both men's and women's), and tuition for all student athletes on scholarship at the in-state rate.

These recommendations were accepted by the board at its May 1992 meeting. This was a major change in how intercollegiate athletics would be funded at Oregon's three universities. It was a paradigm shift.

THE REVOLVING DOOR FOR ATHLETIC PERSONNEL

PERSONNEL CHANGES in athletics are different from personnel changes in academics, but emotionally no easier. On the academic side of the institution, poor performance in teaching and research can be factors in dismissing nontenured faculty, but elimination of faculty positions is most often due to declining budgets. In athletics, a coach's win-loss record is ultimately the deciding factor in the coach's longevity at an institution. For athletic directors, the deciding factors can be more complicated, involving win-loss records of the many teams in athletic competition, but other factors can be how coaches treat their student athletes, promote diversity, and adhere to Title IX requirements. The financial stability of the athletic program, the athletic director's general management skills, and compliance with NCAA standards also come into play. The success of the overall athletic program is the athletic director's responsibility. Selection of the athletic director is the president's responsibility, and the athletic director serves at the pleasure of the president.

Lynn Snyder took over as athletic director at a difficult time. As financial pressures increased, it became obvious that Lynn needed help. Several consultants were brought in to evaluate the athletic department. They identified a number of management problems, and Dutch Baughman was hired as associate athletic director to handle much of the management of athletics.

As Dutch addressed a number of pressing management problems within athletics, Lynn's presence became less visible. As one colleague put it, "Lynn seems to have developed a 'siege mentality.' He avoids people and seems to disappear when he may be needed." At a crucial decision time, Lynn disappeared for two weeks. I was convinced it was time for new leadership in athletics. I did not renew Lynn's contract, and Dutch Baughman took on the role of athletic director, a position he held during the remainder of my time as president.

Win-loss records are important in determining the longevity of coaches. In some cases, it took a coach a few years to implement his particular style of offense and recruit new players who would fit it, but in the third year or so, people start expecting a respectable win-loss record. This was the case for both Dave Kragthorpe and for Jerry Pettibone, the coach who succeeded Kragthorpe. During Dave's first year in 1985, the team won only one game, the legendary upset of the Washington Huskies. By the third and fourth season, the team's record had increased to four wins and seven losses, and although the 1989 season was only four and seven, Dave was selected as the Pac-10 coach of the year. Unfortunately, during the two subsequent years, his record fell to 1–10, and Dave realized he was not going to turn the football program around. He resigned as coach. His win-loss record while at Oregon State was seventeen wins, forty-eight losses, and two ties.

In 1991, Dutch Baughman, as the new athletic director, selected, with my approval, Jerry Pettibone to succeed Dave as football coach. Jerry's offense was significantly different from the passing offense employed by Dave. It relied instead on the running game, particularly the triple-option play, in which the quarterback has the option to pass the football, run with the ball, or lateral the ball to another back. Early attempts at this option frequently resulted in fumbles, which were frustrating to the team and the fans. The records for Jerry's teams were similar to those of Dave's teams—losing seasons, but improving in the third and fourth seasons. One year after I retired, Jerry stepped down as coach with a record of thirteen wins and fifty-two losses.

In men's basketball, the situation was different. Ralph Miller, who had coached men's basketball at Oregon State since 1970, was one of the winningest coaches in college basketball. He elected to retire at the end of the 1989 season with a record of 359 wins and 186 losses. Dutch Baughman chose Jimmy Anderson to succeed Ralph. Jimmy had played basketball for Oregon State under Slats Gill and then went on to be an assistant coach under Slats Gill, Paul Valenti, and Ralph Miller.

Both Dutch and I were of a mind that such dedication must be rewarded, in this case, with a five-year contract as men's basketball coach. It did not detract from Jimmy's record that he had helped to recruit a player from Oakland, California, named Gary Payton. Payton had a year remaining at Oregon State and then went on to become one of the great professional basketball players of all time. Jimmy's first year was very successful, and he was selected Pac-10 Coach of the Year. After Payton left, Jimmy's win-loss record deteriorated, and alumni began to call for a new coach. I was dismayed by the attitudes of many alumni. It appeared

No matter what was happening on the court, it was fun being part of the "wave" at an OSU basketball game (ca. 1987). It gives a sense of togetherness. (OSU Special Collections and Archives Research Center)

that all that mattered was winning. What the man had contributed to Oregon State basketball over the years didn't seem to be all that important to the press or to a number of alumni.

Dutch asked to meet with me to discuss the basketball coaching situation. He was under pressure to make a change in basketball from a number of alumni, some of whom had made significant financial contributions to the athletic program. I had already made up my mind with respect to Jimmy Anderson and OSU basketball. I let Dutch make his case for keeping Jimmy Anderson. He recounted Jimmy's basketball biography, what Jimmy had done for Oregon State basketball, the win-loss record, the pressure from alumni. Then he said, "He has only one more year on his contract, and with your permission, I would like to honor that contract."

Yes, yes. Dutch had said exactly what I would have insisted on. The word was soon out that Oregon State was going to honor Jimmy Anderson's contract and not fire him. Sports journalists were surprised; they had assumed Jimmy would be gone as men's basketball coach. I like to think some of the journalists were even pleased that at least one institution, Oregon State University, had separated itself from the procedure of casting losing coaches aside even in the midst of a contract. We had stayed with principle. We had honored a contract. I like to think we handled the situation in "the Oregon State way."

The non-revenue-producing sports were sufficiently successful to maintain OSU's competitive image in the Pac-10 and nationally. Baseball had always been competitive, was well supported by donors, and had survived the budget nightmare. Wrestling, under coach Dale Thomas, had always been successful. Coach Thomas was instrumental in bringing the sport of wrestling to statewide prominence as well as bringing the OSU wrestling team to national recognition, contending for national honors and guiding his wrestlers to national championships. Dale and I became longtime friends, and he would often call on me to address his annual wrestler's banquets. On one occasion, when I was unable to address his banquet because of a scheduling conflict, he called on the president's wife. Shirley gave the address, and she includes that event as one of her many good memories of being the president's spouse.

Rowing was something I had always wanted to try, and through a somewhat unusual series of events, I did try it. At the beginning of each academic year, it had been the custom for the president to host a reception for all university faculty and staff in the president's home. For exercise, I had a rowing machine in one of the rooms of the house. During the reception of September 1985, Dave Emigh, the rowing coach, noticed the machine and said to me, "Why don't you come down to the crew dock on the river and we'll teach you how to really row?"

So I did. I went down to the crew dock at six in the morning, and Dave took me out on the river in one of the recreational shells, a double, and instructed me in the proper way to row. I really enjoyed it and was soon rowing a recreational single shell by myself. Being on the Willamette

River in the early morning, with only beavers and great blue herons as company, was pretty special. My personal involvement in rowing led me to watch OSU in as many regattas on the river as possible. The crew rewarded my attention to rowing by naming a new shell for the women's rowing program the "John V. Byrne" shell.

The three women's sports that created indelible memories for me were softball, basketball, and gymnastics. Because the softball memory is not a good one, I'll consider it first. During my stewardship as president and Dutch Baughman's as athletic director, the softball team had an interim coach named Vickie Dugan, who, unfortunately, had a difficult time coaching the team to a winning record a number of years in a row. Her overall record was 64 wins and 201 losses. In the Pac-10, the team's record was nine wins and 112 losses.

Dutch stuck with Vickie as the "interim coach" for six years, but when members of the team began to complain about how they were treated— about the coach's inability to coach—and when the record in 1994 came in at zero wins and 24 losses, Dutch terminated Vickie's contract and hired a new coach, Kirk Walker. The team began to win, eventually making it to the women's softball World Series under Coach Walker.

Vickie claimed that she had de facto tenure in the position and therefore her contract could not be terminated. She sued the university. She alleged discrimination and retaliation for her efforts to improve the situation for women's softball at Oregon State. She claimed that softball did not have the support of the Oregon State administration and that she was being retaliated against for her role in a Title IX review of OSU athletics. The case was handled by the State of Oregon's legal department before the federal court in Eugene. The all-woman jury saw the case Vickie's way and awarded her $1.3 million, later appealed and negotiated with Vickie out of court to about $1.1 million, which was paid by the state of Oregon.

Vickie's contention that softball was on the chopping block may have been a logical allegation. Track and field had already been eliminated, and the budget situation for athletics did not begin to change until after 1992, when the Board of Higher Education's mandate regarding financial support for intercollegiate athletics was changed. Vickie's salary may have been less than that of some male coaches; however, the losing record of softball may have had something to do with that. I do not believe that Vickie was intentionally discriminated against or punished for her role in the Title IX review. I don't think Dutch was the sort of person who would do that. In fact, I think he was just the opposite; if anything, he was soft-hearted. Rather than terminate Vickie after a year or so of losing softball, Dutch kept her employed as an interim coach for too long. If there is a lesson here, it involves the balance between reason and emotion. When in doubt, go by the book. If termination is proper, do it with kindness, but do it and help the terminated person move on to a new situation.

For women's basketball and gymnastics, it is the coaches who stand out: Aki Hill for basketball and Jim Turpin for gymnastics. Aki once told me that while growing up in Japan, she was fascinated by American college basketball and was particularly impressed by John Wooden, the men's basketball coach at UCLA. Aki wanted to study under Wooden in order to be a successful American women's basketball coach, and she eventually found a way to do just that. Aki was certainly successful during her seventeen-year career at Oregon State, with a win-loss record of 274–206. After leaving basketball, she completed her Oregon State career in the international education program, where she served for three years in charge of Japan-related activities, including recruiting and summer programs for Japanese students.

Jim Turpin served as the women's gymnastics coach from 1986 through 1997. He was highly successful, winning 317 out of 462 meets and bringing the gymnastics team to ten consecutive NCAA Championship appearances and to the "Super Six" in 1995 and 1996. It was a privilege to watch how he attended to each gymnast before and after each individual event, regardless of the outcome. It was obvious he cared personally about each of his athletes and did everything he could to instill confidence in them.

Jim brought the team to two national team championships and coached eight gymnasts to national championships. Ninety-two of his athletes were awarded All-American status. Those of us who have seen Joy Selig balance herself on the beam using one hand, Chari Knight doing a backward bend on the beam until it seemed she would break in half, or Amy Durham scoring a perfect ten in the floor exercise at the NCAA championships will never forget the excellence of Turpin's gymnasts and of his coaching.

ATHLETIC FACILITIES ENHANCEMENTS

DURING THE ELEVEN YEARS I served as president, there were three major additions to athletic facilities: the Gladys Valley Gymnastics Center, the Valley End Zone Complex, and new skyboxes and a press box for Parker Football Stadium. All were paid for with private donations.

I was back at the NCAA awards banquet in 1991 to present the
NCAA's Top Gymnast of the Year Award to Joy Selig (Petersen), OSU '92.
If you have ever seen Joy doing her one-hand stand on the balance beam,
I'm sure you'll never forget it. But if you do forget it, there's a statue on
campus of her doing it, outside the Valley Gymnastic Center.
(NCAA/OSU Special Collections and Archives Research Center)

The Gladys Valley Gymnastics Center was the latest incarnation of
a wooden building constructed in 1898 as the college gymnasium and
armory. Over the years, it was used for a variety of activities, including
as an ROTC armory but mostly as a gymnasium, until 1951, when it
became the Mitchell Playhouse for dramatic presentations. In 1990, after
the building had been used for theater productions for many years, a
review by the fire marshal put a stop to the theater productions: if a fire
broke out in the basement while a play was under way, we would never
get the audience out alive. I immediately closed the building. Eventually
the unused dairy products laboratory in Withycombe Hall was converted
into an acceptable theater and has been in use as such since 1991. In
1992, the former Mitchell Playhouse was converted into a practice gymnasium for the gymnastics team. The building was renamed the Gladys
Valley Gymnastics Center in honor of its benefactor.

For a great many years, the press box at Parker Stadium, later renamed
Reser Stadium, was probably the worst in the Pac-10 conference. It was
awkward for an OSU president to entertain guests in this facility. Before

each football game, box lunches were distributed to presidential guests in a very crowded room in the press box. After eating their sandwiches and cookies, guests walked down to assigned seats under the press box in the last two rows of seats in the stadium. At halftime, staff members brought down doughnuts, hot coffee, and hot cider in paper cups.

The luncheon procedure changed with the opening of the LaSells Stewart Center in 1981, where guests were served a meal before each game. The viewing of the football games changed in the late 1980s. Ed Coate envisioned a stadium similar to those enjoyed by most Division I football teams, with a modern press box and skyboxes for the president, athletic director, and major donors. The remodeling of Parker Stadium put a roof over many of the seats in front of and below the skyboxes as protection from rain. Ed marshaled the construction of this facility, which was completed and put into use several years before I retired. The box lunches disappeared; guests were served hot meals in the main reception area in the LaSells Stewart Center, across the street from the stadium. Following lunch, guests assembled in the president's skybox to watch the game, converse, and otherwise enjoy the afternoon or evening.

The next step in the Parker Stadium improvement project was the creation of an end zone complex, subsequently named the Valley Football Center. This facility included a locker room, weight-training facility, and football coaches' offices. The remodeling of the stadium, including the construction of the football center, was funded largely through donations from the Valley Foundation and other private donors. The center was subsequently expanded. Although we had a rule that certain potential major donors were to be approached only by the president, it didn't prevent the potential donors from asking faculty, coaches, or other OSU personnel what they needed or wanted. Such was the case when Gladys Valley, on a tour of athletic facilities, asked the football coach what would make his life easier and the football program more successful. Result: a major donation and the construction of the Valley Football Center.

Although the intercollegiate athletic programs at Oregon State were not perfect, there were enough great memories to satisfy. The football program continued to have problems, and men's basketball started to slide downhill, but the nonrevenue sports kept Oregon State at the forefront of athletics nationally. Baseball was saved from the financial chopping block, and eventually the track and field programs were restored.

The most significant change in intercollegiate athletics during the Byrne years was the recognition by the Board of Higher Education of the need to change the method by which intercollegiate athletics could be funded at the three major universities. Permission to use institutional funds in support of intercollegiate athletics was a major change. It recognized the importance of intercollegiate athletics to the major institutions of higher education, and it paved the way for the possibility of a competitive Oregon State athletic program in all sports and at all levels. With the improvement of athletic performance by teams and individuals, it is inevitable that athletic facilities will continue to improve. Competition in intercollegiate athletics is not limited to the playing field.

CHAPTER 18

Budget and Finances

Money, money, money

OSU ATTEMPTS TO DO many things for many people, and it all takes money—a lot of money. It took $240 to $349 million per year during my time as president. The major sources of income for OSU were state appropriations (30–40 percent); gifts, grants and contracts, mainly for research (30–40 percent); and student tuition and fees (12–18) percent. The rest of the income, often on the order of 25 percent, came from federal and county appropriations, sales and services, and auxiliary enterprises such as food services.

Expenditures included instruction (about 25 percent), research (30 percent or more), public service in the form of the statewide services (10–15 percent), and everything else (30–35 percent). The statewide services included the OSU Extension Service, the Agricultural Experiment Station, and the Forest Research Laboratory. These are separate line items in the state budget, which means that funds provided to those services cannot be used to support other university functions. "Everything else" included the library, physical plant, scholarships, services that are not part of the statewide services, and administration from top to bottom.

During good times, the expenditure budget varies only slightly from year to year. But when income to the university suffers, reductions can be significant and percentages can change. On the other hand, a significant increase in federal support of research will increase the percentage of research money, thereby producing a percentage decrease in other categories, such as state support.

The budget process started in the chancellor's office, where general guidelines for our budget preparation were formulated and then approved by the board. Using these guidelines, we put the OSU budget together, "we" being the vice president for finance and administration, the provost, and the president, with input from the academic deans and other unit heads. The OSU budget was combined with the budgets of the other institutions and the chancellor's office to form the state higher-education budget, which was then submitted to the Board of Higher Education for approval. Occasionally the board asked us to defend parts of our budget, particularly if we were eliminating or adding programs.

With the board's approval, the system budget was submitted to the governor's office for approval or modification. Then it was submitted to the legislature, and then the institution presidents and other administrators defended their parts of it before the Joint Ways and Means Committee, which made its recommendation to the general assembly. There were a few line items in the budget, such as the statewide services, which were defended individually as part of the overall budget.

Once the budget was approved, funds could not be shifted from one category to another. For example, monies allocated for facilities maintenance, improvement, and construction could not be used for other purposes within the university. Occasionally, the joint Ways and Means Committee added a budget note, which gave directions for the use of certain funds.

Depending on the general economy of the state, additional funds sometimes became available during the year and were distributed by the chancellor's office to the institutions. These were rare occasions, but when they did occur, I intended to use such extra funds judiciously to solve problems and correct underfunding. Early in my tenure, at a meeting to discuss how we would use one such windfall, Tom Parsons, then vice president for finance and administration, said, "I guess we should send out a memo telling folks these funds will be distributed equitably across the university." I immediately jumped in with, "No, sir, we're not going to do it that way. We'll decide where the funds are most needed and allocate them accordingly." We were going to manage the institution with an eye to improving every aspect of Oregon State University. I wanted everyone involved to realize early that a new management style was in play.

The 1985–1986 budget I inherited on my arrival continued the budgetary traditions of the past. Insufficient funds were allocated to the library, very little was set aside for computing, and there was only a hold-the-line budget for the Educational Opportunities Program (EOP). The library, which was used by students and faculty from all academic disciplines, had been underfunded for years. My intent was to build up its base budget, starting with the current budget. The rapid growth of computing everywhere was obvious to anyone paying attention to what was happening in the business and educational world. The major problem was that computers were expensive and, due to technological advances, became obsolete in a very short period of time. Further, Oregon State was woefully behind in its computing capability and was keeping up with change only in those research areas funded by the federal government. We had to improve our computer capability.

The Educational Opportunities Program had been established to assist students who were disadvantaged in one way or another—students who needed extra help. Most of the students who benefitted from EOP were minorities or were poor, and these students were at high risk of failing. As our student body became increasingly diverse, more and more students needed help in adjusting to the academic world. EOP was essential to their success in meeting graduation requirements.

To meet these needs, we had to adjust the base budget. Having just come from NOAA, where budget reallocation was a way of life, I decided to do the same at Oregon State. I consulted with Tom Parsons and a few others, and then reduced the budgets of each academic school by a small percent. I put the accumulated funds in the library, campus computing, and Educational Opportunities Program budgets—all areas that I thought were crucial to the success of the university. I received no complaints from the academic deans or anyone else; the reallocation was a success. It was the only self-directed budget reallocation during my time as president. Subsequent budgets were the creations of my administrative team, albeit often under extreme external pressures, with reallocations forced by overall budget reductions.

THE GOLDSCHMIDT REDUCTIONS

NEIL GOLDSCHMIDT, elected governor in 1986,[1] was politically experienced, and it didn't take him long to realize that Oregon was trying to do too much with the financial resources available to it. The state was living beyond its means. At the same time, an anti-tax movement was developing. In his judgment, it was time to bring the state budget, including higher education, under control.

Goldschmidt mandated that, in order to meet the salary increases of two percent for each of two years, each department of state government, including the institutions of higher education, must eliminate two per-cent of its programs. "Eliminate" was the operative word. Once programs were eliminated to the satisfaction of the governor's office, the funds were returned for use in the remaining 98 percent of programs.

It was fundamentally a forced reallocation of the budget, and for OSU it amounted to a $2.3 million cut made by reducing or eliminating pro-grams. Although the process was painful, I think we did it properly. We faced this reduction in an orderly manner: first by establishing general guidelines, and then by developing specific guidelines to address the elimination, reduction, merging, or maintenance of programs.

We honored OSU's mission as a land-grant university, keeping the balance of teaching, research, and service in mind, and above all con-sidering the importance of those academic programs that were central to undergraduate education. The guidelines reminded us that, whatever we did, we must protect academic freedom and the tenure system, and we must continue to strive for diversity among our faculty and staff. It was also important to consider the uniqueness of programs. Finally, we needed to retain university autonomy and our capacity to act as a con-structive force in society. As we reviewed these guidelines, which had been developed specifically for the reallocation process, we realized that they were useful guides for the daily life of the university at any time.

For each program, we considered our options: eliminate, reduce, merge with other programs, or maintain. We asked ourselves questions such as: How important is the program to Oregon State's mission? What effect would the elimination of this program have on other programs? What effect would its elimination have on the accreditation of Oregon State? What about the quality of the program—does it have a national reputation? Is it in demand—do many students rely on this program? What about the future need for this program? Does the cost of the pro-gram justify continuing it? Is it similar to other programs with which it might be merged? We used the same criteria and asked similar questions concerning the administrative and management units.

Knowing of the faculty's concern, I sent to all faculty and staff a memo (June 5, 1989) that laid out some basic concepts. There would be no elimination of tenured faculty. Students would be able to complete their degrees. Prior commitments would be honored, and the impact on other state system institutions would be considered. There would be a freeze on vacant positions; no new faculty or staff would be hired except under special circumstances. All programs were vulnerable; there would be no across-the-board cuts. An early-retirement arrangement would be implemented. Any new funds (not likely) would be allocated to the library, to university relations, and to the Educational Opportunities Program. Finally, if we could do it, most of the reductions would be in administration.

On June 15, 1989, we made our proposals to the state Board of Higher Education. The list was lengthy. It included budget reductions in the president's office, the physical plant, media and communications, the Memorial Union, and the provost's reserve. Targeted for elimination were the soil science department, the Environmental Remote Sensing Applications Laboratory, the management science option in the College of Business, and a number of programs in speech in the College of Liberal Arts. We proposed several mergers of programs in the College of Agriculture, reducing majors from sixteen to five or six and cutting five faculty positions and twenty courses. In the College of Forestry, the departments of forest recreational resources and forest management were merged. The College of Home Economics proposed reducing the number of departments from six to three. The College of Liberal Arts lost the geography department through a merger with the geology department, which became the department of earth sciences, which was assigned to the College of Science. The board approved all of our proposals.

In consultation with the provost, Graham Spanier, and the dean of the College of Education, Bob Barr, we decided that the joint College of Education between OSU and Western Oregon State College (WOSC) was not working out as well as we had hoped. WOSC's president, Dick Meyers, concurred and the program was discontinued.

At about the same time, we made a decision designed to strengthen the preparation of high school teachers through a master-teacher program at OSU. The undergraduate major in education would be eliminated, and those students wishing to teach subject matter at the high school level would be required to major in a subject-matter discipline at the undergraduate level and then take a fifth year of education courses. We were convinced that this type of teacher preparation program would result in teachers who would be stronger in the discipline they would teach. For students wishing to become elementary school teachers, a cooperative program in elementary education was established with the child development program of the College of Home Economics.

The timing of the implementation of the Master Teacher Program was unfortunate. Because it occurred at the time of other program eliminations, the impression was generated in the minds of many outside the university that Oregon State University was getting out of the teacher-preparation business when just the opposite was the case; we were improving teacher preparation.

My cabinet spent considerable time preparing carefully for the Goldschmidt cuts. We felt our decisions should be shared simultaneously with all OSU faculty and staff. We held an all-university meeting in Austin Auditorium at the LaSells Stewart Center, sharing with Extension offices and agricultural experiment stations throughout Oregon by video transmission. The script was carefully edited. We believed the reductions and mergers were part of a worst-case scenario. I concluded my remarks by saying I hoped we would never have to go through this again.

What I couldn't know at the time was that these budget reductions were merely practice, a dress rehearsal, for what was to come as a result of the passage of Ballot Measure 5—the 1990 property tax limitation measure that effectively transferred the burden of K-12 school support from local communities to the state. As election day 1990 approached, there was no question in my mind and in the minds of everyone involved in higher education that the passage of Measure 5 would have severe impacts on public higher education as funding for K-12 education was added to the state budget. We were concerned, and so were our students.

Four or five months before the November election, the student representatives to the University Cabinet[2] wanted to know what they could do to help defeat Measure 5. I suggested they do something that would grab the public's attention—something newsworthy. They were at a loss to know what that might be and asked for a suggestion.

I said, "Well, if students on every campus of the State System of Higher Education were to demonstrate and take over the president's office on every campus simultaneously, that might be newsworthy. For that to happen, you would need to coordinate activities with your counterparts on each of the campuses. But don't let on that it was my idea."

About five o'clock on the afternoon of November 1, 1990, thirty or forty students came to my office and told me they were there to take over my office in protest of the possible passage of Ballot Measure 5. They had brought a video camera and were prepared to record this event. I asked them if this was happening on other campuses. They weren't sure, but they didn't think so.

Well, I thought, this demonstration would still be newsworthy, at least locally. Inasmuch as they were about to record the event, I asked them if they would like to take turns sitting in the OSU president's chair and making a statement as to what effect the passage of Ballot Measure 5 would have and why they were opposed to its passage. Further, I pointed out they needed the attention of the media, at least the Portland and Eugene television stations. They asked permission to use my phone—they asked permission! Some demonstration, I thought.

A few more students joined the group. The group seemed to be having trouble getting the attention of the TV stations. At about seven thirty, I called a meeting of the demonstrators for the president's conference room. I introduced two plainclothes university security officers, who would be there all night. I pointed out that if there was any damage to the office or if this demonstration got out of hand, the security officers had been directed to call the state police, and the students present would be apprehended. Then I told them that I was going home. I wished them well in attracting media attention, and then I left.

When I returned to my office at about seven fifteen the next morning, I noted several large plastic bags stuffed with pizza boxes, paper cups, and plastic bottles outside my office. Next to the small television on the end table next to the sofa in my office was a videotape of *The Little Mermaid*, which I assumed they had watched during what must have been a long night for them. They had cleaned my office.

I learned later that they did reach one or two television stations and were interviewed by phone. I also learned that mine was the only president's office occupied as a protest against the passage of Ballot Measure 5. There may have been demonstrations of one sort or another at other campuses, but to my knowledge, they weren't picked up by the news media. The talk-show host on a local radio station said he hoped the students would not be punished, as they hadn't caused any damage and were simply engaging in civil protest of an electoral issue.

Unfortunately, in spite of this demonstration, Ballot Measure 5 passed, with 52.4 percent of more than one million votes. The effect was at least twofold. Because the state's income did not increase, all state agency budgets needed to be cut to accommodate support of local schools as a new part of the state budget. Further, because all school districts would be obtaining funds from the same source, funds would be distributed on the basis of the number of students in a district. The result was that the more affluent schools would be treated the same as those in poorer districts.

For higher education, Ballot Measure 5 was devastating. For Oregon State University, the total reduction of state support over the subsequent six years was 35 to 38 percent. In the first year, 1991–1992, the OSU budget was reduced 20 percent—ten times what we had been through with the Goldschmidt reductions.

State reductions in funding allocations to higher education tend to be offset initially by raising tuition for students. These tuition increases have their own consequences. During the period of state budget reductions, 1988 to 1995, undergraduate tuition for in-state students more than doubled, from $1,603 to $3,312 per year. Partly as a consequence of this tuition increase, Oregon State's undergraduate enrollment dropped from 16,048 to 14,261. Many students who might have come to Oregon State opted to start their higher education at one of Oregon's community colleges or to seek higher education outside the state.

If there was anything positive about the reduction, it was simply that we had already developed the criteria we would need to use, and we'd learned how to merge and eliminate programs. If there was anything we wanted to do to reform the university, this was the time to do it. Unfortunately, we had to do a number of things we really didn't want to do, and we had already done the relatively easy things during the 2 percent reduction. We scrambled for every dollar we could find, no matter how seemingly insignificant.

The process for identifying areas to be eliminated started with suggestions from the deans. Some of their suggestions were accepted, some were not. The agriculture dean wanted to eliminate the joint program between OSU and Eastern Oregon State College (EOSC) in La Grande. I rejected this suggestion immediately. There was no way I was going to jeopardize the survival of another institution in the system. The OSU Agriculture program at EOSC was one of the most popular programs at that institution. Had we eliminated it, EOSC would have had difficulty surviving.

The College of Liberal Arts proposed cutting its programs in technical journalism and broadcast media. I went along with those suggestions. It didn't take me long to realize that closing those two programs was one of the biggest mistakes I had made as president. What I hadn't thought through at the time was the long-range implication of eliminating programs that produced graduates who might be future media leaders, influential in shaping the news about higher education. Our faculty and alumni had occasionally complained that the University of Oregon had an advantage over OSU because it had a journalism school. At that time, they were convinced the *Oregonian*, a statewide newspaper based in Portland, was biased in favor of the U of O because the newspaper's leaders were U of O journalism graduates. Perhaps.

Eliminating the two media programs was a mistake, but we were looking for dollars wherever they could be saved. We eliminated the marching band at football games, reasoning that we needed something visible that would get the attention of the citizens. Other than marching band alumni, no one seemed to notice. I considered this another of my mistakes. In part to demonstrate that I had no personal bias against the band, I made a $500 personal contribution to enable the band to travel to Eugene for the 1991 Civil War football game. This received some positive attention, particularly because the band was present at one of the rare victories of the Beavers over the Ducks in Autzen Stadium.

Some of the more academically insignificant cuts seemed to draw the most letters of complaint from outside the university. Horner Museum was one of these. It had been a fixture at Oregon State for seventy years until it became the victim of Ballot Measure 5. John B. Horner had come to Oregon Agricultural College in 1891 to teach English and history. During his tenure, he collected all sorts of interesting artifacts, and as people learned of his collection, they gave him many more. He established the museum in 1925 to store and show his collection. I closed it.

The museum was a favorite of many local residents and their children. Favorites included a stuffed moose and a mineral collection that glowed under ultraviolet light. In 1994, at the time of its intended closing, we discovered there was no inventory of the collection. The following year, the museum was closed to the public while museum director Lucy Skjelstad and part-time helpers inventoried the collections, which were then transferred to the Benton County Historical Museum. I received many letters questioning the need to close the museum and regretting its loss to the public. I agreed with the letter-writers; I would certainly have kept Horner Museum open if it were financially possible.

There were other adjustments during Measure 5 years. Two that come to mind were the elimination of the department of religious studies and the demise of the program in hotel, restaurant, and tourism management. The religious studies department was small, with three or four faculty members. The nontenured faculty positions were eliminated, and the tenured faculty were made members of the philosophy department, which continued to teach religious studies courses.

The hotel, restaurant, and tourism management program had originally been administered jointly by the College of Home Economics, where food-system courses were offered, and the College of Business, which presented the usual business courses, finances, management, and so on. Early in my tenure, I changed that. I believed a single line of oversight was more efficient than one that involved reporting to two administrators. After making a number of phone calls to the CEOs of hotels and restaurants in the Portland area, I followed the universal advice I received: that education in business management was more important than that in food preparation. I assigned the administration of the program solely to the College of Business.

It was an important program for a land-grant university, but we were looking for savings wherever savings could be made. Technically, we eliminated the program, but in actuality what disappeared was the title of the program, one faculty member, and one survey course. All of the courses needed to prepare for a career in the hospitality industry remained in both the College of Business and in the College of Home Economics.

We achieved additional budget reductions by cutting back on administration and management at every level. We had been in a budget-reduction mode for the better part of seven or eight years. What we were going through, and had gone through, was a period of austerity that was noted by other academic institutions and would eventually be manifested throughout the United States. We were simply ahead of the curve, and as a result we became acknowledged experts in the field of budget reductions. A number of universities actually sent representatives to Corvallis to learn what they could from our example and the procedures we had followed. It was nice to be an acknowledged leader in something; too bad it was in how to reduce the budget.

FUNDRAISING

ALTHOUGH THE STATE portion of the OSU budget decreased due to Ballot Measure 5, funding for research continued to increase, and the OSU Foundation became increasingly successful in raising private funds. External grants for research and related instructional programs increased from $72.8 million in 1988 to $111.6 million in 1995. During that same period, the assets of the OSU Foundation grew fourfold, from $52.6 million to $221.4 million, and annual receipts almost tripled from $14.5 million to $43.3 million.

During the decades of the 1980s and 1990s, private fundraising by public university presidents and development officers increased in importance throughout the United States. Fundraising became a more and more important function of university presidents in both private and public institutions. Public universities became increasingly similar to private ones as fundraising became a major factor in the convergent evolution of higher education in the United States. The increasing limitation placed on state funds for higher education made it incumbent to raise funds from private individuals, corporations, and foundations for student scholarships, faculty professorships and endowed chairs, equipment, buildings, and other facilities.

The OSU Foundation, created in 1947, was and remains a private organization with the mission to receive gifts that enhance the quality of Oregon State University. There are advantages to maintaining private accounts for use by the university and its administrators. Gifts made directly to the university, a state entity, become part of the state general fund and are subject to state policies, rules, and regulations. Funds maintained in the private OSU Foundation are not subject to the same oversight and control, and thus can be used in more flexible ways.

PROJECT FOURSIGHT

In 1981, before I left to join NOAA, OSU's major fundraising effort and the construction of the LaSells Stewart Center had been completed. The Stewart Center included two auditoriums, several meeting rooms, and a reception and art gallery area. It was an important addition to the campus, used by both the university and by the community, thereby enhancing the relationship between town and gown. Loran L. "Stub" and Faye Stewart were brothers who had made their names, and their money, in the forest products industry. As major donors for the construction of the building, they requested that the center be named in honor of their father, LaSells Stewart.

After the LaSells Stewart Center opened in the spring of 1981, the question for the president and the foundation became, What should we raise money for next? President MacVicar invited recommendations from the faculty, and ultimately Project Foursight was created. It targeted four areas for development: gene research and biotechnology, advanced materials research, marine studies, and a Center for the Humanities. Funding for Project Foursight had not been completed when I returned to OSU as its president. I wanted to complete it before we took on other fundraising projects.

The Center for the Humanities part of Foursight gained my interest. I have already mentioned my role in obtaining what became Autzen House as a home for the center. Fundraising for the other three areas of Foursight—all scientific in nature—seemed to be proceeding well, but fundraising for the Center for the Humanities was lagging behind. The National Endowment for the Humanities had offered an endowment grant, a one-for-three challenge to Oregon State, promising $700,000 for a Center for the Humanities endowment if we could raise $2.1 million from private sources, thereby creating a $2.8 million endowment for the center.

Endowment grants from federal agencies were unusual and, as a challenge, were important in stimulating other gifts. If the center's endowment could be created, the proceeds from the endowment would make it possible for faculty in the liberal arts to obtain release time from teaching in order to pursue scholarly research. It would also be possible to attract scholars from other institutions to spend time at Oregon State to teach and conduct scholarly research for months at a time. In order to meet the NEH challenge, OSU needed to acquire another one million dollars. That had my attention.

When I arrived as president in late 1984, Jim Dunn was the director of the OSU development office and an ex-officio member of the executive committee of the OSU Foundation. Jim learned I would be traveling to the San Francisco Bay area for a meeting of the Pac-10 presidents, athletic directors, and faculty representatives. He suggested that while I was in the Bay Area, I might visit with Wayne Valley.

Wayne Valley grew up in Oakland, California, and came to Oregon State College in the 1930s to gain a college degree and to play football. He was intent on graduating from Oregon State with a degree in business, or commerce, as it was then called, but the only business degree Oregon State offered at the time was in secretarial science. Wayne played football for the Beavers, then transferred to the University of Oregon for his senior year and received his diploma there. But he remained a Beaver at heart. He went on to start a successful construction business, and he and his wife, Gladys, became significant financial contributors to Oregon State. However, over the years, for a variety of reasons, the Valleys became disenchanted with Oregon State and were alienated from OSU. I think Jim Dunn was hopeful that I might be able to bring the Valleys back into the "OSU fold."

Wayne Valley and I met for dinner in Oakland and discovered that we had enough in common that another meeting to include our wives was in order. We had that dinner and discovered that we enjoyed each other. "Cultivating" donors is now part of every president's job. It involves developing a personal relationship with potential donors, educating them about the values of your institution, and discovering which of their interests can be matched with activities within the institution. I always enjoyed making friends with potential donors, and I always tried to meet them in their office or home, knowing that I would learn more about them than if we met on my turf. Often the cultivations led to friendships that have lasted long after I retired from the OSU presidency.

The Byrnes and the Valleys got together several times. In late 1985 or early 1986, I traveled to San Francisco to ask the Valleys, specifically Wayne, for a gift of $1 million to meet the challenge established by the National Endowment for the Humanities. I imagined that Wayne might not have much interest in the humanities, but hoped his business experience would lead him to recognize the financial value of meeting a matching-fund challenge.

Wayne and I had lunch in his favorite Italian restaurant. After we ordered, Wayne asked me, "What can I do for you, Doc?"

I responded, "I'm looking for a million dollars, Wayne, and hope you can help." I explained about the FourSight Project, the Center for the Humanities, and the NEH challenge grant.

Wayne said, "Oh, I don't think so, Doc. My business is going through some changes right now, and I don't see any possibility for a gift that size at this time. No."

I accepted his response and thought, Well, we'll have a nice lunch in any case. So we did have a nice lunch.

After the second glass of wine, I excused myself to go to the men's room. When I returned to the table several minutes later, Wayne said, "Doc, I think I figured a way to give you the million-dollar gift, but I won't know until next week. I'll call you on Monday or Tuesday." I enjoyed the remainder of lunch even more than I had anticipated.

On Tuesday, Wayne telephoned me to say he was transferring Singer Sewing Machine Company stock to the OSU Foundation in lieu of the $1 million I was seeking. He explained that he had been a principal owner of the Singer Company and was divesting himself of that stock holding. He was pleased he could make a gift of that size. When the OSU Foundation sold it, the Singer stock produced several thousand dollars more than the $1 million. It was the first million-dollar gift ever received by the OSU Foundation. And, probably of greater importance, the Valleys were back in the fold. They had just become one of the largest supporters of Oregon State University. With the help of Wayne Valley, Project Four-Sight was completed.

Before Wayne died, later in 1986, he and his wife, Gladys, established the Wayne and Gladys Valley Foundation. Gladys continued to manage the foundation until she died a dozen years later. The Valley Foundation became a major donor to Oregon State, with gifts that made possible the Valley Football Center, the Valley Gymnastics Center, the Valley Library, and an endowed chair in marine science. The Valleys had indeed come back to the "OSU fold."

CHANGING DEVELOPMENT AND OSU FOUNDATION OPERATIONS

"ALL FUNDRAISING will be done from the president's office." That was the mandate I inherited when I arrived as president. I had lived with it when I was in the oceanography department and when I served as dean and vice president for research. With the OSU president, the OSU Foundation kept close control of fundraising and asset management in order to ensure there were sufficient funds to maintain foundation operations.

The fundraising mandate was not well liked by the academic deans. When I first arrived in 1985, I asked the deans to list, in priority order, the things they would like to see changed at Oregon State. At the top of many lists was "permission to raise private funds for my college."

I realized that if we allowed the deans to do this, we would still need to exert centralized control, increase the number of development officers, and arrange a system that provided funds for the individual colleges and also supported the foundation. I envisioned an organization similar to a large law firm, in which each client is assigned a representative who sees to all his or her needs. In our case, the OSU Foundation would act as the law firm and would assign a development officer, who was a member of the foundation, to assist each college in raising funds for that college.

The first challenge was to convince the OSU Foundation leaders that this was a good thing to do. I envisioned that Oregon State could benefit substantially from making this change, but convincing the "old hands" on the foundation's executive committee wasn't easy. They objected that the funds raised for the colleges would be restricted for use by the colleges and would not include money for the operation of the foundation. I countered by saying the new scheme would bring in more money to

Oregon State University overall, and we should be able to work out a system that would provide money for foundation operations as well.

In the end, we created a University Fund of unrestricted gifts for the president's use and charged a small fee on each gift, designated for foundation operations. The problem with the fee idea was that most donors wanted their whole gift to be used to benefit the college for the purpose they had in mind. Initially, we set the fee at 10 percent of the gift. After receiving many complaints by the deans and the donors, we reduced the fee to 5 percent.

Adopting this constituency fundraising system required expanding the development staff significantly to provide a development officer (fundraiser) for each college, or at least one for every couple of colleges. There were two problems with this. First, neither the university nor the foundation had the funds to pay the development officers for each college. And second, if the colleges paid for the fundraisers' salaries with state funds, any legislator could legitimately question why a university employee—an employee of the state of Oregon—had any business raising money to be deposited in a private entity, the OSU Foundation.

We addressed the first problem by asking each dean to pay the salary of the development officer assigned to their college. The deans grumbled, but those who could provide the salary dollars did so. We ignored the second problem and hoped that no one outside the university would notice. I suspect that only the university president worried about the second problem.

The initial result was the creation of a university development office responsible for raising money, and an OSU Foundation that continued to manage the money once it was received. I hoped that the foundation would eventually be in a position to raise money and then manage it. Later, after my tenure as president, the OSU Foundation took over both the fundraising and the management of gifts.

We knew we needed an orderly means of allocating prospective donors among the colleges and the president's office. We decided that the president would approach the major philanthropists for gifts that would benefit the entire university. After that, the colleges were permitted to identify prospective donors, who in most cases would be alumni of their college. In the event of duplication by colleges, the development office made the final assignments.

A reporting system was established in which each of the collegial development officers identified prospects to the director of development and reported back on the results of their approaches to the prospective donors. As this system was put into practice, the development officers learned it was in their best interest to share information. In one case, sharing information resulted in a gift establishing an endowed chair in another college. The OSU Foundation officers eventually accepted this system, and the relationship between the development office and the foundation became harmonious.

I was aware that other college and university foundations were operating businesses on the side, such as local farms and other businesses. Why didn't the OSU Foundation do something similar? This became a possibility with two proposals submitted by OSU alumni. In 1985, Nat Giustina indicated he was prepared to contribute funds to complete a long-standing dream, an OSU golf course along the Willamette River. And, in 1987, Glenn and Mildred Harvey, both OSU alums, indicated they would like to deed their twelve-hundred-acre ranch in south-central Oregon to OSU, if the university would continue to operate the ranch.

The idea that the foundation should operate profit-making businesses—a ranch and a golf course—for the benefit of the university seemed logical to me. It was not warmly received by several members of the foundation's executive committee, though. I think some of them worried that the foundation's tax-free status would be jeopardized. Resistance was overcome when it was pointed out that income unrelated to the purpose of the foundation was permissible under existing tax law without jeopardizing the foundation's tax-free status, but federal and state taxes would need to be paid on the income from those two businesses.

As it happened, OSU owned 175 acres of agricultural land along the east side of the Willamette River that President A. L. Strand had acquired in 1951 for a university golf course. Nat Giustina, a supportive alumnus, wanted to see Strand's vision achieved; he wanted a public golf course for use by OSU students and the public. Nat was an avid golfer, and he had been instrumental in developing the Tokatee Golf Club on the McKenzie River near Blue River, Oregon. He was eager to build one for OSU.

Construction began in 1986, and Nat came almost every day to supervise. The Trysting Tree Golf Course—named after the campus "trysting tree" memorialized in the old Oregon Agricultural College song and still OSU's alma mater—opened to the public in late 1988.[3] I had the honor of hitting the first drive during the dedication ceremony, a three wood (spoon) shot that went sufficiently far to avoid my embarrassment.

The highly regarded seventy-two-par course, more than seven thousand yards long, has an associated three-hundred-yard driving range with three target greens and a practice bunker. The OSU Foundation hired a manager, created an advisory board of foundation trustees, and has operated the Trysting Tree Golf Course successfully since its opening. The course, home for the OSU golf team, has been the site of many NCAA golf tournaments. Additional donations by the Giustina family in Nat's name have endowed a professorship in turf management as well.

Nat Giustina wishes me well as I prepare to hit the opening golf shot at the Trysting Tree Golf Course in the spring of 1988. OSU Foundation board member John Fenner looks on somewhat apprehensively. (OSU Special Collections and Archives Research Center)

Using a "spoon" (a three-wood to those of you new to golf), I hit the first ceremonial drive at the opening of the Trysting Tree Golf Course—successfully! (OSU Special Collections and Archives Research Center)

The Harveys owned twelve hundred acres near Paisley, Oregon, and had grazing rights on adjacent public lands. Their Harvey Ranch had been producing beef cattle since 1917. Today the ranch is operated and managed under the guidance of the OSU Foundation and is available to students for hands-on experience in preparation for careers in the beef industry. The ranch provides opportunities for students from various fields to work together and for graduate students and faculty to conduct research in watershed management and various aspects of ranch management. The Harveys also provided an endowment for a professorship in animal science and several scholarships.

A MAJOR FUNDRAISING CAMPAIGN

ON A DRIZZLY Saturday morning shortly after I became president, during a meeting of the OSU Foundation Trustees at Welches Resort near Mt. Hood, Bob Lundeen, a chemical engineering graduate of Oregon State and the CEO of the Dow Chemical Company, invited me to take a walk with him. During that walk, Bob asked me, "If you had a large amount of money, how would you use it?"

Without hesitating, I replied, "I'd put it into the library. We are way behind where we should be in terms of acquisition, and we are seriously out of space. In fact, many of our holdings are stored off campus. Mel George, our librarian, has made the need pretty clear. We can either build another library or expand the current Kerr Library."

Apparently that was the kind of answer Bob was looking for. It was the beginning of a major campaign to raise money for the expansion of the existing Kerr Library. The fundraising goal was about $40 million. The campaign for the library would become "Byrne's fundraising project."

Before initiating a campaign, John Evey, the foundation's chief development officer, brought in a well-known fundraising consultant, who spent a few days at Oregon State examining our records and talking with people who would be important to the project. I remember the final dinner with him and John Evey at the Gables restaurant in Corvallis. When I asked him if we should take on such a project—the largest the university and the foundation had ever attempted—he hesitated.

"I'm not going to tell you to start the campaign, or not," he said. "I will tell you, however, that libraries are among the hardest projects there are to raise funds for."

"Thank you," I said. There was no question in my mind. We would go for it. We needed a bigger and better library.

As the idea of a major campaign for the library began to gel, we put together a steering committee chaired by Bob and Betty Lundeen, Bill and Sara Kimball, and Keith and Pat McKennon. Sara Kimball and Keith McKennon, both alumni, were also major contributors to OSU. Sara was a major supporter of the College of Business. Keith was an administrator in the Dow Chemical Company and a close friend of Bob Lundeen. After we were under way in identifying potential donors, it was decided that Linus Pauling would be a good choice to serve as honorary chairman of the campaign. The major fundraisers for the campaign were John Evey, Ober Tyus, and Cliff Dalton, and much of the credit for the success of the campaign must go to them.

Tony Van Vliet, a forestry professor who served as a representative in the Oregon legislature, also deserves credit for making the project a success. He played a major role in stimulating matching funds from the legislature at a time when state funds were limited. As Tony told me the story, in March 2013 he and George Pernsteiner, at the time the associate vice chancellor for administration of the State System of Higher Education, were sitting in the back of the legislative chamber during a late-night meeting of the Joint Ways and Means Committee. It was in 1993 or 1994. They put their heads together to come up with ideas that would make it possible to fund construction of buildings on the campuses of the state universities and colleges.

According to Tony, George recalled that the University of Oregon was faced with a similar problem in 1989. At that time, George had approached Mike Thorne, president of the Oregon Senate, to see if there was some way in which private funds could be used to meet the match included in the capital construction statute. That law provided that 11G state bonds could be issued for construction if these private funds were matched fifty-fifty by general fund monies. Apparently, however, any private funds raised could be used only if they were added to the state's general fund, which would put them at risk of being used for other purposes.

Tony and George came up with an idea to change the statute in a way that protected the private funds so they could not be used for other purposes once converted to the general fund category. Tony managed to orchestrate a change to the statute so that the OSU Foundation's funds, once converted, would be placed in a special account that could be used only for the expansion and construction of the OSU library.

Tony and George targeted a match of $20 million for expansion of the Kerr Library if OSU could raise an equal amount. Tony took the idea to the Joint Ways and Means Committee and then to the full legislature, where it was approved. Private matching funds were raised and transferred to the state under the capital construction statute provisions, with the promise that the issuance of the bonds would be authorized by another legislative action.

This final legislative action was scheduled to be addressed by the legislative emergency board at the same time Oregon State was celebrating University Day in September. (The emergency board handled legislative business when the full legislature is not in session.) We had arranged to have someone in Salem monitor the action of the emergency board and then relay the information immediately to someone at OSU, who would then signal me from the rear of the auditorium so that I could announce the outcome to the assembled audience.

It worked. We received the go-ahead, and I was able to make the announcement to the University Day attendees. My announcement was a positive one, but, as I learned later, it was not a sure thing. Senator Mae Yih of Albany had objected to the issuance of bonds that would mature at some time in the future—possibly a financially uncertain future. Senator Kevin Mannix reportedly took the opposite position: he stated that the legislature had made a bargain with OSU and OSU had satisfied its side of the bargain. Further, the credibility of the legislature would suffer if the bargain was not kept. Whether that report is accurate or not, we had the needed match and could go ahead with the planning and remodeling of the library.

We had anticipated that the library expansion would cost in the neighborhood of $40 million, so, including whatever the legislature could provide, $40 million was our target. It was the largest fundraising goal the OSU Foundation had ever taken on—and at a time of considerable financial uncertainty. The expansion of the library, completed in 1999, cost about $47 million, $7 million more than originally estimated, with the excess over the original estimate coming largely from private gifts, including $1 million pledged by the students of Oregon State University.

A significant part of the fundraising effort pertained to naming opportunities. Donors were given the opportunity to name hallways, rooms, meeting areas, and the like, with the idea that the larger the gift, the more important the area or object being named. The largest gift could be the key to actually naming the library.

Toward the end of the campaign in 1995, a number of us were meeting with the library architects in Portland. John Evey came to the door and beckoned to me. From his expression, I could tell it was important. I excused myself and left the room. He told me, "The Valley Foundation Board is meeting in San Francisco right now, and they have asked to speak with you. Steve Chandler, executive officer of the Valley Foundation, is on the phone."

I picked up the phone, identified myself, exchanged a few pleasantries, and then Chandler asked me, "How much will it cost to name the library?" I covered the phone and whispered to Evey, "How much to name the library?"

We had asked the Valley Foundation for $5 million, but Evey must have been thinking about it, because without hesitation he held up two hands with fingers spread, ten. "Ten million, Steve," I told Chandler.

There was a short period of silence, but it seemed much longer than it actually was. Then I heard, "The Valley Foundation would like to contribute ten million dollars for the expansion of the OSU Library, the OSU Valley Library."

With profound thanks, I concluded our phone call and gave the phone back to John Evey to work out the details. Then I returned to the meeting with the architects to consider details of the newly named OSU Valley Library.

There is more to the story. Before a major library fundraising campaign could be put into full swing, Oregon State hired Joy R. Hughes as associate provost for information services, a position that included oversight of the library. Joy made a major impact on the nature of the proposed new library space. She was brilliant, a visionary who knew high technology. She focused on the future and played a major role in transforming the concept of the library from one of simply more space to one that made the OSU library a modern information center for use by students and faculty preparing for life in the twenty-first century.

As a result of Joy's input, the architects were forced to think anew and to alter their original concepts for the expanded library. Students and faculty have continued to benefit from OSU's state-of-the-art library.

When Kerr Library was renamed the Valley Library, the name of William Jasper Kerr was transferred to the administration building in which the leadership of the university is housed. Kerr had been the president of the Oregon Agricultural College/Oregon State College for twenty-five years during a critical time of its development during the first part of the twentieth century. It seemed appropriate that the major administrative building at OSU should carry his name.

The financial austerity we faced caused us to work harder at acquiring funds from nontraditional sources, private contributions, and external grants and contracts. And we were successful. We learned that the university can and will survive. During these hard financial times of 1989–1995, we increased private donations and external grants significantly, added fourteen new buildings to the campus, purchased the first supercomputer in Oregon, and raised $40 million for remodeling what was to be the state-of-the-art Valley Library.

Financial adversity had unified the campus. As George Edmonston, editor of the *Oregon Stater* alumni magazine, put it, "We showed that you can't budget for pride."

Four OSU presidents with their wives at the OSU Foundation's 1985 Presidents Dinner: Shirley and John Byrne (1984–1995), Robert and Clarice MacVicar (1970–1984), James and Chris Jensen (1961–1969), and Marilyn and Roy Young (1969–1970). (OSU Foundation)

CHAPTER 19

The Chancellor, the Presidents, and the Legislature

"Is this a Washington Monument?"

WHEN I ARRIVED AS president in late 1984, the State System of Higher Education had eight separate institutions: Portland State University, Oregon State University, the University of Oregon, the Oregon Health Sciences University, Western Oregon State College, Eastern Oregon State College, Southern Oregon State College, and the Oregon Institute of Technology.

THE CHANCELLOR

THE SYSTEM was presided over by Chancellor William E. "Bud" Davis. Before becoming chancellor, Bud had been president of the University of New Mexico, the interim football coach at the University of Colorado, and an officer in the US Marine Corps. An English major in college, Bud took pleasure in writing, particularly humorous accounts of his exploits as a football coach and as a university president.

At the time of budget submission before the Joint Ways and Means Committee of the legislature, Bud used the presidents as he saw fit, possibly as he'd coached the football team at Colorado. The Joint Ways and Means Committee had great influence over our budgets, so impressing the committee was a high priority. Bud frequently started our testimonies with the statewide public services operated by Oregon State University: the Extension Service, the Agricultural Experiment Station, and the

Forest Research Laboratory. Because these three units provided excellent service to the citizens of Oregon, they were highly regarded and generated strong political support. Bud and all the presidents were convinced it was important for the Ways and Means Committee to start their deliberations with a good feeling about higher education.

The procedure for budget formulation was always the same. The presidents received marching orders from the Board of Higher Education, via the chancellor, regarding the general formulation of our institution's budget proposal. Our actual proposal was then reviewed and approved or modified by the board, and then folded into an overall budget for the entire state system. The chancellor, some of his staff, and the presidents of the institutions always met well in advance of the hearings to work out strategies. We met again on hearing day for any last-minute adjustments.

Because OSU operated the statewide services, we were usually the first on the docket. I opened the presentation and then introduced the deans of the Colleges of Forestry and Agriculture and the director of the Extension Service, or their representatives, who made detailed presentations. We then proceeded to the educational aspects of the OSU budget, frequently featuring faculty and students as part of our presentation. The legislators seemed to relish hearing from students, even more than they liked hearing from the faculty. It is safe to say that our requests for funds always exceeded what the Ways and Means Committee was able to recommend to the full legislature.

During Christmas week 1987, an event transpired that shed light on the character of the chancellor, the board of higher education, and possibly the governor himself. My reaction to the event brought me into the ensuing controversy. It started when Chancellor Davis was summoned to Salem to meet with Governor Neil Goldschmidt to discuss higher education issues. As Bud interpreted what happened, he and the governor disagreed on a number of educational issues, and the governor then indicated Bud's services as chancellor were no longer required. In short, he was fired, at least that was Bud's impression of what had happened.

Whether that was what the governor actually intended is not certain, but to Chancellor Davis, a former marine officer accustomed to taking orders from his superior officers, there was little question that the governor wanted to see him gone. In the week after Christmas, Bud resigned.

I was shocked when I learned about this. My understanding was that according to Oregon law, authority to hire and fire the chancellor and the university presidents was vested in the Board of Higher Education, not the governor. I expected the Board of Higher Education to erupt at this news. Chancellors were appointed by the Board of Higher Education and were in reality the staff of the board. The board's primary functions were to set higher education policy, monitor the finances of the State System of Higher Education, and appoint the chancellors and institutional presidents.

Not a whisper was heard from the board. No voice was raised in protest of Bud's decision to resign, no word was shouted that the governor did not have the authority to fire the chancellor. Nothing was said. Perhaps the event was missed in the festivities of the holiday season, but it certainly was not missed by the presidents of Oregon's institutions of higher education. It was not missed by me. I simply could not believe that the board didn't take the governor to task, but it didn't.

A short time later, answering questions after a talk at a local Rotary luncheon, I was asked to comment on the "recent firing of the chancellor by the governor." I responded that I thought the Board of Higher Education had abrogated its responsibility in maintaining its authority of hiring and firing the chancellor. I explained the law as I understood it and noted that it was set up specifically to protect higher education from this sort of political interference.

My response to the question was direct and honest. It didn't occur to me that my public comments would get me into trouble with the board. In any case, I said what I said, and the *Gazette-Times* reporter in the audience did not miss it.

A short time after my comments were shared with the newspaper-reading public, I received a call from Bob Adams, a local engineer and friend of mine who served on the higher education board. He invited me to have coffee with him. Apparently the chairman of the board had asked Bob to talk to me about my public comment.

We had coffee and I explained my thoughts. Bob accepted my comments but didn't reveal his own opinion on the matter. That was the last I heard about my public comment—almost. A couple of years later, I had a conversation with another board member, a Eugene businessman who had been on the board at the time of Bud's departure. He said, "You know, I've thought a number of times during the past year about Bud Davis and what you said about the board abrogating its responsibility. You were right."

Bud and his wife, Polly, were charming people, fun to be with. Bud's sense of humor was far above average. It was always entertaining to hear him recount some of his adventures as the football coach for the

University of Colorado or his accounts of life as the president of the University of New Mexico. Shirley and I looked forward to Bud's holiday letters, which always made us chuckle. Polly delighted in talking of their children, particularly their twins. The fact that Shirley and I had twin daughters helped us develop a special relationship with the Davis family.

This relationship was enhanced after Bud's termination as chancellor. After one higher education board meeting, Dick Hensley, chairman of the board at that time, pulled me aside and asked if Oregon State could find a position for Bud for a year or so. I responded immediately, "Absolutely!" We took Bud on as a part-time faculty member in the College of Education, and we had the opportunity to welcome Bud and Polly socially to Corvallis. They left after a year or so when Bud became the chancellor of Louisiana State University at Baton Rouge. I have no doubt that he developed a new collection of funny stories about his time in Louisiana.

With the departure of Bud Davis, and in spite of my public comments, I was asked to serve on the search committee for the next chancellor. The search committee interviewed a number of people we thought were qualified for the position, but our search was ultimately unsuccessful. Whereupon the board effectively said, "We gave you a job to do, and you haven't done it. Find a chancellor." The search committee renewed its efforts.

We felt the system needed stability at the chancellor's level, and there was a certain amount of anguish and hand-wringing between the two searches. During this period of uncertainty, Paul Olum, president of the U of O, tried to persuade me to volunteer for the job. Paul and I had been friends for some time, going back to a few years before either one of us was the president of a university. We respected and liked each other.

Paul had gone through a troublesome period with the board and with Bud Davis and, under board pressure, had agreed to retire in 1989. I think he was convinced that he and the University of Oregon could get along better with me in the chancellor's office than with an unknown.

I told Paul no way and that I thought he was my friend. I was not interested in being chancellor; I wanted only to be the president of Oregon State University.

The search committee started the search again by reviewing our notes about some of the candidates we had interviewed the first time around. Tom Bartlett had been in the first pool, and we felt perhaps we should interview him a second time. Tom was an Oregonian, having grown up in Salem. With a PhD in political science from Stanford, he went directly to a position with the United Nations, then over a period of twenty-four years he had been president of the American University in Cairo, president of Colgate University, president of the Association of American Universities (AAU), and chancellor of the University of Alabama system. On the basis of Tom Bartlett's experience, it is difficult at this time to understand why we didn't propose him for the job the first time around.

At the second interview, Tom mentioned the first interview and our collective failure, ours and his, to recognize the possibility that he might be the right choice. He said that obviously he didn't convince us that he was the man for the job, nor did we, as a committee, convince him the chancellor's job was designed for him. In any event, with the search committee's recommendation, Tom Bartlett was selected by the board to succeed Bud Davis as chancellor.

Tom's management style was collegial. He kept the presidents fully informed, discussed issues, and sought our counsel. During his tenure, he restructured the OSSHE office, enlisting the help of several vice chancellors. Although his open style of management may have been time-consuming, it was welcomed by all of the presidents. With the guidance of a vice chancellor for academic affairs, the provosts of the institutions met regularly to iron out academic problems before they came to the attention of the full board. The same procedure was followed by the vice presidents for administration. The system of public higher education functioned harmoniously under Chancellor Bartlett.

Tom Bartlett retired a couple of years before I did and was succeeded as chancellor by Joe Cox, president of Southern Oregon State College, now Southern Oregon University. While serving at Southern, Joe had developed good relations with legislators from southern Oregon. He played the political game well, which may have been a factor in his selection as chancellor. My tenure as president while Joe was chancellor was brief. I knew him better as the president of SOSC. Joe and his wife, Regina, were always pleasant to be with, interesting to work with, and fun to travel with.

THE PRESIDENTS

BOARD OF HIGHER EDUCATION meetings occurred three or four times a year and usually lasted two days. Committees met prior to the board meeting to work out agenda details that eventually would be presented to the board. The location of the board meetings rotated among the institutions, and at each board meeting, the host institution was given half a day to demonstrate programs the institution wanted the state board to be aware of. Usually the host put on a dinner at the end of the first day, again using the opportunity to show off some aspect of its institution.

Generally, relations between board members and university presidents were harmonious, but occasionally tension could be high, particularly when budget reductions were discussed. There was little question that the board and the chancellor set the tone for the meetings and determined the specific issues to be addressed. It seemed to me the board became most involved in facilities issues and least involved in academic matters, leaving decisions on the latter pretty much to the institutions. I think they were correct in doing so.[1]

The three universities had much in common administratively even though their academic missions were significantly different. There were probably minor feelings of distrust on many issues, but our common challenges helped us maintain good relations and a feeling of coherence among our universities.

Oregon State's relationship with the three smaller state colleges was in some cases closer than our ties with Portland State and the University of Oregon. OSU and Western shared a joint College of Education whereby the OSU dean of education was responsible to both institutions. The tie with Eastern was equally direct, as Oregon State faculty were stationed on the Eastern campus to conduct an agricultural program for which students received credit at either OSU or Eastern. For students, it was a significant program. Under its innovative president, Dave Gilbert, Eastern was a pathfinder in distance education despite its location in a sparsely populated part of the state. Dave developed imaginative programs to reach students who could not come to La Grande.

Like Eastern, Western suffered from close-to-the-edge finances. Western adopted a police academy, which pulled in financial support from parts of the state budget other than that reserved for higher education. Both Southern and Western aspired to be the public small-college liberal arts institution of choice for Oregon students. Eastern was clearly a natural-resource-oriented school. All three were financially vulnerable, as was the Oregon Institute of Technology in Klamath Falls, to which Oregon State was tied through our College of Engineering.

I enjoyed all my colleagues who served as presidents—Paul Olum, Myles Brand, and Dave Frohnmayer of the University of Oregon; Judith Ramaley of Portland State; Dick Meyers of Western Oregon; Joe Cox of Southern

Oregon; Dave Gilbert of Eastern Oregon; and Larry Blake and Larry Wolf of Oregon Institute of Technology. I think we all learned from each other, and we respected each other. I don't think it's an exaggeration to state that the adverse financial environment for higher education and the open leadership of Chancellor Bartlett enhanced the cohesion of the state system.

THE LEGISLATURE

AS THE PRESIDENT of Oregon State University, I had the privilege of meeting a number of truly hardworking legislators, honest men and women who were making personal sacrifices to spend months in Salem every other year, often working late into the night seven days a week, attempting to keep the state on an even keel, usually without adequate funds to do so. I also enjoyed the opportunity to meet those legislators in their home territory when traveling around the state.

During my tenure, OSU was fortunate to have two of its faculty members serving in the legislature, Senator Cliff Trow, a Democrat, and Representative Anton "Tony" Van Vliet, a Republican. We didn't receive special favors from these two legislators, but they kept us informed of the general tenor of the legislature and any special aspects of legislation we should be aware of. Tony was a member of the Joint Ways and Means Committee most of the time I was president.

By and large, Oregon legislators supported higher education. They were faced with the perennial problem of not having enough money to maintain all the government services beneficial to the people of the state. The Oregon Constitution requires that the budget be balanced. Partly because higher education is considered an investment in the future of the state and funds are not required for the immediate support of Oregonians, the higher education budget is often reduced in order to fund more immediate state needs.

"Is this a Washington Monument?" The question was directed to me by Grattan Kerans, Democratic representative from Lane County, during a meeting of the Joint Ways and Means Committee in 1991. I had just told the committee that OSU was proposing to close the College of Veterinary Medicine.

I replied, "No, sir. We are prepared to close the college."

My response was honest, although I hoped we would never have to do that. When Kerans asked about a "Washington Monument," he was referring to a political tactic frequently used in Washington, DC, whereby a favorite entity, such as the Washington Monument, is proposed for elimination in order to meet a budget total. Such monuments are popular with the public, and a politician's political career could be over if it were actually eliminated. So it is saved by moving funds from elsewhere, thereby jeopardizing some other part of the budget.

The veterinary school was under discussion because the chancellor had asked us, when preparing our 1991 budget, to eliminate our most expensive degree program, in our case, the degree in veterinary medicine. When we presented our proposed budget to the Board of Higher Education, minus funds for the College of Veterinary Medicine, board member Mark Dodson asked me directly, "Is this a good decision?"

I replied, "According to the guidelines we were given, it is the right decision. From the perspective of the people of Oregon, it is a terrible decision." Although I did not say it at the time, it meant that veterinarians who were needed in Oregon would no longer be educated in Oregon.

"I understand," was Dodson's rejoinder, and I knew he did.

We submitted the budget to the legislature. In the meantime, Provost Graham Spanier and I had met with the veterinary-medicine faculty, staff, and students to tell them of the circumstances under which their college was proposed for elimination. We told them that every member of the faculty and staff would receive a "letter of timely notice" informing them that within one year of the passage of the budget by the legislature, each of their positions would be eliminated, and in most cases they would be out of a job. We explained why this was necessary, and that during the ensuing year, we would do everything we could to see that the college was not eliminated. We needed their help if we were to achieve this goal. It was not a happy occasion.

Following that meeting, the dean of veterinary medicine and his associates contacted every veterinarian in Oregon, informed them of the situation, and asked for their support and active help. Pet owners throughout the state were asked to contact their legislators and request that the proposed budget be rejected. The livestock industries of the state weighed in. Farmers, pet lovers, and 4-H kids demonstrated at the state capitol building. Llama owners brought their llamas up the Capitol steps. Members of the Joint Ways and Means Committee were inundated with letters of protest and requests that the college be funded. People all over Oregon were upset. Eliminating "their College of Vet Medicine" was preposterous. No way could that be allowed to happen.

The members of the Ways and Means Committee received the message from the public, they understood the message, they agreed with it. In the end, the legislature fully funded the College of Veterinary Medicine, even to a better extent than the rest of higher education, at least for the first biennium under Ballot Measure 5. During that year of grassroots politics, only one vet-med faculty member left to take a position at another university.

The college continued to struggle for financial support during the next biennium. Similar tactics were employed, and I was informed that pygmy goats were actually brought into the hearing room. I suspect they must have been smuggled in. They did their part, and veterinary medicine continued to be funded.

The legislature didn't always support what we thought was in the best interest of the people of Oregon. If a legislator didn't agree with what was happening in higher education, we certainly heard about it, usually by way of the chancellor's office or the Board of Higher Education. A major example: in 1987 or 1988, the board made a decision to convert the academic calendar of the entire state system from the quarter system to the early semester system.

An early semester usually starts in August and is completed before Christmas, then starts again in January and finishes in May. Many faculty at a number of the institutions favored the semester system because they felt that they could cover course material in greater depth than is possible under the quarter system. Those favoring the quarter system, including most faculty at Oregon State, preferred the flexibility that three shorter academic quarters allow. Three shorter quarters permitted more different topics to be covered than was generally the case with two longer periods. In a sense, the arguments were academic flexibility versus academic depth.

We argued forcefully to remain on the quarter system, but to no avail. The whole state system would be required to convert to the semester system. We argued that there might not be enough time to do this properly before the 1989 legislative session because it would require us to evaluate and change the entire academic calendar. We saw the conversion mandate as an opportunity to assess our entire curriculum and alter it to meet the changing needs of society. Such an assessment would take time.

We began with a complete evaluation of our curriculum. Every quarter-length course needed to be reconsidered; semester-length courses needed to be designed; a new academic calendar needed to be developed; a new course catalog needed to be written and printed. It was a big job, if it were done properly, and we intended to do it properly. We did not panic, but we started on the task immediately and seriously. OSU led the other institutions in preparing for the change. By the time the legislature was preparing for the 1989 session, we were ready.

However, the legislature wasn't ready. Some legislators argued that in earlier years, perhaps the early 1900s, college students helped in harvesting crops during September. The forceful leader for this position was Republican representative Elizabeth VanLeeuwen, a farmer from Linn County. Liz was convinced that the conversion to the early semester, which started in August, would be a devastating blow to farmers who depended on college students to help at harvest time. We tried to convince her that our research of the agriculture manpower situation indicated that mechanized harvest techniques had virtually eliminated the need for student labor at harvest time in September. She was not convinced.

Each of the colleges and universities had worked extremely hard to be ready to convert to semesters. The evening before the Board of Higher Education would make its final decision, the presidents of the institutions gathered to draft a statement indicating their universal approval of the conversion. We worked hard, had a drink, and then went to bed.

At breakfast the next morning, we were relaxed and ready for the board meeting, when suddenly Dick Hensley, the board's chairman, appeared in the doorway of the dining room. He seemed to be looking for someone. When he spotted me, he motioned for me to join him outside the dining room.

He had news. He informed me that while the presidents were drafting their statement of approval during the previous evening, the board decided it was not going to approve the conversion to semesters. The political pressure was too great to risk it.

Liz VanLeeuwen and political pressure had prevailed. Oh boy!

At the official board meeting, the board formally rejected the conversion and then went on to other agenda items. Our provost, Graham Spanier, called Bruce Shepard, who had been in charge of the conversion preparation, and informed Bruce of the board's final decision.

Later that afternoon, when Graham and I returned to campus, we immediately sought Bruce, hoping he had not done anything rash. Bruce seemed calm, composed. He told us that when he received the news, he erupted, hit the ceiling, and then went for a long walk. He then returned to his office and began to alter the new semester curriculum to fit the existing academic quarter system.

When other faculty learned the news, their reaction was similar to Bruce's—emotional at first, and then calm and reasoned. We certainly had a great faculty. Later we surveyed our students and discovered that virtually none of them participated in the harvest of agricultural crops. All of them would have been available for the start of an early semester system in August.

There was a two-fold silver lining to this episode: we had completely evaluated our existing curriculum, and the esteem in which I held our faculty was enhanced significantly. Incidentally, Bruce Shepard went on to become the president of Western Washington University.

A UNIQUE GIFT

I MADE my final testimony to the Joint Ways and Means Committee in early 1995. The thought occurred to me that each committee member needed a memento after they left the committee chamber—something to take back to their offices that would remind them of the good things Oregon State University did for the people of Oregon. Not a pamphlet or piece of literature; that would not do it. The legislators would simply put any paper aside to be buried under all the other paper they accumulated. My gift needed to be a unique reminder of how OSU benefitted the people of Oregon.

Then I thought of the perfect symbol. It would be a testament of the innovation of OSU's faculty, a reminder of OSU's land-grant roots and profound influence on Oregon's agriculture industry, and an affirmation that we were proud of our heritage as "aggies," as a "cow college."

I would present each member with a stalk of the Stephens variety of winter wheat.

Stephens wheat had been developed in 1978 by one of Oregon State's legendary faculty members, Warren Kronstad. It was widely adopted by growers, and by 1995, Stephens wheat represented about 90 percent of all the wheat grown in Oregon.

I obtained a small bundle of Stephens wheat from the OSU crop science department. Arriving a bit early at the hearing room, I placed a stalk of wheat at each legislator's place. During my presentation, I told the committee about this variety of wheat and how important it was to the state of Oregon. I told them about Warren Kronstad and how he had worked with farmers in Oregon and in Mexico to achieve two growing seasons in one year for the development of this strain of wheat. I told them how proud I was of Oregon State University. I pointed out that this stalk of Stephens wheat was only one manifestation of OSU's many contributions to the citizens of Oregon.

The stalk of wheat got their attention. I heard comments such as, "I've heard about this wheat. I'm glad to have this" and, "So this is Stephens wheat." I watched one of the legislators leaving the room holding his stalk of wheat and looking at it as he walked out. I think my testimony made an impression, or perhaps I would be more accurate if I said that the Stephens wheat made an impression. As I left the hearing room, I thought, Thank you, Warren Kronstad.

Later Chancellor Bartlett told me that Carolyn Oakley, chair of the Joint Ways and Means Committee, had told him, "I don't ever want to see John Byrne testify before this committee again." She got her wish: I retired before the next legislative session. But I wonder why she said that. I don't think I insulted any of the committee's members, nor do I think I abused my privilege of testifying. It occurred to me that one of Representative Oakley's objectives was to keep the higher education budget under control. Could it be that my testimony, with the Stephens wheat, didn't help her attain her objective? I hoped so.

I was only doing my job.

CHAPTER 20

Students, Faculty, and Staff

It's all about people

CRITICAL TO OSU'S SUCCESS as a university is its relationship to the people it serves—students and Oregon citizens—and to the people who are the university: its faculty, staff, and administrators. There are others: parents, the chancellor, the board and other institutions in the state system, the legislature, and Congress. But most important are OSU's students, faculty, and staff. For the university to be successful in its mission, it must maintain optimum relationships with individuals in these groups. The president, as the personification of the university, is the key to those relationships. Harmonious relations are relatively easy if the president is a "people person;" if not, there can be problems. I considered myself a people person, but even in the best of all worlds, agendas occasionally clash.

STUDENTS

I DID FAIRLY WELL with students, but we did sometimes differ. On occasion, my relationship with the students of the University Cabinet was strained. At one meeting, the students brought up an issue concerning student participation on decision-making committees of the faculty or administration. They wanted a decision-making role in matters that would transcend their tenure at the university. We wanted them on committees for their perspective and advice as students, but not to make decisions that would be effective long after they had left the university.

The discussion lasted longer than it needed to. Faculty and administrators explained as clearly as possible why it was not appropriate for students to make decisions that would affect faculty and staff as well as students. The students persisted. I became impatient, slapped the table hard, and said when we put students on faculty-student committees, unfortunately the students frequently did not come to the meetings. My action essentially stopped further discussion, and the meeting was over. Apparently the ASOSU president took my intervention personally. Later that day, I received a copy of a letter, on ASOSU letterhead, written by the president of ASOSU to the chancellor of the State System of Higher Education, calling for my dismissal as president of Oregon State University. Nothing came of the letter or of the incident.

Another issue where some of the students and I parted company had to do with senior final exams. It had been the custom at OSU that at the annual commencement ceremony, each graduate was presented with his or her actual diploma. This is quite an undertaking, particularly when the undergraduates scheduled to receive diplomas numbered in the several thousands. It also required that the diplomas be stacked in the exact order in which graduates crossed the platform to receive their individual diplomas. This required last-minute adjustments as students dropped out of the proceedings or showed up at the last minute. It was important that everyone, staff and students, be serious about the procedure.

Here I'm joining the dance at the annual Hawaiian student night (ca. 1988). I didn't realize at the time that my experience in Tahiti would prepare me for this aspect of being a university president. (OSU Special Collections and Archives Research Center)

I conducted commencement exercises eleven times. Here I am on the platform in about 1990. I often left the platform to conduct the band while undergraduates trooped across stage to receive their very own diplomas. (OSU Special Collections and Archives Research Center)

Traditionally, seniors did not take final examinations during the spring quarter of their senior year, and commencement was held during the weekend before examination week for all other students. Because senior records were completed well before the commencement, the staff had ample time to set up the procedure for providing individual diplomas during the commencement ceremony. Commencement weekend was traditionally a festive time on campus. The seniors celebrated having satisfied all the requirements for their degrees, and the rest of the students had one final fling before the ordeal of final exams.

Imagine the travail on the part of the seniors when the Faculty Senate changed the rules and required seniors to take final examinations and wait until after examination week for commencement. This rule change precipitated a major debate between seniors and the Faculty Senate. Making no progress in the debate, the seniors turned to the "all-powerful" president of the university, the Great Oz—me—to overturn the senate's ruling and return to the tradition of the past.

Of course, I did not do this. Seniors were required to take final examinations and attend commencement following the end of examination week. A number of the seniors were quite upset, although their parents and other family members seemed not to notice. There were several unanticipated consequences. On commencement weekend, most undergraduates had left campus, so the campus was quiet and relatively unoccupied except for the graduating students and their families. The parties that took place were quiet family affairs.

The biggest change, however, took place during the commencement ceremony itself. There were virtually no incidents of graduates consuming alcohol during the ceremony. Previously, the consumption of alcohol during the ceremony had been a significant problem, often with several graduates becoming sick and even unable to cross the platform, disrupting the orderly distribution of diplomas. The tradition initiated during my watch resulted in a more dignified commencement ceremony, one of which Oregon State University was justifiably proud—and so were the families of the graduates.

FACULTY

WHEN I ASSUMED the presidency, I had been on the OSU faculty rolls for twenty-four years and still thought of myself as a faculty member—sort of. To some colleagues, I referred to myself as a "former faculty member confined to the tower." The administration building where the president's office is located was often referred to by faculty as the "Power Tower."

Governor Neil Goldschmidt was interested in and supportive of higher education and decided he wanted to meet one-on-one with the presidents of each public university. After my meeting with him, I decided the faculty, as well as the deans, should be informed about our meeting. One way to spread the word to faculty about my meeting with the governor was to have a series of breakfasts with faculty from across campus. The first several breakfasts of the series were with the department chairs, and the rest were with other faculty. Faculty were selected in a quasi-random fashion so that eventually we would have representation from all departments. Fifteen to twenty faculty members met with me in a boardroom in the Memorial Union. Often the faculty did not know one another. I tried to hold these breakfasts as often as possible.

The breakfasts, continental in style, were scheduled for an hour and a half starting at seven. By eight thirty, they were usually going strong, and it was often difficult to end the meetings. We started with self-introductions, allowing each person a few sentences—not too many semicolons, please. Following introductions, I told them what was on my mind, my session with the governor or whatever I thought was important for them to know. Then we talked about whatever was on their minds. Although some of the faculty messages were challenging, they were often based on insufficient information from the administration. In case the conversations were slow, I had a couple of questions to throw out to stimulate discussion.

On one occasion, I asked them to consider an idea I had about creating a series of faculty groups, such as a "faculty of human creativity," a "faculty of systems development," a "faculty of sustainability," and so on. The idea was not new to me; when I first arrived at Oregon State in 1960, there was a group of faculty who referred to themselves as the "faculty of ecology." They came from departments of biology, forestry, geology, and geography and met for lunch about once a month. This was the type of faculty group I had in mind when I brought the idea up at breakfast. I never mentioned anything about substituting them for departments or colleges—I was thinking only about creating an opportunity for faculty to communicate across disciplines with other faculty who had related interests.

By one o'clock that afternoon, the rumors were spreading on campus that Byrne wanted to eliminate departments and colleges and create these new faculties. The spread of these rumors suggested the grapevine worked rapidly, though often with some distortion of the issues. It also suggested that the breakfasts were an effective means of communicating directly with faculty. I noticed at the breakfasts that the messages I received directly from faculty were often different from those conveyed by the academic deans.

I particularly enjoyed the give and take with the faculty, and I think many of them enjoyed it as well. The diversity of faculty backgrounds and interests at the breakfasts impressed on those present how comprehensive and complex Oregon State University was. There is no question in my mind that my relationship with faculty benefited from these occasions.

It seemed important to me to operate in accordance with established procedures. I was careful not to exert presidential authority by mandating actions that violated existing protocols, particularly those that faculty might consider important to faculty governance. I suppose I violated this self-imposed restriction when it came to the naming of the oceanography building. Everyone in oceanography at Oregon State knew the building could be named for only one person: Wayne V. Burt.

Wayne was responsible for the very existence of oceanography at Oregon State University. The original Department of Oceanography

I help John Fryer, chair of the department of microbiology, break ground for the construction of the Salmon Disease Laboratory in 1989. The lab was later named the John L. Fryer Aquatic Animal Health Laboratory. Fryer pioneered the important fish-disease research program at OSU.
(OSU Special Collections and Archives Research Center)

headquarters was built during the 1960s and referred to as the oceanography building ever since. I was confident I could do something about renaming the building for Wayne while he was still alive, even though it was policy not to name a building for a living person unless that person had provided a significant sum of money.

I contacted Doug Caldwell, dean of the College of Oceanography, and told him I thought it was time to name the building Burt Hall. Doug and I agreed it would be best if the proposal to name the building came from the oceanography faculty. We knew exactly who should submit the proposal: Vern Kulm. He was my first graduate student in oceanography, my first student to receive the PhD. Vern stayed on as a faculty member in oceanography and became one of the senior faculty leaders.

Vern wrote a letter to Doug Caldwell recommending that the oceanography building be named Burt Hall in honor of Wayne Burt. With the unanimous support of the oceanography faculty, Dean Caldwell followed up with a proposal to me and at the same time obtained the support of the Faculty Senate. I submitted the renaming request to the State Board of Higher Education for their approval, which they granted. In 1987, Wayne and his family were present at the naming ceremony, and they were quite moved. My relationship with the oceanography faculty continued to prosper.

STAFF

WHEN I WAS a faculty member in oceanography, I learned how important the staff are to the university. I relied on them for routine support of my teaching and research. When special events occurred, the staff provided special support. It was obvious to me that the staff cared as much about the oceanography department as the faculty did. After I became department chairman, everyone in the department—faculty, students, and staff—was invited to our regularly scheduled department meetings.

Those were my thoughts when, as a new university president, I faced my first Faculty Day in 1985. Faculty Day was how Oregon State had traditionally opened the academic year: an all-university meeting of faculty to which staff were not invited. Faculty honors and awards were announced at the meeting.

That all changed in 1986, when I called for all faculty and staff members to attend the first University Day, at which the achievements of faculty *and* staff were announced. Being a Beaver was not limited to the faculty, nor was the Beaver Champion award. As was the case in oceanography, many staff members were more dedicated to OSU than many of the faculty were. Furthermore, the faculty couldn't do their jobs without the support of the staff. We all were Oregon State University.

The University Day program often included a greeting from the chancellor. The president of the Faculty Senate gave a talk, and awards were presented. In my own address, I reviewed accomplishments of the previous year, congratulated the faculty and staff on the excellence of their achievements, forecast some of the challenges of the coming year, and perhaps gave a bit of a pep talk about what was needed to meet those challenges. I usually completed my talk with the surprise announcement of the Beaver Champion Award. Enthusiasm was always high. It was a good beginning to the academic year.

While I was president, the Oregon Public Employees Union (OPEU) had about eighteen thousand members throughout Oregon. About a thousand Oregon State staff were members of OPEU; about seven hundred were not. In April 1995, my final year as president, the state leaders of OPEU argued for statewide increases in wages and pension benefits from a state that was severely stressed by the effects of Ballot Measure 5 passed nearly five years earlier. Statewide OPEU leaders called for a strike vote. At OSU, 291 members of the union voted in favor of striking, and twelve voted in opposition.

On May 1, I issued a "Dear Colleagues" letter to our staff and faculty saying that a strike was quite possible within the week. The last paragraph of that letter read: "Our mutual respect for each other as colleagues and friends may be tested in the days ahead. I hope our example will help others to understand how much we care about Oregon State University, our students and each other."

The strike was called for the morning of Monday, May 8. Staff who were members of OPEU gathered to picket the university at selected locations around the perimeter of the campus. They had no idea how long they would be on the picket line.

It was time for me to show my support of them as staff of Oregon State University, as people who were caught up in an issue over which they had little control. I left my office and approached the group that was picketing in front of the administration building. We had a friendly chat, and I decided to approach the next group, located several blocks away, near the engineering complex bordering Monroe Street at the north edge of the campus, and so it went all the way around the margin of the campus. I was well received by each group of picketers. Fortunately, for them and for me, the weather was clear. I discovered in a physical way how big our campus really was.

I repeated my "picket tour" each day of the strike. On one day, I was offered coffee and doughnuts at a nearby coffee shop and was given a box of a dozen or so donuts. I shared them with the first group of picketers I encountered. This act grew in public awareness far beyond the size of the actual event. Word was soon out that I had bought coffee and doughnuts for all of the OSU staff on the picket line. Not so!

On the fourth day of the strike, it occurred to me that I was ignoring the staff who had not struck, but who had stayed on the job, in many cases doing the tasks that would ordinarily be done by their friends on the picket line. Those staff members were dispersed throughout the campus and were not clustered, as were the picketers, and so my contacts with them were not nearly as effective as my meetings with the strikers. But the word was out to all OSU staff, union members or not, that Byrne cared about them. Serendipitous or not, that act of walking the picket line probably did more to benefit my relationship with the employees of OSU than anything I did during my eleven years as president.

I learned later that some statewide nonunion leaders thought my action with the strikers was inappropriate for a manager. Those leaders did not fully understand how important every member of Oregon State—faculty and staff—was to our effectiveness as a university, a university that served all of the people of Oregon. I was proud of the staff members who did not strike, and I was equally proud of those who had no choice and found it necessary to strike.

The strike lasted seven days. On Monday, May 15, a bargain was reached between the union and the state. At OSU, all staff members were back at work, together.

CHAPTER 21

Race and Diversity at Oregon State

Trying to improve conditions

THE FIRST RACIAL INCIDENT I became aware of at Oregon State occurred during the university's centennial celebration in February 1969. I was the chair of the oceanography department at the time. Dr. Linus Pauling had returned to his alma mater to present a centennial lecture celebrating the one-hundredth birthday of the institution Pauling had graduated from in 1922—then known as Oregon Agricultural College.

Pauling's talk was to be delivered in Gill Coliseum, the only inside seating area of any size on campus at that time. As the program was about to get under way, thirty members of the Black Student Union and some white sympathizers crowded in front of the speakers' platform and requested to use the microphone to address the assembly about "the Fred Milton Affair."

Fred Milton was a member of the Beaver football squad, coached by Dee Andros. Milton and Andros had encountered each other on campus, and Andros noticed that Milton was growing a mustache and goatee. Even though it was not football season, Andros told Milton to shave off the facial hair, inasmuch as facial hair was a violation of a team policy established by Andros. Failure to do so would result in dismissal from the football team.

Milton refused to shave off the hair, claiming it was a cultural matter for him, and sporting a beard was one of his "human rights." True to his word, Andros cut Milton from the team. Milton reported the issue to the Black Student Union on campus, and a racial incident was born. There were demonstrations, petitions, meetings, and inflammatory comments on both sides of the issue. All forty-seven black students on campus boycotted classes.

President Jensen handled the event in Gill Coliseum on that February morning professionally. While Linus Pauling chatted with the demonstrators, President Jensen listened to the leaders of the group and then agreed to give them the microphone to address the audience, if they would then leave the building in an orderly manner.

The microphone was handed to the leader of the group, who explained the Milton incident and its cultural implications to black students. He made a request to the OSU administration to make changes in the way blacks were treated on the OSU campus. Then the demonstrators marched out of Gill Coliseum, and Linus Pauling gave an address that the demonstration had clearly upstaged.

Subsequent to that demonstration, President Jensen created a Commission on Human Rights and Responsibilities, consisting of faculty and students, minorities and others. The commission met several times and made its report to the faculty and the administration, a report which apparently pleased no one.

During the entire episode, there was no violence or physical injury to anyone that I am aware of. What may have been missed during the turmoil was the value of the Fred Milton affair in enhancing awareness of racial differences at Oregon State. It was a learning opportunity for a predominantly white university in a predominantly white community, a community with virtually no cultural support for African American students and other minorities. Although racial awareness was increasing at OSU, the university and the community were not spared from racial events.

AFFIRMATIVE ACTION

TIMES WERE CHANGING, but slowly. The university made efforts to enhance the visibility of cultural differences and to diversify its faculty, staff, and student body. These efforts were only marginally successful. Affirmative action seemed to be gaining steam nationwide during the 1960s and 1970s, but at Oregon State, affirmative action was clearly more process than result.

I had a direct experience with affirmative action in the late 1960s and early 1970s when I served as chair of the oceanography department. The OSU affirmative action director was an African American named Ron

McClain. Ron, who came to OSU in 1973 shortly after the affirmative action office opened, did his job well in forcing OSU administrators, largely department chairs and deans, to comply with the affirmative action procedures he had established. Unfortunately, the results didn't seem to be consistent with the efforts. When I wanted to hire a new oceanographer, I was required to make an extra effort to locate and hire a minority, such as a black oceanographer. I tried to convince Ron that there simply were not many, if any, black oceanographers in the United States, even in the graduate programs at the nation's oceanographic institutions.

Ron's response was "Prove it." So I wrote to the directors of all the major oceanographic institutions in the United States; there were only ten or so. I explained to the directors, all of whom I knew personally, about affirmative action at Oregon State and asked if they might be facing a similar situation. I asked them to share with me how many faculty, staff, and students they had in their institutions who could be classified as minorities.

In exchange for their information, I told them, I would share all of the data sent to me for all of the institutions, but I would identify the institutions by a letter code. To each director, I would reveal only the identity of his own institution and of Oregon State. Each director saw all of the data for the entire academic oceanographic community.

I repeated this procedure every couple of years. The results of the survey showed that there were no minority faculty or staff represented in the accumulated data and only one or two minority graduate students preparing to be oceanographers in all of the major oceanographic institutions.

I showed the results to Ron, but he wasn't convinced, or at least he didn't indicate to me that he was. I learned later that, unknown to me, he challenged other departments to do what oceanography was doing. The survey I carried out came to be known nationally as "the Byrne survey of minorities in oceanography." There was no other similar survey of minority oceanographers. For OSU oceanography, the procedures of affirmative action were not effective, nor were they, I think, effective for the entire university. When I returned to OSU from NOAA as president, I was convinced we could diversify the faculty and staff of Oregon State, but we would need to do it in a different way.

A NEW APPROACH FOR ACHIEVING DIVERSITY

SHORTLY AFTER becoming president, I called OSU's affirmative action officer, Pearl Spears Gray, and asked her to see me. I shared with her my concern about the effectiveness of our affirmative action procedures. I asked her to give thought to other things we might do to increase diversity on campus and otherwise improve the climate for minorities at Oregon State. I wanted results.

A week or two later, Pearl returned with a plan that might work to generate new ideas for us. She proposed that we improve our communication with minority leaders in Oregon, starting by hosting meals in the Portland area for leaders of four key minority groups: African Americans, Asian Americans, Hispanic Americans, and Native Americans. She proposed holding the meals at or near the Portland Airport and inviting twelve or fifteen leaders of each group.

As an African American, Pearl was well respected in the minority communities around Oregon, and she was effective in getting acceptance from the leaders we invited to the meals. Pearl and I both signed the letters of invitation. The invitations explained there would be no commitment on the part of those invited to the meetings, or by us for actions resulting from our conversation; we simply wanted to share ideas and to get to know one another. We held the meetings during a two-day period in April 1986.

We had much to discuss with the African American group: racial incidents that had occurred in the past, the lack of a supporting culture in Corvallis, and methods we might use to attract more African American students to OSU. I learned about some of the day-to-day cultural problems faced by blacks in Corvallis; for example, the lack of a barbershop that could provide African American hairstyles, and the dearth of grocery stores that sold food specialties that were common in African American cuisine.

The Asian American group was next. We had difficulty getting the participants of that group to speak up and share their thoughts. Finally, one person stood and addressed the group, urging them to speak and share ideas. "This man is trying to improve conditions for all Asian American students at Oregon State University. He wants us to share ideas from our perspective. He can't improve things for our sons and daughters unless we share with him our concerns." That seemed to open up the discussion.

This group may have been the most difficult to engage in conversation because of the diversity within the population we identify as Asian American. Nevertheless, it was a useful conversation.

The next morning, we met with the Hispanic leaders. They were ready. There was no reticence to speak, and in fact the major challenge was to maintain some semblance of order to the conversation. They had a great many suggestions for how we could make Oregon State a more welcoming institution for Spanish-speaking people.

Finally at lunch, we met with the Native Americans. Their understandable distrust of "government"—us—seemed palpable. The discussion started slowly until they understood where we were coming from and what we were attempting to do. Oregon State, through its Extension Service, had developed good relations with the tribal groups throughout Oregon. When those present at the luncheon understood that those of us from Oregon State identified with the OSU Extension Service, the discussion became more fruitful.

All of the conversations were useful. Each discussion was different in substance and in style. There were common themes: we could do a much better job of actively recruiting in the communities where minorities were concentrated; we needed to develop ethnic awareness courses as a required part of our curriculum; academic counselors should include minorities; there should be a permanent administrative structure offering ethnic support; a program should be implemented to enhance faculty and staff awareness of ethnic differences and sensitivity. All four groups commented on how quiet Corvallis was and mentioned the lack of nighttime entertainment. They thought Corvallis was a dull place for minorities to live. Minority students could feel very isolated in Corvallis.

There was uniform agreement that meetings like the one we had just had were important; there was no substitute for open, frank, and respectful discussion. We concluded the meetings by asking them to share in writing what they considered the most important issues we addressed, what had been omitted, and what we at OSU should be doing next. I asked them to share their thoughts with Pearl. We received a number of laudatory comments. Several indicated they did not know of any other university that had held such meetings. In exchange for their thoughts, Pearl and I sent everyone who had attended the meetings a summary of the meetings as we saw them.

A board of visitors

PEARL AND I concluded that the meetings were worthwhile and that we needed to follow up with specific actions. One suggestion that surfaced during several of the meetings was that we needed to maintain contact and continue to have such discussions. I concluded that one way to do this was to create a board of visitors for minority affairs. I don't recall if this was my idea or Pearl's, or if it had surfaced in the discussions, but we agreed we would do it. I asked Pearl to suggest who the members of the first such group should be, bearing in mind that it should include leaders from each of the groups we had met with in Portland.

Pearl did a great job, and in July we identified and named a twenty-five-member board of visitors for minority affairs. Members would commit to a three-year renewable term and would receive a stipend of $50 per meeting plus travel expenses. Once identified, the board held a two-day retreat in Newport in January 1987, including a facilitator who had been present at the meetings in Portland. At the retreat, the board elected a four-person steering committee with a member from each minority group. Phyllis Lee represented the Asian American group; Annabelle Jaramillo, the Hispanics; Rudy Clements, the Native Americans; and Kathleen Sadat, the African Americans. Those present at the Newport meeting clarified the role of the board, drafted a mission statement, and formulated a plan of action to help OSU recruit and retain minority students, faculty, staff, and administrators.

The board met three times in 1987. The chair of the steering committee kept me informed of their progress. By December, the board had completed its report and forwarded it to me. I shared it with OSU faculty and administrators. The report, "Working Together for the Future: Toward Racial and Cultural Diversity at Oregon State University," included the assessment that the OSU environment was indifferent and insensitive to the needs of minorities. The three goals with supporting strategies included in the report called for OSU to increase the numbers of minority students graduating; increase the number of minority employees; and create supporting and accepting environments for minorities, including the creation of an Office for Minority Affairs.

Using the specific suggestions under each of the goals, I charged the academic deans and other university officers to report on the present situation in their units and to specify how they planned to implement the suggestions of the report. In May 1990, their achievements were reported in a Minority Action Program Summary.

In 1991, I authorized the provost to create an Office of Multicultural Affairs, in lieu of the minority affairs office called for by the board of visitors. The concept for this office evolved from the original goals of the board. It would promote cultural diversity and awareness of cultural differences. Following a national search for a leader of that office, I selected Phyllis Lee, an original member of the board of visitors steering committee, to lead and manage that office. Much of the subsequent improvement in the cultural sensitivity at Oregon State is a direct result of Phyllis Lee's leadership.

RACISM

AT TWO O'CLOCK on a Saturday morning in mid-October 1990, Jeff Revels, coordinator of the Black Cultural Center, was crossing the parking lot of a local watering hole when a shout from a van in the parking lot rang out: "Hey, nigger."

The van swerved close to Revels and then drove away. Revels noted Sigma Chi stickers on the van. He followed the van to the Sigma Chi house on Twenty-Fifth Street, where he reported the incident to someone in the house. Then he left a note in the van requesting an apology and leaving his phone number. Later, he received a call from the driver of the van, who claimed he was not a member of Sigma Chi, admitted that those in the van had been drinking and that he, the driver, did not have to apologize to Revels.

The call offended Revels. Subsequently, in protest over the incident, Revels closed the Black Cultural Center indefinitely. He demanded that the OSU administration do something about racist incidents on the OSU campus. In response, I called a town hall meeting for noon on October 31 in the Memorial Union lounge.

As I walked up to the MU from the administration building, I commented to the couple of vice presidents who were with me, "This will give folks an opportunity to yell at the president," and that's exactly what happened.

The MU lounge had been set up as an auditorium, with chairs filling the lounge and with two aisles through the chairs. A microphone had been set up in each of the aisles. There was a standing-room-only crowd of about two hundred students and faculty, mostly students.

I moderated the meeting, explaining to the attendees why we were all there—to hear their thoughts about racism at OSU and their ideas of what could be done to counter racial incidents here. I permitted speakers to alternate between the two microphones. This alternate arrangement of speakers provided some order to the event, even though many of the comments were intemperate and emotional.

The president of the Associated Students of OSU (ASOSU) led off with, "We know there are students, faculty, and administrators who are bigots. We need to kick them out." Other comments called for the wholesale resignation of the administration. Others made comments such as: "We don't see anything being done about racism at OSU; how long has Byrne known about racism on campus?"

To which I responded, "I've been at OSU since 1960, and there has been racism here since then."

One person said, "Corvallis is no better than OSU; the city council and the mayor should hear what we're saying and take it to heart."

A student said, "President Byrne, you can stand up there with a smug smile, looking like this matters to you, but we know better."

I think this was the only time I lost my temper. I rejoined, "I'm not smug, and no one in this room wants racism at OSU to disappear more than I do." I learned later that that student suffered some form of mental illness. Had I known that at the time, I think I would have reacted differently.

Jeff Revels said, "We want to see some commitment from you, Mr. President." We had already created the board of visitors and decided to create an office for minority affairs. I think I did not mention what we had already done, but I did say, "Judge me by what I do, not by what I say!" It seemed obvious the group wanted me to make proclamations that were as emotional as the statements I was being subjected to. I concluded by stating that we would take the comments we had heard to heart and would be doing something about them. The meeting, originally scheduled for one and a half hours, lasted close to three hours. That evening, a videotape of the meeting was shown in its entirety on Beaver TV.

The word quickly spread about the meeting, and faculty who had not been there watched the TV broadcast. Many of them wrote notes of support to me and expressed a willingness to help address the problem.

Subsequently I created a commission of faculty, students, and staff to address the problems of racism on campus.

A week later, on November 8, under guidance from student leadership, a group of students drafted a list of demands. They wanted a policy of zero tolerance, including dismissal of faculty and staff and suspension of students who engaged in racism. They called for academic courses that addressed cultural and ethnic diversity, an educational program in minority issues for faculty and staff, a commitment to maintain the cultural centers, the creation of an office of minority affairs, and an annual review of the office of affirmative action.

We were already doing most of these things. We had started doing them in 1987. Unfortunately, one racist incident by a single individual can quickly expand into a major trouble-generating, attention-grabbing event. Racist events are ugly. They are counter to everything we stand for in our quest for a humane society. They still take place. Three months after I retired from the presidency of Oregon State University, several racist events in Corvallis involving students led to a major demonstration on campus and an all-OSU boycott of classes organized by the black students of OSU in reaction to those events.

When I was president, I saw it as my responsibility to support continuing efforts by the university to counter discrimination, enhance diversity, engender understanding and sensitivity to cultural differences, and create an atmosphere in which individuals were accepted for who they were and not stereotyped as belonging to a particular race or group.

Furthermore, I believed then, and believe now, that every leader in the university at the rank of department chair and above has the same responsibilities as the president. With the valuable assistance of the board of visitors for minority affairs, we made changes at Oregon State to develop an environment of understanding of the value of every individual regardless of race, color, or cultural background. I think we made progress with the Office of Multicultural Affairs. The Oregon State community became more diverse and increasingly aware of the value of diversity. But there was, and still is, a long way to go.

CHAPTER 22

President Emeritus

Staying busy? No problem!

WHEN I SIGNED ON AS PRESIDENT, I thought I would serve for ten years. Ballot Measure 5 caused me to change that estimate. I couldn't imagine leaving the university I had committed my career to until it was once again financially sound. That took an additional year. By 1994, I thought I could see light at the end of the tunnel; by the beginning of 1995, it was obvious to me the university would recover financially before the end of the year. After discussions with Chancellor Bartlett and then Chancellor Cox, I announced my intention to retire at the end of 1995 or at such time as my successor could take over. As it turned out, that time would be December 31, 1995.

Once I made my retirement plans public, a variety of volunteer opportunities began to arrive. Some of these fit my interests; others did not. There was no question I could stay busy if I wanted to. Prior to my actual retirement from the presidency, I put together a list of activities I thought I would like to pursue once I was retired: fly-fishing, learning to play bridge, taking up painting, and so on.

Two years into my retirement, I realized that nothing on the list had happened. I was too busy. When people asked me about retiring, judging from my own experience, I told them, "Put your helmet on and get your head down low. More opportunities to stay busy will come to you than you can possibly handle."

Before I left the president's office, I received a request from Phil Keisling, Oregon's secretary of state, to chair a commission on whether the state should adopt a system of vote-by-mail. I told Keisling I would serve on the commission if he wanted me to, but I would not be chairman.

Retirement stimulates memories. One of my favorite is playing the saxophone during halftime at an OSU basketball game while I was president. (OSU Special Collections and Archives Research Center)

I did participate on the commission, which advised the secretary of state to adopt a vote by mail system; this system was subsequently adopted.

Also, before I left OSU, Peter Magrath, president of the National Association of State Universities and Land-Grant Colleges, asked me to serve as the executive director of the Kellogg Commission on the Future of State and Land-Grant Universities. The Kellogg Commission, funded by the

W. K. Kellogg Foundation, comprised the presidents of twenty-five public universities who worked together to stimulate reform in public higher education. I told Peter I would take the job if I could do it from Corvallis.

The commission held its first meeting in early 1996 and its final meeting in March 2000. The work occupied much of my time through 2000 and beyond. It was virtually a full-time job, or perhaps I made it a full-time job because I thought the commission was important and it was something I enjoyed doing.

I was also appointed to the National Sea Grant College Advisory Board. Members met several times a year and traveled to a number of Sea Grant universities to assess their programs. It was time-consuming, but interesting and enjoyable. In addition, I did a certain amount of consulting for universities, often as a result of my association with the Kellogg Commission and with the Association of Governing Boards, a nongovernmental organization designed to help the boards of colleges and universities do their jobs.

At the same time, I served on a number of advisory committees at OSU: the Honors College, Valley Library, College of Oceanic and Atmospheric Sciences, the Department of Art. Partly because of Shirley's interest in music, I chaired a committee to raise money to buy a new Steinway piano for the LaSells Stewart Center. This led to more leadership as the first chair of a committee to ensure there were public piano recitals using the new Steinway piano. We created the Steinway Piano Series, which in turn led to the creation of the Corvallis–Oregon State Piano International (COPI), a committee dedicated to creating a "culture of piano" in Corvallis.

Added to these voluntary assignments were others outside higher education: the Corvallis Public Schools Foundation Board, the Corvallis-OSU Symphony Society (COSUSS) Board, and others of an ad hoc nature. These were all activities I was interested in, but I did have my helmet on, and I did turn down requests of less interest to me.

As activities related to the Kellogg Commission eased, I let Joe Hendricks, the dean of Oregon State's Honors College, talk me into offering a colloquium on leadership. The weekly colloquium focused on the tools of leadership that could be useful to student leaders. With help from my assistant, Carol Mason, I offered this colloquium for several years. I drew on my experiences as the leader of a research group at the Humble Oil and Refining Company; as department chairman, dean, vice president and president of OSU; and as the administrator of NOAA and US commissioner to the International Whaling Commission. I had between six and twenty students for each colloquium I taught over the five-year period.

At the first session, I told the students, "This experience is about you, who you are, what you do, who you will become. The focus will be on how each of us develops as a person and as a leader. We will start with that end in mind. This experience, which we will create together, should help us to better understand the world and our relation to it and to its people. Where each of us ends up will depend largely on our own individual efforts. We will explore several concepts of leadership, and we will practice several tools effective leaders use." There are many quotes about leadership, and I used many of them, including this favorite:

> *"Leadership is the capacity to translate vision into reality."*
> —Warren G. Bennis

I covered such topics as the attributes of leaders, the nature of change, the future, vision, creativity, passion, values and ethics, good habits, planning, relationships, attitudes, and motivation. Tools for learning and leading were in the areas of communication (reading, writing, listening, talking), awareness (seeing, hearing, noticing, feeling), and budgeting (time and finances).

I required the students to purchase, read, and use *The Elements of Style* by William Strunk Jr. and E. B. White. I believed then, and do now, that one cannot write without thinking, and I wanted them to think about the topics we covered. I wanted them to be learners. As the philosopher Eric Hoffer said, "In times of change, it is the learners who will inherit the earth, while the learned will find themselves beautifully equipped for a world that no longer exists."

The philosophy for the colloquium was that the activities relative to organizational leadership could be developed and applied to each individual personally. To start, I asked them to write a short paper on how and why each of them personally was unique, unlike anyone else in the world. I wanted this to be the basis for each student's personal plan, setting goals and objectives for themselves. Subsequently we focused on setting goals, defining objectives that supported those goals, and planning activities to achieve the objectives and consequently the goals.

> *"A goal without a plan is just a wish."*
> —Antoine de Saint-Exupéry

I wanted them to forecast the future from daily news reports and prepare themselves for such a future.

"The tracks of the future lie in the sands of today."
—Harold Hodgkinson

We practiced "reconnaissance reading," a technique for skimming a book in five minutes and knowing pretty much what was generally in the book, if not the specifics.

The students gave many short talks to their colloquium-mates and were critiqued by those mates. For some, it was their first attempt at public speaking, and they were terrified. Collectively, using Strunk and White, we reviewed examples of their writing.

"Omit needless words."
—*The Elements of Style*

We practiced managing resources (budgeting), primarily managing our time.

"Time is a nonrenewable resource."

Leaders are generally broad-gauge people, aware of many things. To stretch the students' horizons, I brought in faculty from the worlds of business and the arts to challenge them. I also required them to select one piece of art in the Valley Library that they reacted to, positively or negatively, and write a short paper on how and why they reacted to it.

We covered many topics, learned about ourselves, and concluded that effective leaders are able to assess reality, create a vision, and communicate that vision to others. Leaders set goals and make plans to achieve their vision.

Anyone can become a leader.

CHAPTER 23

What's Best for the University

... a president's responsibility!

As president of Oregon State University, I recognized it was my responsibility to know what was best for the university. The changes my colleagues and I introduced in the university's substance and structure were designed to position Oregon State for a productive future. My main role was to guide others as they joined me in making the university more effective. I had a vision for the university, and others came to share that vision. I was the cheerleader, the promoter, and others were the implementers.

My overriding goal was to bring OSU into the late twentieth century and to prepare it for its future in serving students. I am confident that by my decisions and actions, OSU is more in harmony with the times than it was when I assumed the presidency. Through the efforts of all of us, Oregon State University survived difficult financial threats, grew stronger as a university, and was better prepared to meet global challenges.

Students and graduates of tomorrow will live in a world of ever-increasing population and greater disparity between the haves and have-nots, in a climate significantly different from that of today, and with shortages of critical natural resources. Knowledge is increasing faster than ever before, and communication is virtually instantaneous worldwide. Natural-world challenges will be greater and more complex and will be associated with economic, social, and political problems of equal or greater magnitude and complexity. The universities of tomorrow, including Oregon State University, will need to find new ways of preparing students to face this challenging future. The successful universities will prepare students to be active learners who can face the uncertainties of a world constantly in crisis materially, intellectually, socially, and politically.

OSU has always done reasonably well as a site of student learning. The future will require that OSU do even better. I have a vision for the future Oregon State University, of its graduates and of the education that will prepare them for the challenges and opportunities tomorrow's world will present.

As a public state university, OSU will admit any person who can meet its entrance requirements, regardless of personal characteristics. All students admitted will be capable of graduating—and if they need help, they will get it. Learning will be a basic element of all university activities, curricular and extracurricular. Students, professors, and staff will combine to form learning communities in which all participants learn from each other. Students will learn how to learn, and as OSU graduates, they will continue to learn, to keep pace with the increases of knowledge long after they leave OSU.

The university will recognize its responsibility to assist every student to be a responsible citizen. To that end, the curriculum will include the liberal arts as a meaningful part of the student's full intellectual, professional, and social development. OSU will promote moral and social values—including civility—in its graduates.

Direct measurement of a student's integrated knowledge will serve to assess student success. The ability to integrate knowledge from different courses will be the measure of their education. The university will provide an environment conducive to learning, including adequate facilities, equipment, and mentors. As new knowledge develops and is integrated into new courses, the cost of education will increase. Student tuition will be indexed to the cost of education, possibly increasing or decreasing annually. When they enter OSU, incoming students will be informed of the continuous nature of tuition increases during their time at OSU. More and more students will be assisted financially through private contributions.

In order to provide the richest intellectual environment for all students, OSU will strive for diversity among the student body, with students of different ethnic backgrounds and international students from countries throughout the world. To prepare students for success on a global basis, OSU will emphasize international studies, including overseas experiences, so that graduates will be aware of opportunities and challenges facing people throughout the world.

The Graduate School will recognize the need for education designed to prepare students for careers in business and government, as well as academe, and will adjust the requirements for individual degrees accordingly. While the research thesis and dissertation are well-established as products of creative thinking for careers in academe, preparation for non-academic careers will benefit from other activities that demonstrate and encourage creativity.

Graduate education continues to represent a pinnacle in formal education. Consequently, if there are to be changes in the nature of education for future generations of undergraduates and graduates, those changes should be included in the education of graduate students now.

As Oregon's major engine of knowledge creation, OSU will continue its many diverse research efforts that create new knowledge and provide learning opportunities for students by involving them in the research.

Since the latter half of the nineteenth century, the land-grant colleges and universities of this nation have led the way in engaging with society to solve societal problems. By reaching out to the citizens of Oregon through the Oregon State University Extension Service, the Oregon Sea Grant College program, and more recently with the adoption of Extended Education as a core part of its mission, Oregon State University will be a leader in the engagement of higher education with the people of Oregon. OSU will be one of the outstanding land-grant universities in America.

In fact, it already is.

Acknowledgments

A GREAT MANY PEOPLE made a contribution to this memoir and in fact to my life. As I have been engaged in this writing, I have reflected on those who were significant in shaping my life: my parents, my mentors, my friends, those who initially were not friends but became friends, colleagues at work, students I may have influenced, my family, and the persons who made significant contributions to the shaping of this work—friends and acquaintances who have influenced me in some small or not-so-small ways. All were, and are, important; all deserve to be acknowledged.

My parents, Frank E and Kathleen Byrne, provided the basic principles and values that provided the path along which my life evolved. I hope they realized how much they were loved and how much I value what they have done for me.

During each phase of my life, I have been privileged to know and to have learned from a number of individuals who provided more than a simple education. Teachers who stand out were Ethel Getman and Morris Ottman in elementary school and Sylvia Kurson, Alice Barry, Jean Fenn, and Herbert Oakes at Horace Greeley High School. At Hamilton College, those who stand out were Phil Oxley, Cecil Schneer, both geologists, and Samuel Obletz, who provided wisdom well beyond the Spanish language he taught. Phil Oxley became a lifetime friend. In graduate school, I had no greater mentors than Norman Newell and K. O. Emery. Harold N. Fisk, for whom I worked at the Humble Oil and Refining Company, must be included as one of the great mentors in my life. At Oregon State University, I learned from Wayne Burt, Roy Young, and Robert MacVicar, among many others. All had a hand in influencing and shaping who I became; all affected the life I write about.

Closer in time and place are those individuals who contributed directly to this memoir. No one put more pressure on me to write my memoir than Brooke Collison. Whenever I encountered Brooke, he asked me how my memoirs were coming, even though I had not begun to write. He urged, cajoled, and never let up. There were others who prompted me to write this work, but none with the intensity and persistence of Brooke. Thank you, Brooke.

Advice comes easily, and many people provide it. It is usually of value, and none is more valuable than the advice by wise people who have been over the same ground. At the early stage of writing, I received sound advice from my longtime good friend, Joe Creager. Joe and I first met at Columbia University as graduate students. Later we kept in touch when he was my counterpart in the oceanography program at the University of Washington. My time at the National Science Foundation was a direct result of a timely invitation from Joe to succeed him as a program manager for oceanography. I mentioned to Joe that I was writing my memoir. Joe had written his own and graciously sent copies of chapters from his work, accompanied with advice. The advice was useful, and I followed some of it. Joe, I have always enjoyed our association.

Other useful advice, mainly editorial, came from Linda Fleming. She and her husband, Bob, have been traveling companions on several birding trips. I sent Linda a draft of a section of this memoir dealing with an excursion into Mexico. Linda became interested in the story and provided editorial advice on sections of the manuscript I sent to her regularly. Her editorial suggestions were useful and were incorporated into the draft text.

My story before becoming president of OSU is based essentially on my memory. The part about being the president of Oregon State University is based on memory, my notes, and the material stored in the university's archive. The archived material was essential to stimulating my memory and occasionally correcting it. Larry Landis, OSU archivist, and his dedicated staff provided outstanding assistance. Their efforts on my behalf deserve special recognition. My thanks to all the staff, including Elizabeth Nielsen, Chris Petersen, Trevor Sandgathe, Anne Bahde, Rachel Lilley, Tiah Edmunson-Morton, Natalia Fernandez, Ruth Vondracek, and Ryan Wick. Thank you, Mike Dicianna, Mike Mehringer, and Adam LaMascus, the student assistants whose efforts were also of great help.

I also appreciate very much the useful discussions I had with the late Emery N. Castle, OSU distinguished professor emeritus. Emery, whose entire career has been devoted to the land-grant concept and to natural resources, shared with me his understanding of land-grant universities and of Oregon State University. While I was president of OSU, I relied on Emery for his suggestions concerning the Extension Service and the role OSU should play in extended education. As I prepared this work, I relied heavily on Emery's memoir, *Reflections of a Pragmatic Economist*, published by OSU Press, and used it as a model for my own tale.

Tony Van Vliet and George Pernsteiner provided essential information about how private donations could be used safely in matching state funds for the bonds needed to remodel the OSU Valley Library. Bill Robbins, a great friend and OSU distinguished professor emeritus of history, shared his knowledge of the history of various events affecting Oregon State University and was a steadying hand as I entered the wilderness (for me) of book publishing.

Longtime friend Gwil Evans provided the cover photo that so clearly reflects the tone of much of my story. Thank you, Gwil. Mike McInally came through with the necessary permission to use the "retirement" photo that ran on the front page of the Corvallis *Gazette-Times* two weeks after I retired from the OSU presidency. Thanks, Mike, and the *GT*, too, for accurate reporting of my presidential years.

I have been so fortunate during my retirement from the presidency to have the best, albeit the smallest, office of my career at the Center for the Humanities, Autzen House . . . and the finest hosts, too: the late Peter Copek and David Robinson. Thank you, all.

Carol Mason, my longtime valued assistant, was particularly helpful throughout the writing of the original manuscript in helping to make it a readable document. Special thanks to George Mason, Carol's brother, who served as mediator when Carol and I couldn't agree on something grammatical and who suggested the title of this work. George, you will probably never realize how important you were to this enterprise.

Gail Wells, whom I will always consider "my editor," was invaluable in guiding me as I, make that we, molded the original draft into this document. Both Gail and Carol helped educate me on the ways editorial assistance is critical to an acceptable document. Many thanks to them both.

A special kind of appreciation and thanks to the champions of the Oregon State University Press: Mary Braun, Marty Brown, Micki Reaman, and Cheryl McLean. Mary played the critical role in making this story possible through the OSU Press. If Mary had not shepherded me, and this document, through the publication processes, you would not be reading this now. I also thank Mary for introducing me to Gail Wells, who taught me much about the ways of editing and added fun to the editing enterprise. Marty chose the cover, for me a wonderful choice, and orchestrated marketing activities. Micki was responsible for seeing that all of our efforts became a book, an attractive one. (I hope you, the reader, think so, too.) Cheryl, the ultimate editor, put the icing on the cake. Thank you so much, all of you representing the OSU Press. I can't conceive of any other publisher for my story.

None of this would have been possible without the constant encouragement, support, and patience of my best friend of more than sixty years, Shirley Byrne. Shirley has been my partner through most of my life, sharing the good and the not-so-good parts of it. Her family guidance and critical evaluation of this narrative helped to shape this story.

To all, I offer my sincere thanks. Words are inadequate. You have all added a significant dimension to my life. To all of you, I want to say, I love you. I realize that I really do. Thank you, all!

Notes

CHAPTER 1

1. The Precambrian eon is the geologic time from the formation of earth 4.6 billion years ago till the Cambrian period, when hard-shell fossils first occur, about 541 million years ago. The Manhattan schist and the Fordham gneiss, together with the Inwood marble, are Precambrian metamorphic rocks exposed in the New York City area of New York.

2. A vast continental glacier, the Laurentide Ice Sheet, covered much of the northeast United States from 110,000 to about 12,000 years ago. When the ice melted completely, the gravel and rocks enclosed in the ice were deposited at the site of the ice's final location.

3. Horace Greeley High School is named in honor of Horace Greeley, who maintained a summer residence nearby in the 1860s. Greeley was the founder and editor of the *New-York Tribune* and is credited in 1865 with the advice: "Go West, young man, and grow up with the country."

CHAPTER 2

1. The roots of Hamilton College go back to the end of the eighteenth century. In 1793, Samuel Kirkland, a missionary, created the Hamilton-Oneida Academy for the education of Indians and whites on a hill overlooking the Mohawk Valley. He named the academy after Alexander Hamilton, who served on its first board of trustees. In 1812, the academy was chartered by the state of New York as Hamilton College. The college remained all-male until 1978, when it merged with the neighboring all-female Kirkland College, founded in 1968.

CHAPTER 3

1. Ted Pyfrom kept a complete set of charts of Bahamian waters in the Carib Shop, and when a Bahamian from an outer island came into the shop, Ted got the appropriate chart down from a shelf behind the counter and quizzed the person about the area he came from. Ted would ask about the kind of ballast he used in his boat. If the answer was "pebbles," Ted's interest increased. *Pebbles* was the term often used for basalt cobbles and boulders, rocks foreign to the Bahamas and used as ballast in Spanish galleons. "Where did you find the pebbles? Please, show me on this chart." Once the location was marked on the chart, Ted had a clue as to where an ancient Spanish ship might have sunk and where he might look to find treasure.

2. Chickcharnies are imagined to be forest-dwelling elfin creatures resembling birds. Their nesting sites are constructed by joining the tops of two pine trees. Their piercing eyes are red. They have three fingers, three toes, and a tail, which they use to suspend themselves from trees. They can be good or evil.

3. The Permian geologic period lasted from 298.9 to 252.1 million years ago and was the last geologic period of the Paleozoic era. The end of the Permian period was marked by the earth's most severe extinction event, with a loss of about 98 percent of all marine species and 70 percent of all terrestrial vertebrates.

4. The Columbia University geology faculty disciplines: Kay (stratigraphy), Newell (paleontology), Strahler (geomorphology), Behre (mining geology), Poldervaart (petrography), Ewing and Worzel (marine geophysics), Kulp (geochemistry), Press (geophysics/gravity). Press subsequently became president of the National Academy of Sciences and President Jimmy Carter's science advisor.

5. By "Runyonesque" I mean, resembling the Broadway bars described by the American writer Damon Runyon in his stories about Broadway and the New York underworld, made famous in the 1931 musical *Guys and Dolls*.

6. The *Kon-Tiki* expedition of 1947 was designed by Thor Heyerdahl to prove it was possible for Polynesians to travel from South America (Peru) by balsa raft to the Polynesian Islands. Heyerdahl's team floated for 101 days until the raft encountered the reef on the windward side of Raroia atoll.

7. A bathymetric chart is a chart or map of water depths that uses contour lines to represent equal water depths. In general form, a bathymetric chart is similar to a topographic map of a land area, only showing water depths rather than land elevations.

8. Norman D. Newell, "Geological Reconnaissance of Raroia (Kon Tiki) Atoll, Tuamotu Archipelago," *Bulletin of the American Museum of Natural History* 109, Article 3, 1956.

CHAPTER 4

1. Beno Gutenberg and Charles Richter were a pair of outstanding seismologists in America during the middle of the twentieth century. Gutenberg and Richter carried out fundamental studies in seismology at the California Institute of Technology. Their studies led to many fundamental laws of seismology and included the development of the Richter scale of earthquake magnitude, expressing the release of energy from an earthquake.

CHAPTER 5

1. A turbidity current is a gravity-driven, high-density underwater current of sediment-laden water that moves rapidly down a slope. As the turbidity current slows to a stop, it deposits the materials making up the flow. Deposits from turbidity currents are frequently graded vertically from coarse grains at the bottom to fine grains at the top.

CHAPTER 6

1. Corvallis, located at the junction of the Marys River and the Willamette River, was originally settled and platted in 1845–1846. It is the county seat of Benton County. The name Corvallis, adopted in 1853, means "heart of the valley." During the nineteenth century, Corvallis was the head of navigation for steamers on the Willamette River.

2. In 1862, President Abraham Lincoln signed the Land Grant College Act proposed by Senator Justin Morrill of Vermont. Under the act, the federal government granted to each existing and new state a parcel of land, the sale of which would provide funds to be dedicated to the "support and maintenance of at least one college, where the leading objective shall be, without excluding other scientific and classical studies and including military tactics, to teach such branches of learning as are related to agriculture and the mechanic arts…in order to promote the liberal and practical education of the industrial classes in the several pursuits and professions in life." The act required that each state accept its terms within two years of its enactment, which the Oregon legislature did on October 9, 1862. In October 1868, the legislature designated Corvallis College, which had existed since 1858, as "The Agricultural College of the State of Oregon until other provisions can be made." This temporary designation was made permanent by the legislature in October 1870. Passage of the federal Hatch Act in 1887 added agricultural research, and in 1914 the Smith-Lever Act added the Extension Service to Oregon State's responsibilities as a land-grant college. On March 6, 1961, Oregon State College was designated Oregon State University.

3. The Office of Naval Research, a department of the US Navy, was authorized by Congress and approved by President Truman in 1946 to plan, foster, and encourage scientific research deemed to be of value to the navy. Following its creation, it was the foremost supporter of oceanographic research at America's universities and colleges.

4. Louise Burt and Miriam Ludwig, *Oceanography at Oregon State University: the first two decades, 1954–1975*. Self-published; supported by the College of Oceanic and Atmospheric Sciences, Oregon State University, 1998.

5. A Secchi disk is used to measure the relative clarity of surface water, considered to be a measure of the surface turbidity. The disk is white, thirty centimeters in diameter, and is lowered into the water until it is no longer visible. The depth of water at this point, or Secchi depth, is a general measure of the turbidity. A bathythermograph is a torpedo-shaped instrument with a pressure (depth) sensor and a temperature recorder. It is used to make a vertical measurement of water temperature at various depths. It can be used while a ship is under way and was an aid in the search for submarines during World War II.

6. At that time, I learned a hard lesson about talking to the press. On one occasion, I was privy to information I had learned, some of which came from an oil-company colleague. I was questioned by a journalist about what I knew. I told the newsman something, which he agreed to keep "off the record." In the next day's *Oregonian*, I was shocked to see what I had told the journalist appearing as a minor headline in the business section. Lesson: with the press, nothing is ever completely off the record. A corollary lesson I learned somewhere along the line was that once something is committed to ink on paper, it should be regarded as public information. It is interesting to me how easy it is to leak information to others once that information is preserved on paper.

7. LORAN (Long Range Navigation) is a radio navigation system that enabled ships and aircraft to determine their position and speed from low-frequency radio signals transmitted from fixed land-based transmitters and received by a receiving unit. LORAN has been replaced by satellite navigation and global-positioning systems.

8. As state geologist, Hollis Dole moved in political circles. When Richard Nixon was elected president, Hollis, who had spent time with Nixon in the navy during World War II, was appointed assistant secretary for minerals in the Department of Interior. During Nixon's first term, Hollis used his influence to have me appointed to a committee charged with preparing the Department of Interior to receive all the federal civil marine agencies—essentially what later became the National Oceanic and Atmospheric Administration (NOAA) in 1970. The committee worked hard and was one meeting short of releasing its plan when Interior Secretary Walter Hickel had a falling out with President Nixon over Nixon's handling of the war in Vietnam. Possibly as a result, the president decided on short notice that NOAA would not be assigned to the Department of Interior. By executive order, he assigned NOAA to the Department of Commerce, where it has been ever since. After his reelection, the president cleaned house in a number of cabinet departments, including Interior. Hickel and all his subordinates, including Hollis, were fired. Subsequently, Hollis joined the Atlantic Richfield Oil Company in its Colony Shale Oil Project, a joint venture in western Colorado. When

the company pulled out of that project, Hollis became its lobbyist in Washington, DC. During his time with Atlantic Richfield, Hollis became well acquainted with Dick Bressler, a vice president in the company. In the early 1980s Bressler left to become president of Burlington Northern Railroad, which owned extensive real estate and natural resources throughout the West. Bressler used Hollis as a special consultant to the company. At Hollis Dole's recommendation, Bressler invited me to join the Burlington Northern Railroad's board of directors in 1987. At the first board meeting I attended, Bressler recommended splitting off the Burlington resource companies into a separate company, Burlington Resources Inc. I was appointed to the Burlington Resources board of directors, a position I held for twelve or thirteen years. While I was on the board, Dick Bressler established an endowment in his name at Oregon State recognizing senior faculty with longtime service who have demonstrated a major commitment to undergraduate instruction.

9. Coastal upwelling occurs along the Oregon coast when winds from the north drive surface waters westward. Waters driven offshore to the west are replaced by the upwelling of cold, nutrient-rich water from depth. The presence at the surface of the cold upwelled water is frequently accompanied by fog. The nutrients in the upwelled water stimulate biological productivity as a base for fisheries productivity.

10. The Area Redevelopment Administration (ARA) was established in 1961 as a demonstration project designed to enhance area economic development in severely depressed areas. Among other things, the ARA provided funds for local facility development. The success of ARA led in 1965 to the creation of its successor, the Economic Development Administration.

CHAPTER 7

1. The National Science Foundation was established by the National Science Foundation Act of 1950. Its stated mission is "to promote the progress of science; to advance the national health, prosperity, and welfare; and to secure the national defense." (from Wikipedia)

2. John Byrne, "The National Science Foundation," *Geotimes* 13, no. 8, 15–19, 1968.

CHAPTER 8

1. Louise Burt and Miriam Ludwig, *Oceanography at Oregon State University: the first two decades, 1954–1975*, self-published, supported by the OSU College of Oceanic and Atmospheric Sciences, 1998.

2. Report to the President of Oregon State University from the Commission on University Goals. Corvallis, August 1970.

CHAPTER 9

1. Manganese nodules are rock concretions up to three or four inches in diameter, about the size of a baseball, of layered manganese and iron hydroxides with contained nickel, copper and cobalt. They occur in vast areas of oceanic abyssal plains. In the 1960s and 1970s, they were thought to have considerable value for their nickel content. The exclusive rights to their collection was a major factor in Law of the Sea negotiations.

CHAPTER 10

1. The Research Office personnel ensured that a faculty member submitting a grant proposal had complied with all of the institutional, system of higher education, state, and federal regulations pertaining to his or her research. Responsibility for doing this resided with the faculty member, who was required to obtain approvals from responsible authorities within the university. If the intended research involved the use of human subjects, laboratory animals, radioactive materials, etc., the proposal needed to be reviewed by the person responsible for each of those categories and initialed on a checklist. The proposal's budget was checked in the Research Office to ensure it included the appropriate indirect cost and was otherwise financially accurate and that all clearances had been obtained. The dean of research then signed the proposal, thereby committing the university to carrying out the research in the manner indicated in the proposal. The faculty member submitted the required number of copies of the signed proposal to the funding agency. The action of preparing and clearing a proposal for submission was vested in the individual faculty member, who would serve as the principal investigator of the research if a grant were made. When a proposal was approved for funding by an agency, copies were filed in the Research Office and in the university office responsible for financial management of the grant. Officially, the grant was made to Oregon State University with management of the research vested in the faculty member who had written the proposal, would carry out the research and would serve as the principal investigator (PI). The PI was responsible for filing a final report when the grant expired. The Research Office kept track of all proposals and about twice a year issued a summary report listing all the active grants at Oregon State University.

2. At this writing (2014), the Agricultural Experiment Station in Oregon has eleven branch stations in fifteen locations.

CHAPTER 11

1. The National Oceanic and Atmospheric Administration (NOAA) was created in 1970 by executive order of President Richard Nixon. Assigned to the

Department of Commerce, NOAA was a consolidation of the Environmental Sciences Service Administration (ESSA), which included the US Coast and Geodetic Survey and the Weather Bureau, with the Bureau of Commercial Fisheries. Subsequent to its formation, I simplified the organization of NOAA into the National Ocean Service (NOS), the National Weather Service (NWS), the National Marine Fisheries Service (NMFS), the National Environmental Satellite Data and Information Service (NESDIS), and the Ocean and Atmosphere Research laboratories (OAR).

2. The notes for this speech are in the OSU Archives.

3. The US Office of Management and Budget (OMB), a major part of the president's executive office, is charged with producing the president's annual federal budget. OMB also monitors the quality of agency programs, policies, and procedures to ensure they comply with the president's agenda.

4. The National Sea Grant College Program, administered by NOAA, consists of a national network of thirty-three Sea Grant colleges and universities engaged in research, education, training, and Extension to enhance the conservation and wise use of the coastal areas and nearshore waters of the oceans and Great Lakes of the United States.

5. The Dall's porpoise is a north Pacific species weighing three hundred to five hundred pounds and attaining six or seven feet in length. Named by American naturalist W. H. Dall, the porpoise gained public attention when it was caught in large numbers in fishing trawls. Attention increased when it was noted that Japanese hunters killed upwards of forty thousand Dall's porpoises the year after the commercial whaling moratorium went into effect. (from Wikipedia)

CHAPTER 12

1. Tom Garrett served as deputy US whaling commissioner prior to my appointment. Tom was a dedicated environmentalist who had grown up on a ranch in Garrett, Wyoming, where the occurrence of dinosaur bones generated his interest in huge animals, the last of which are the great whales. Tom represented the United States at the 1981 IWC meeting as the United States joined other nonwhaling nations in mounting a case for the moratorium.

2. The countries voting in favor of the moratorium on commercial whaling were Antigua, Argentina, Australia, Belize, Costa Rica, Denmark, Egypt, France, Germany, India, Kenya, Mexico, Monaco, Netherlands, New Zealand, Oman, St. Lucia, St. Vincent, Senegal, the Seychelles, Spain, Sweden, the United Kingdom, the United States and Uruguay. The seven countries voting against the measure were Brazil, Iceland, Japan, Norway, Peru, South

Korea, and the USSR. Chile, China, the Philippines, South Africa, and Switzerland abstained.

3. Bowhead whales are among the largest whales by tonnage, although individual whales may be only forty to sixty feet in length. The bowhead is a baleen whale similar to the right whale. They received their name because of a high-arched lower jaw said to resemble an archer's bow. These whales occur only in Arctic waters, migrating northward through leads (cracks) in the ice during spring months, feeding in Alaskan and Canadian arctic waters in summer, and returning through the Bering Strait to the Bering Sea in late fall. Eskimos in northern Alaska hunt them as they swim north through open leads in the ice. Management of the bowhead hunt is the major task of the Alaska Eskimo Whaling Commission, created in 1981.

At one time there may have been as many as thirty thousand bowhead whales. By 1981, commercial whaling had reduced that number to fewer than a thousand, causing them to be listed as an endangered species, though this low estimate was probably due in part to a lack of information about the bowhead stock. By 2012, additional research and careful management had increased the estimated population to more than seven thousand.

The whales were harvested under the aboriginal-subsistence provisions of the ICRW, administered by the IWC. The quota for the taking of bowhead whales has two overlapping parts: a strike quota for harpooning the whales, and a smaller quota for whales that are actually killed. A strike occurs when a whale is harpooned and wounded. Once a whale is killed, it is counted as part of the kill quota, and once the kill quota is reached, whaling ceases for that season. Management of the two quotas is assigned to the Alaska Eskimo Whaling Commission, which allocates the quota to individual villages in northern Alaska. Thus the commission might assign ten strikes and seven kills to Barrow and six strikes and four kills to Gambell or Wainwright, villages on the north slope of Alaska.

Bowhead whales were important to traditional Eskimo culture. An aged former Eskimo whaling captain told a number of us of the legend the Eskimos believed in:

> At some time in the ancient past, Eskimos were starving. One brother decided that in order to survive he would live in the sea, which was rich with food. He became the bowhead whale. Then, as a whale, he recognized that life on land was difficult and that his land-brothers were frequently starving. He decided then that he would offer himself up to his brother as food. Believing in this legend, to be an Eskimo whaling captain was, and is, a position of great prestige and responsibility. The captain throws the harpoon into the whale, his brother. To harpoon and kill the whale in order to feed brothers on land is

considered noble. To only strike the whale and not kill it was considered an act of shame.

CHAPTER 13

1. During the relatively short time we spent in Washington, DC, Shirley and I met people who continued to be good friends long after we left. In addition to the many friends we made at NOAA, others outside the normal business circle played an important role in enhancing our social lives. Shirley taught music at Janney Elementary School and indirectly met Joanie Hollander, who became a longtime friend and piano partner. Together they played piano duets, frequently at retirement homes. Joan and her husband, Bernard "Bernge," kept in contact with us, and on the occasions when we returned to Washington, they were always dinner partners.

Another couple we visited with socially after leaving the District was Jack Botzum and his partner, Priscilla Capra. Jack was the owner and editor of numerous weekly newsletters concerning various aspects of the marine environment, published under the aegis of Nautilus Press. He was always fun to talk with about literature. Priscilla had been involved in the motion picture industry and had been married to Frank Capra; she was extremely knowledgeable about the entertainment industry.

Because both Shirley and I enjoy jazz, particularly piano jazz, we frequented one of the piano lounges where John Eaton played. Eaton grew up in Washington, attended Yale University, studied classical piano, and became a familiar figure in DC jazz circles. He and his wife, Penny Karr, became close friends of ours, and they have been on our must-see list whenever we return to Washington. After Penny died in 2013, John has come to Corvallis many times to give jazz lecture-concerts. He has become a favorite of local jazz fans.

We came to know Charlie and Judy Bussmann because of an ocean connection. Charlie was the publisher of a monthly news magazine, *Sea Technology*, about oceans and the technology involved with learning about and using the resources of the sea. Judy was a recognized designer of fashionable dolls. I first became acquainted with Charlie at a lunch we had together in the Washington Hotel. During our conversation, we talked about a way to have ocean-related organizations publicize their programs as part of a domestic "Year of the Ocean." Activities of the year would be organized under the auspices of NOAA. Diane Boratyn, who had organized and run a major publicity program for the fisheries service, was put in charge. Under her direction, March 1984 till March 1985 was designated "The Year of the Ocean," a year of celebration for the oceans and their importance to the people of the United States. Diane was effective in obtaining congressional funds for the yearlong celebration.

CHAPTER 14

1. The schools of agriculture, engineering, forestry, home economics, pharmacy, business, health and physical education, education, veterinary medicine, and oceanography, as well as the Reserve Officers' Training Corps (ROTC), were recognized as professional schools.

2. Space-grant colleges are institutions that are members of a network of fifty consortia formed for the purpose of outer space-related research. Each consortium is based in one of the fifty states, the District of Columbia, or Puerto Rico, and each consists of multiple independent institutions, with one of them acting as the lead. OSU is the lead institution for the Oregon consortium. NASA administers the program and first took that role in 1989. (From Wikipedia)

3. Oregon State University is a member of the Sun Grant Association, a group of six US universities that serve as regional centers of the Sun Grant Initiative, established by Congress in the Sun Grant Research Initiative Act of 2003. These universities research and develop sustainable and environmentally friendly biobased energy alternatives. (From Wikipedia)

4. University searches for academic or administrative personnel are time-consuming affairs. The first step is to decide whether the search will be internal or external, national or international; internal searches can be faster than external searches. Second, if the search is to be external, will a search firm be employed to help with the search? Search firms, or "headhunters," are frequently used in searches for upper-level administrative personnel, vice-presidents, and presidents. Such firms can help with preparing announcements, applicant screening, and seeking qualified applicants. Employing headhunters is usually expensive. We elected not to employ a search firm but to do the entire search ourselves.

   Another decision is the selection of the search committee, which is needed regardless of how the search is conducted. The composition of search committees for university-level positions usually includes representatives of the academic deans, possibly a department chair, faculty, occasionally an alumnus or two, a community member, and often a student leader or two. The search committee determines the qualifications required for the position and prepares the announcement of the position, which is sent to a number of outlets, including the *Chronicle of Higher Education*. The committee also solicits nominations directly from a number of sources, including acquaintances at other universities, and receives and reviews all applications. The committee makes the initial selection of possible candidates; determines the schedule for initial interviews (usually conducted by only the search committee and frequently taking place at a neutral site such as a hotel near an airport); and selects a number of semifinalists, who are invited to campus. The candidates are then interviewed by others and are often requested to give a public talk. The search committee receives input from the campus community and selects the finalists, who are again invited to campus. Finally, the committee receives additional input and makes recommendations from among the finalists to the appointing authority, in this case the president, who selects the individual for the position.

5. Graham Spanier was provost at Oregon State University until 1991. He left OSU to become chancellor of the University of Nebraska, a position he held until 1995, when he left Nebraska to become President of Penn State University. In 2011, he was forced to resign as president in the aftermath of a child sex abuse scandal in Penn State's intercollegiate athletics program. In March of 2017, Spanier was convicted of failing to inform child welfare authorities of sex-abuse allegations against Jerry Sandusky, an assistant football coach at Penn State.

CHAPTER 15

1. I was among the first (possibly *the* first) oceanography leaders nationwide to add an Extension agent to oceanography, in this case as faculty in the Department of Oceanography. This action predated the development of Extension within the Sea Grant College System, which has served the entire nation well. Further, after I joined NOAA as its administrator, I thought NOAA could be more effective in serving its stakeholders if it had its own Extension Service. I worked with the Department of Agriculture, which included the Cooperative Extension Service, to have Dan Panshin assigned to NOAA to initiate and develop a NOAA Extension effort. Dan had been the Extension agent I added to the Department of Oceanography at Oregon State. He'd left Oregon State to assume an Extension position at the University of Minnesota and then had moved to the Extension Service in the Department of Agriculture in Washington, DC. I left NOAA before I could complete the development of a NOAA Extension Service. Fortunately, the earlier passage of the Sea Grant College Act in 1966 provided for Extension and outreach to the coastal areas of the United States.

2. Emery N. Castle, *Reflections of a Pragmatic Economist: My Intellectual Journey*. Corvallis: Oregon State University Press, 2010.

3. Emery N. Castle. 1993. "On the University's Third Mission: Extended Education: Final Report to President John V. Byrne on the Placement of the Oregon State University Extension Service within the University." Also, *Reflections of a Pragmatic Economist*, 151–157.

4. The Kellogg Foundation, established in 1930 by breakfast-cereal pioneer W. K. Kellogg, is one of the nation's largest philanthropic foundations. Its mission centers around the well-being of children.

5. "Returning to Our Roots: The Engaged Institution," Kellogg Commission on the Future of State and Land-Grant Universities, 1999.

CHAPTER 16

1. Emery N. Castle, *Reflections of a Pragmatic Economist: My Intellectual Journey*. Corvallis: Oregon State University Press, 2010.

2. The United States Agency for International Development is the federal agency responsible for administering US foreign aid.

CHAPTER 17

1. Title IX is the portion of the Equal Opportunity in Education Act (2002) that states "no person in the United States shall on the basis of sex be excluded from participation in, be denied the benefits of, or be subjected to discrimination under any education program or activity receiving federal financial assistance." For athletics, it means that women and men must have equal opportunity to participate in sports (i.e., the same number of sports).

2. We maintained the baseball program, and in 1995, the last year of my presidency, we hired a baseball coach, Pat Riley, who ultimately took the Beavers to national championships two years in a row, 2006 and 2007.

CHAPTER 18

1. Neil Goldschmidt served as secretary of transportation under President Jimmy Carter from 1979 to 1981. He was elected governor of Oregon in 1986 and served until 1991. He disappeared from public life in 2004, when he confessed to having had sexual relations with a minor during his first term as governor.

2. The University Cabinet was a quarterly meeting of student leaders and upper administrators. The student leaders included the president and vice president of the Associated Students of Oregon State University, the president and vice president of the Memorial Union Program Council, and others. The university was represented by the president's cabinet, including the president and elected officers of Faculty Senate. The cabinet usually met at noon on a day near the beginning of the academic quarter. To a great extent, the agenda was set by the students, with information items added by the administration.

If there were major events that would affect the university and the students, these events dominated the agenda.

3. The poplar tree had been christened the Trysting Tree by the class of 1901 in reference to the students' use of the tree's shade for romantic encounters. It was memorialized in the university's alma mater by Homer Maris: "I love to wander on the pathway, down to the Trysting Tree. For there again I see in fancy old friends dear to me."

CHAPTER 19

1. We presidents often worked more with the staff of the system office than we did with the chancellor himself. The staff impressed me as dedicated and effective. Over the years, the staff I became most familiar with were Bill Leman, who served as the interim chancellor after Bud Davis resigned; Shirley Clarke, who was brought in to serve as the vice chancellor for academic affairs under Tom Bartlett; Weldon Ihrig, vice chancellor for finance and administration under Bartlett; George Pernsteiner, associate vice chancellor for finance and administration; and Virginia Thompson, who held together much of the day-to-day business. Virginia took care of the details of the three or four annual meetings of the state board, which were moved from one campus to another. The Board of Higher Education members with whom I became most familiar during my eleven-year tenure as president included John Alltucker (Eugene), Loren Wyss (Portland), Jim Petersen (La Grande), Mark Dodson (Portland), Dick Hensley (Medford), Les Swanson (Portland), Herb Aschkenasy (Albany), Bob Bailey (The Dalles), Tom Bruggere (Wilsonville), Diane Christopher (Medford), George Richardson (Portland), Jim Willis (Salem), and Janice Wilson (Portland).

Index

Note: Photographs are indicated by an italic page number or span. Material from the Notes section are indicated by an italic "*n*" and note number following the page number.

About the Author

JOHN V. BYRNE is president emeritus of Oregon State University, one of American's leading land-grant universities, where he served as president for eleven years, from 1984 to 1995.

His experience includes service to higher education, government, and the private sector. After joining Oregon State in 1960, Dr. Byrne served for sixteen years in OSU's oceanography program as faculty member, department chair, and dean. Subsequently he was OSU's dean of research, graduate dean, and vice president for research and graduate studies. During his thirty-five-year tenure at Oregon State, he took leave twice to serve the United States government in Washington, DC, first as a program director for oceanography at the National Science Foundation and later as the administrator of the National Oceanic and Atmospheric Administration and US commissioner to the International Whaling Commission. Prior to joining OSU in 1960, he worked for three years as a research geologist with the Humble Oil and Refining Company in Houston, Texas.

As president of OSU, he guided Oregon State through a period of turbulence caused by severe state budget restrictions resulting from a property tax-limitation ballot measure. During this period, OSU continued to grow in programs, facilities, and external funding. Dr. Byrne was one of the first to introduce Total Quality Management techniques to higher education. He emphasized the importance of international education for students at OSU and was a supporter of significant academic reform in higher education, including extended education as part of OSU's mission.

After retiring from OSU's presidency, Dr. Byrne served as executive director of the Kellogg Commission on the Future of State and Land-Grant Universities from 1995 through the Commission's conclusion in March 2000. The Kellogg Commission comprised the presidents and chancellors of twenty-five major public universities dedicated to the reform of American public higher education. Dr. Byrne has also served as a consultant on various aspects of higher education to more than a dozen major public universities. He assisted university governing boards with board-president relations, presidential assessments, and presidential searches. He has served on several corporate and nonprofit boards, including the National Sea Grant College Advisory Board. For a number of years, he was a member of the board of the Harbor Branch Oceanographic Institute in Fort Pierce, Florida, and of the Oregon Coast Aquarium. In retirement, he continued to assist Oregon State on a number of committees and as an instructor in the Honors College.

He also served on a number of corporate boards, including the Benjamin Franklin Savings and Loan Co., Burlington Railroad Co., and Burlington Resources and its subsidiary company boards, including the Plum Creek Timber Co. board.

Dr. Byrne has been recognized for his contributions to education and to science by community colleges and private and public institutions of higher education.

His degrees in geology are from Hamilton College, Columbia University, and the University of Southern California. He resides in Corvallis, Oregon, home of Oregon State University.